TEARS OF

My Mother

TEARS OF
My Mother

THE LEGACY
OF MY NIGERIAN
UPBRINGING

Wendy Osefo, PhD

GALLERY BOOKS

New York   London   Toronto   Sydney   New Delhi

G

Gallery Books
An Imprint of Simon & Schuster, Inc.
1230 Avenue of the Americas
New York, NY 10020

First Gallery Books hardcover edition September 2022

GALLERY BOOKS and colophon are registered trademarks
of Simon & Schuster, Inc.

Some names and identifiying characteristics have been changed.

For information about special discounts for bulk purchases,
please contact Simon & Schuster Special Sales at 1-866-506-1949
or business@simonandschuster.com.

The Simon & Schuster Speakers Bureau can bring authors to your live event.
For more information or to book an event, contact the Simon & Schuster Speakers
Bureau at 1-866-248-3049 or visit our website at www.simonspeakers.com.

Interior design by Davina Mock-Maniscalco

Manufactured in China

10 9 8 7 6 5 4 3 2 1

Library of Congress Control Number: 2021953263

ISBN 978-1-9821-9450-5
ISBN 978-1-9821-9452-9 (ebook)

This book is dedicated to any first-generation child who ever felt like they were not enough, who felt that they never belonged. Our story is unique, but that is what makes it so beautiful. In this moment, I hope you feel seen.

CONTENTS

TEARS OF

My Mother

I sat in a green armchair in the corner of my kitchen, fiddling with my hair as my mom stood at the kitchen island, cutting fresh okra. Recently, my mother, Iyom Susan Okuzu, had volunteered to cook dinner for my family of five: my husband, Eddie; our older son, Karter; younger son, Kruz; and baby daughter, Kamrynn. She was going to make her signature spicy, comforting palm oil okra soup with pounded yam. Once she'd organized all the soup ingredients—okra, red onion, spinach, a habanero pepper, crayfish, assorted meats and spices, ogbono seeds from the African market—the chopped onion and crayfish went into a pan with hot oil. The room filled with an aroma that instantly took me back in time.

Nigerian food is hearty, rich, and humble, and it dominates my childhood memories. I'd see Mom standing in front of the stove, stirring two, three pots of fragrant stews or soups with a slotted spoon. Many nights she'd come home exhausted from a twelve-hour nursing shift at the hospital and head directly to the kitchen to fry up meat or fish. The movement in our home always originated in the kitchen. In any Nigerian home, it's where the action is. You can have a twenty-room house, but 90 percent of the time, the people who live there will be in the kitchen.

Smelling the sizzling onions, my two sons came barreling in, tossing a football. Their toddler sister, a new walker, tried to keep up. Karter, the spokesman of the group, asked, "What's for dinner?" All three kids circled their grandmother, the boys tall enough to peer into the pan. They do the same with me at 4 p.m. when I cook dinner. I make tacos and spaghetti and love experimenting with international cuisines, but cooking Nigerian food makes my heart sing. The fact that my kids' favorite dishes are Nigerian—like Mom's okra soup and my grandmother Angela's fried plantains (crispy on the outside, soft and sweet on the inside, and spicy when dipped in palm oil)—is a testament to the techniques I learned from them when I was a child.

"It's not ready yet," said Mom, shooing the kids away with a laugh. The two boys ran out of the kitchen as quickly as they had rushed in. Kamrynn hung back, wanting to help. The highest form of love in our culture is preparing a family meal, and my daughter had instinctively sensed its importance. "Go play with your brothers," I told her. I was hoping for some alone time with my mother. I had something to ask her, and to tell her.

We watched Kamrynn toddle out. Mom flashed me a smile and I flashed one back. Then silence.

Stalling, I asked, "How's Jordan doing?" My brother, eighteen years my junior, was a sophomore in college.

"He's doing well," she said. "I'm very proud of him."

I nodded, swallowing a lump. Not that we weren't all proud of Jordan, with good reason. He'd grown up well, despite the loss of his father (Jordan and I had different fathers). I just couldn't recall the last time Mom told me that she was proud of me. The expectations for Nigerian girls are so much higher than they are for boys. A girl is considered a failure if she doesn't cook expertly, keep house, marry a good Nigerian man, have children, care for the elders, look fabulous, *and* be a doctor or a lawyer. Nigerian boys only have to avoid getting a girl pregnant too early and eventually provide for their families. But even then, if boys miss the mark, they're cut a lot of slack. They're given dozens of chances to get back on track, reach their potential, and achieve success. Girls, not at all. Our missteps aren't brushed off, and we don't get pats on the back for doing the right thing. It's expected of us, and any failure is met with disapproval by our demanding parents.

I glanced around at my glorious chef's kitchen, the gleaming stainless steel appliances, the hammered copper pots and pans Mom was using. My gaze drifted into the living room, with its creamy walls and yummy plush couch, the colorful accent pillows I'd carefully chosen. Just outside the back door, we had ten acres of rolling green lawn and trees for the kids to play in. Two new cars were parked in the driveway. Eddie, the kids, and I had been living in our new house for just over a year, and it felt like home. Buying it was the culmination of our years and years of hard work, first earning our degrees, then proving ourselves in the workplace. Our family oasis was an objective symbol of success, and it felt good, validating, for my mother to spend time here and see the payoff of all her hard work raising me. It'd be even better if she acknowledged it.

When I was growing up in North Carolina, Mom always made our homes look beautiful, even when we lived in more modest places. Our apartments got bigger and nicer as Mom's income grew. She started as a nurse and eventually became the director of nursing at major metropolitan hospitals. Still, although we were comfortably middle-class in terms of income, Mom had never figured out how to manage her money. In Nigeria, cash is king. So when Mom came to America, she didn't have the savvy to use credit well and wound up with a bad credit score. Even at fifty-something, she struggles with that financial culture gap.

I got out of the chair and walked to the counter. "Can I help?" I asked her, sounding a lot like my own daughter. A pot of water was boiling on the stove, just waiting for yam flour to be poured in, the first step in the process of making pillowy, springy pounded yam balls to dip in the soup. "I want to help," I said.

"It's all under control," said Mom, sending me back to the chair. I sat down, feeling dismissed, which took me back to childhood again. This scene had played out in the kitchen throughout my life when I offered to stand at her side and cook with her. She would refuse the offer, every time. I never pushed it.

My mother had long proven her capability as a woman who didn't need help. Gifted, gutsy, and brilliant, she first came to America at seventeen and single-handedly put herself through college, eventually earning *two* master's degrees. Not too shabby for an immigrant. She arrived here bright-eyed and bushy-tailed, ready to grab her slice of the American Dream. Then she suffered heartbreak and had to grow up quickly in a country that was not her own. These tragedies made her wiser, but they hardened her, stealing her optimism and the spark in her that I remembered from childhood. Her suffering showed her that the world is often cruel, and never wanting her own children to sulk or be blind to the cruelty of the world, she did not go easy on my older sister, Yvonne, and me.

Watching Mom stir the yam flour in the pot to smooth out the texture, I noticed a slight sheen on her forehead. She made a noise, a "hmph," the sound I'd heard a million times—her exasperated noise.

"Is something wrong?" I asked.

She shot me an annoyed expression, another hallmark of hers. Every Nigerian mother has a repertoire of facial expressions and distinctive sounds that show how they feel without having to utter a single word.

"What?" I pressed.

Finally, she said, "Wen," using my nickname, "you don't know what I'm going through."

"So tell me," I said.

She shot me another look, the one that said, "I'm just overwhelmed."

"If you're tired, you don't have to cook for us," I said.

"Well, I'm doing it," she said, her tone short, anger creeping in.

Now *I* was annoyed. "You offered to come over here and cook. No one asked you to do any of this. You insisted, so why are you doing it with anger?"

The truth was, she was angry at life, had been for a while. I was still trying to understand what my role was in her disillusionment. In our Nigerian culture, parents are only as successful as their children. My whole life, my mother had been adamant about keeping Yvonne and me locked into her vision of success and living our lives the way she wanted us to. We were given two options for our future: doctor or lawyer. Yvo (pronounced ē-voh) became a surgeon and married a lawyer. I got my doctorate and married a lawyer. Our success gave Mom bragging rights for life, but it didn't appear to make her happy.

"Don't live your life for your children like I did," she said. "You'll just wind up alone."

It wasn't the first time she'd said this, and I *wanted* to respond, "Don't take out your frustrations on me. Didn't I do everything you ever asked of me?" But I didn't dare speak the words out loud. Back talk was not part of the Nigerian parent-child contract.

I took a breath. "Mom, if you're upset that you sacrificed so much, don't sacrifice anymore." I walked toward her. "I got this. I can finish dinner." I moved to take her place at the stove, just as one day Kamrynn would take my place.

Susan frowned. "You don't want my food," she said, not budging.

For her, the very suggestion that I didn't want her food was like a slap in the face. I hadn't meant that, and she knew it. It was as if she was determined to misunderstand, to take offense at my attempts to have a real conversation.

My eyes burned. I had to confront my truth, one that I had danced around my entire life: *my mother and I, as close as we are, don't really understand each other.*

How can it be that two people who lived side by side in small houses and apartments, talked every day for decades, went through so much pain and suffering together, could still keep so much hidden? Would we ever really understand each other and become as close as I wished we were?

Mom has always been my role model for nearly everything, but since I'd become a mother, I'd been noticing behaviors of hers—vulnerability, neediness, covetousness—that I didn't want to emulate as a parent or as a woman. As a dutiful daughter, I walked a constant tightrope of meeting my immigrant mother's strict expectations and upholding our Nigerian cultural traditions. But I also wanted to define myself—a first-generation immigrant raised in America—and my parenting style, on my own terms.

Mom and I never talked about past hurts—at all, ever. I wanted to be a different kind of mother, one who was available to talk with her kids about their feelings. Tonight I'd meant to bring up a couple of things, as some old hurts had been nagging me lately. Clearing the air with my mom would go a long way toward healing some of my own feelings.

I also wanted to tell Mom about a major decision concerning my career. And I knew she wouldn't approve. Her parenting style was to use her disapproval like a blunt object. My sister and I succeeded out of fear of disappointing her. I was putting off telling her my news because I knew she'd give me her disappointed look, and I'd feel like I failed her. I was a mother of three, with a career and a marriage. I was thirty-seven years old, and Mom's approval still weighed like an anvil on my choices.

As always, I couldn't quite bring myself to say what was truly on my mind. I told myself, "Come on, Wendy. You can do it!" But then, I set the table instead. I knew rehashing ancient hurts wasn't going to make Mom happy. Her happiness depended on my meeting her expectations for me. However, her expectations and my happiness were not aligned.

All my life, I'd done everything she asked. When would that be enough? When could I start living my life for me? What did I owe my mother *now*?

The food ready, I called in the family. My sons, my daughter, and my husband, Eddie, gathered in the kitchen and we sat down to eat. We ripped off pieces of the pounded yam ball, transforming them into balls with our hands, and dipped them into the soup. Mom watched us all closely as we took our first bites.

"It's amazing," I said.

She said, "I don't know, I used too much salt. I'm not sure if it affected the recipe." Her modesty was a fishing expedition. Food is her love language, and we had all learned to speak it.

"Oh no, no, no, no. It's great!" I said to show my gratitude and appreciation.

Eddie said, "It's delicious. Best I've ever had."

The kids joined in, too, gushing praise until Susan smiled and dipped a piece of pounded yam into her soup to assess what she'd created for all of us.

ONE

Coming to America

When I was three, my mother shook me awake in the middle of the night.

"Get up, Wen," she said. "We have to go."

My sister, Yvo, then six, was standing next to Mom at the foot of my bed. We were in a house at my maternal grandfather's compound in Nigeria. Two weeks prior, we had fled my father's home in Imo State to take refuge at my grandparents' in Anambra State. Mom helped me out of bed, picked me up, and carried me out of the house. Like me, Yvo was wearing just her pajamas. Mom was dressed in her regular clothes, a long skirt and a long-sleeved blouse.

I'd never been awake that late before. Mom helped my sister and me into the back seat of the car. A man I didn't recognize helped Mom load our six suitcases into the trunk. Mom slipped into the seat next to me, and the man got into the driver's seat. "Let's go," she said.

"Where are we going?" I asked, confused.

"Close your eyes," she said.

I dozed off in the car and woke up again in my mother's arms in a white tunnel. Yvo held Mom's hand and walked alongside us. The tunnel ended and we were ushered into a space I'd never seen before, with rows of cushioned seats and bright lights overhead. Mom found our row and buckled Yvo and me into our seats before she sat between us and fastened her own seat belt.

Overtired and excited to be inside an airplane for the first time, I cried when I was forbidden to run up and down the aisle. Eventually, I fell back to sleep and woke up the next morning in another new place, a new country. We were met at North Carolina's Raleigh-Durham International Airport by a woman named Winifred, one of my mother's sisters (she had four sisters, three of whom lived in and around Durham). I was too young to remember meeting my aunts before. Winifred drove us to a town house on Fargo Street. It looked just like all the other town houses on the block.

Mom said, "This is our new home, girls." The house was, as I came to learn, owned by Aunt Ekwy, another of Mom's sisters.

"Where's Dad?" I asked once we were settled, fed, and dressed. The midmorning sun coming through the windows was bright.

"He's fine. Don't worry," said Mom curtly.

"Is he coming here?" I asked.

"He's coming," she said. "He'll be here soon."

A lot was new to me in America: the relatives and friends who came in and out of the house on a steady basis to sit and talk to Mom; the humid climate; the people on the street and in stores who wore strange clothes and spoke with a weird accent. Many of the people were white, which was also a change from what I was used to.

Inside the house, it still felt like being in Nigeria. Mom cooked all our favorite dishes to give us a taste of home. And she spoke Igbo, the dialect of southeastern Nigeria, while she held court in the kitchen, entertaining and cooking for the stream of visitors. I'd never seen her like this before, so free and fun, the perfect hostess with a wooden spoon in one hand and a glass of wine in the other. I came to understand that most of the people who dropped by were our family members, aunts and cousins as well as some friends from the local Nigerian community. Listening to them talk, I soon realized that Mom had lived in Durham before I was born. Even though both my parents were Nigerian born, this was where they had been married in 1981. My sister, Yvo, had been born at Duke University Hospital later that year. Having been born in Nigeria, I was the only member of our immediate family who was totally new to this place—although Yvo's memories of the first two years of her life in America were faint at best. I adapted quickly, as children do.

Thanks to Mom's incredible cooking and open-door policy for guests, Fargo Street was like Grand Central Station. Back in Nigeria, our routine centered on home and the fundamentalist Christian church where my father, Edwin, was a pastor. Our lives before had been circumscribed, with few social gatherings. Now, in Durham, our house was alive with people, music, laughter. It was a place of joy.

For weeks, the newness distracted me from the mystery of why we were here in America at all. I missed my father, but I was okay. As long as my mother was to my left and my sister to my right, I felt secure. It didn't matter where I was.

Over the course of a year, the three of us settled into life in Durham, and I got to know my aunts better. Mom worked odd jobs as a home-care worker and whatever else she could find. After several months, I stopped asking about my father, because Mom always said the same thing: "He's coming. Soon."

And then, out of the blue, Mom called to Yvo and me one random afternoon and said, "Girls! Your father is here."

What? My sister and I ran toward the front door. There he stood, the man I had been starting to forget. I was overjoyed to see him after a year of absence, and dazzled by his huge afro, chocolate skin, electric smile, and soft, sweet cognac eyes. They were shining at me now, and I hugged him as tight as I could.

I glanced back at Mom to check how she felt about this, and I was relieved to see her beaming at him. "Your father is going to live with us from now on," Mom informed us with no other explanation. Whatever made my mother flee with us in the dark of night a year ago had apparently been resolved. I was way too young to understand the emotional adjustments and negotiations that went on between my parents. I was just thrilled to have him back in the house. We moved out of Fargo Street, into a two-bedroom in the Lakewood apartment complex. Yvo and I had bunk beds and shared one room, while Mom and Dad had the other. Our furniture was utilitarian and basic.

At the time, Mom worked at an assisted-living facility and Dad got a job at the Budget car rental at the Raleigh-Durham International Airport. While they worked, we were watched over by family members. All I knew was that I was surrounded by love. Mom made the Lakewood apartment feel like home with decorative touches like fresh flowers by the window and a rainbow array of spice jars on the kitchen counter. Even if it was small, the apartment was always immaculate and smelled amazing. Every home my mother has lived in holds the same two aromas: the scent of her cooking and the fragrance of her perfume, a beautiful floral mixed with amber and vanilla. She has always worn this scent, which remains in my memory and my consciousness. Even the tiniest trace of it makes me think of her—as an adult I've walked into my sister's house, detected a hint of vanilla, and asked, "Was Mom just here?"

My parents' relationship during those years was the happiest I can remember. We were a family, and we needed each other. In that first year, my mom had to have abdominal surgery (for uterine fibroids, as I learned later). My father brought her home after the operation. As she walked into the house, she had one hand on her stomach, and one arm around my father's neck. He helped her walk up the steps slowly, surely. As frightening as it was to see Mom in pain, the sight of my father's comfort and support gave me a warm, secure feeling.

One memorable day, my father took me to work with him. He drove the Budget shuttle bus that picked people up at the different terminals. I sat in the shuttle bus one row back and diagonally across from him so I could see him (and he could see me). All day, I watched him greet people, help them on and off the shuttle. I was fascinated by the lever he pushed to open and close the door. You'd think a four-year-old would get bored sitting on a bus all day. Not me. I loved watching my father do his job. He was making people's lives better, easing their stress. And they showed how much they appreciated him with a smile and warm thank-you. I was bursting with pride.

From what I saw, Mom and Dad were enjoying our life together, too. There was no apparent tension at all between them. But Edwin was increasingly unhappy about living in Durham. I overheard enough of their discussions to know that he wanted to leave and take us with him. Edwin had picked up certain ideas about the behavior of American girls. He thought they were wayward, got pregnant out of wedlock, and were sinful. He considered any woman who lived alone—not with a father or a husband—to be wild. That included Mom during her year without him, and possibly Yvonne and me when we got older, if we stayed in America.

Along with being a pastor, Edwin was a traditionalist: the husband made the decisions for the family and the wife obeyed. However, Mom was *not* a traditional Nigerian wife.

"God told me to go back to Nigeria, and God doesn't want me to be separated from my wife and children," Edwin told Susan.

"I will wait for a message from God to call me home to Nigeria," she countered. "If that happens, I'll go with you. If it doesn't, we're staying, with or without you."

God did not deliver to Mom the same message he was giving my father, and she continued to defy him by refusing to leave. This only increased his demands that we all return to Nigeria.

My aunts came by as usual a few times a week to sit around the kitchen table and talk. Winifred, my mother's oldest sister, told her, "You can go against your husband's word or get a divorce, but people won't like it." By "people," Winifred meant the local Nigerian community, our family, and friends. Culturally, divorce was just not an option. It dishonored both the families. For Nigerians, family honor was everything. Even if a married couple hated each other's guts, they stuck it out or they'd be ostracized from the community.

"I don't care what people say," replied Susan, defiant.

"What kind of life will you have without a husband?" asked Winifred. "How will you support them on your own?"

"I'll figure it out," said Mom.

"You're playing a dangerous game, Susan," warned Winifred.

It wasn't the first or last talk of certain doom between Mom and her sisters. Their concern was real, though. I even felt it as a little kid. On the line was Mom's reputation and the respect of our social circle. Susan didn't have *any* American friends. If she was rejected by the insular immigrant community, she would have no one except us. Also hanging in the balance was Yvo's and my future. As a small child, I wasn't told that if my father left, he would stop contributing financially to our family. Mom would be completely responsible for the cost of raising us.

One sunny, beautiful North Carolina day, I heard my parents arguing in their bedroom. My father yelled, "What are you going to do alone in America with two girls? Who's going to want to be with you?"

Next, my father came into the living room where Yvo and I were playing, kissed us on the head, and said goodbye, like he did when he left for work, and left through the front door. Sensing something was off, I found Mom sitting on the edge of her bed, crying.

"What's wrong, Mommy?" I asked, sitting on the floor at her feet. I'd never seen her cry before, and the sight was alarming.

"Dad is gone," she said.

It didn't seem real. I remember looking out the window to make sure it was still the same view of trees and sky or if the whole world had changed. The sun was still shining, but inside my head, it was dark and cloudy.

He'll be back, I thought. He'd just shown up before. He could walk in the door at any second. "Is this real?" I asked.

"It's real," she said. "And he's not coming back this time."

Edwin returned to Nigeria for good the following year. His parting words—that Mom would be all alone in America—were a warning and a curse. That cruelty made it easier for her to let him go.

I wouldn't see my father again for eight years.

Our father's abrupt departure was a huge blow to Yvo, but perhaps not as much of a shock as it was for me. She was seven, old enough to pick up on undercurrents that I missed. Even if she knew that trouble was brewing, she felt as miserable about his abrupt departure as I did. One minute our father was with us, and the next he was gone. All I understood at four was that I'd lost someone I loved.

I noticed an immediate change in Mom after he'd left. She was sad for a while—had lower energy than usual, and I'd occasionally catch her crying—but eventually she seemed lighter, happier, more determined than ever to build a life in Durham. She started to wear makeup and get her nails done, things my conservative, religious father never would have allowed.

I overheard Mom tell Winifred, "I'm free. I can do whatever I want." For her, sending my father away meant she could choose her own destiny, whether that meant wearing shorter skirts, pursuing a career, or making the decisions for her daughters.

My aunt's warning that Mom would be ostracized by the Nigerian community never came to pass. Why would it? She was feeding them all, and our people are not going to turn down great cooking. When you're an immigrant, you yearn for your community, your culture, and your traditions. Our constant guests were lured by the flavor of home, the conversation about the old days in the village, and news from back home.

Our Lakewood apartment became *the* gathering place for every celebration. Each Christmas, our house was packed with aunts, uncles (Mom had four brothers; three of whom eventually came to live in the Durham area), other families, and friends. Our table groaned under huge ceramic platters of rice, stews, okra soup, plantains, and assorted meats. I remember the press of bodies, my uncles' leather jackets, the sound of wine bottles being uncorked and people laughing, the singing of Oliver De Coque and Nigerian highlife music, the wink of string lights, and the flash of gold chains. There was a buzz in the atmosphere and good vibes from being together.

In America, Mom bucked small traditions along with the big ones. For example, when she was growing up, the tradition was that her father, Albert, ate first and took the best parts of the meat. The next oldest would then choose his or her pieces, and so on down the line until the youngest child in the house was served. In a party situation, the eldest guests eat first. The kids are told to wait in the living room for their turn. Susan always felt like that order wasn't right. So at all the holiday parties she hosted, and at every postchurch Sunday dinner, Mom flipped the script. "My kids eat first," she said. "They deserve the best." I felt privileged and special as I filled my plate before anyone else.

Mom put us first in every way. She chose our freedom over her marriage. Mom was different from the other mothers in the Nigerian community. They answered to their husbands. Mom answered to no one. I've never seen her cower to any man, which served her well. Mom was the queen, and no king would tell her what to do. She was certainly my queen. Mom didn't bend for anyone. I've never seen her give in.

She might've become *too* independent. She loved her siblings, but she never changed her mind if they challenged her. Just the opposite. She'd dig in harder. A child needs to see adults love and support each other, as well as disagree, argue, compromise, and make up. A child learns to see the world from both parents' different perspectives. For me, only one point of view mattered—my mother's. (Thank God my husband is so patient with me, because, before I got married, I had no idea what compromise looked like.)

During my childhood, I didn't see many examples of happy relationships around me. My aunts were single or in distant marriages. Culturally, Nigerian women typically marry older men for the financial stability, either by choice or because their parents make them. Marriage isn't usually rooted in love; it's a practical decision. Many of the Nigerian girls I knew growing up followed that pattern and married some-one ten or more years older than they were. Mom and Edwin bucked convention by being the same age and marrying for love. But they were swept up in the romance of love, American style, the fairy tale of find-ing your Romeo, your Juliet. The fact that they still split up despite being in love chipped away at Mom's idealism. Once that process began, it didn't stop. She became a hardened realist. She never thought she'd be a single parent of two girls, but that's what came to pass. I don't begrudge Mom for doing what was right for her and what she thought was right for us: staying in America, even if she had to sacrifice her mar-riage to do it. I often reflect on how brave it was for her to go it alone. But I felt my father's absence every single day.

It's probably not too surprising that I ended up marrying a man who shares my father's nickname and resembles him. My husband, Edward (Eddie), has my father's deep chocolate skin and those rare cognac eyes. When people ask me, "What's your favorite feature of Eddie's?" I don't have to think about it. Eddie's eyes remind me of my dad's, and he passed on those eyes to Karter and Kamrynn. It's also possible their co-gnac eyes were passed down from my father, through me. It's a very strange thing to see pieces of my father, a man who was not in my life, in my children. Stranger still, I love those pieces despite my conflicted feel-ings about the man.

When I watch my husband with Kamrynn, I feel nostalgic for an experience I've never had. Kam is a daddy's girl. If I say no to her, she immediately goes running to Eddie. Eddie gathers her up and she puts her little arms around his neck. Love lights them up. In his arms, she stops crying (not that they were real tears; she just wanted his attention) and they smile at each other like a besotted pair. I watch her sit on his lap while he's working on the computer, swinging her foot in her baby Nikes, as content as can be. Their mutual adoration melts my heart.

I wish I'd had that.

As glad as it makes me that they have such a sweet relationship, as grateful as I am to have found a good husband who is a devoted father, my envy runs right alongside those positive emotions, and often takes the lead. *Must be nice to have a dad*, I think. Or, as I observe them together, I say to Eddie, "Can't relate." We laugh at the joke, but it's also my truth.

I believe in the phenomenon of the butterfly effect, the theory that a small action (a butterfly flapping its wings in North America) can cause a large impact far away and later on (a typhoon in Asia). My parents' separation, and my mother's decision to stay in America and raise us alone, changed the trajectory of my life. I missed growing up with a father, but who I am and what I am would never have been if Edwin stayed in the picture. Mom applied a lot of pressure on us throughout our lives. But that pressure would have been ten times worse — and far more limiting — under Edwin's traditional, conservative authority.

I am myself because of my mother's painful decision to let my father go. As hard as that was for all of us, the truth is, I'm grateful for it.

Although I've asked her many times, Mom hasn't told me everything about her split with Edwin. "He was very strict," she said. "He never would have let you have a career. You would have been married off as a teenager."

That explanation was undoubtably true, but I knew there was more to the story than that. I wouldn't see the full picture for years to come, but when I did, I was even more grateful that Mom made the choice she did, risking personal and social disaster for our freedom.

TWO

The Narrow Path

Mom's first order of business as a modern, independent woman was to figure out how to be the breadwinner. As she often said, "Some people have jobs, some have careers." To have a career, she needed to go to college, and she decided to go into nursing. It was a viable option. Other immigrants in the North Carolina Nigerian community became nurses, so she knew it was possible. It was also something she'd dreamed about for a long time, ever since she was a child in wartime.

To this day, my mother still remembers the whistling sound of bombs dropping, the concussive force when they exploded, the smell and screams of people burning alive. The stories about my family's trials through the Nigerian Civil War, also known as the Biafra War, were told and retold at gatherings throughout my childhood. They frightened and awed me, so different from the life I experienced. The war broke out in mid-1967 and lasted until early 1970. It was ignited by ethnic and religious persecution between the main tribes of Nigeria (the Yoruba in the west, Hausa in the north, and Igbo in the southeast), government turmoil with one military coup after another, and the battle to control the Niger Delta oil fields. The Igbo of the Biafra region—my people—sought to separate and form their own country. As a consequence, the Nigerian military squeezed the region, cutting off the food supply. Millions died from starvation and bombs.

My mother was four or five when the bombing started. We aren't sure exactly how old she was, because family documents, including birth certificates, were lost in flight and in raids. Because her father, Albert, served in an advisory role in the Nigerian army, he had access to intelligence briefings from the generals and was tipped off that the battle was coming to their village of Nimo, in Anambra State. In the middle of the night, the no-nonsense matriarch of our family, my great-grandmother Mmgbeoye Ogoadigbomma (everyone called her Nne, pronounced *en*-nay), and grandmother Angela fled their village with eight of her nine children. The oldest son, Fred, was in the army.

They had a driver and left by car—Nne, Angela, and all the kids squeezed into it—but it quickly ran out of gas and was abandoned. The family was forced to continue on foot through the woods and along the side of the roads in search of sanctuary. They could walk only at night, because planes swept the area during the day. If they'd been spotted, they would have been shot or bombed. During daylight, they hid in the empty buildings of abandoned villages.

For weeks, my aunt Winifred carried Mom on her back; Angela and her older children carried the youngest ones on theirs. The women balanced parcels of whatever possessions they brought with them on their heads as they passed through bombed villages, stepping around decaying bodies and rivers of blood. My aunts have told me stories about their walking by decimated houses that had been reduced to rubble, seeing the blackened skeletal remains of an entire family sitting around the scorched dinner table.

Planes came without warning, even at night, flying low over the ground, shaking the trees, kicking up blinding dust, the noise splitting their ears. As soon as my family heard one coming, they would scatter into the woods and frantically dig trenches in the dirt to hide in. When the roar of flames died down, the next sound they heard was the cries for help from the survivors. But there wasn't much anyone could do, and most of the time, the survivors didn't last long.

Passing through one town, my family came upon a naked, malnourished, crying child covered in soot and ash. He was around my mother's age, the sole survivor of a raid. My grandmother Angela quickly discovered that the child was deaf, although it wasn't clear if he was born that way or if his eardrums had been damaged in an explosion. She gathered him up, wrapped him in a piece of her own filthy clothing, and carried him in her arms as they kept going. They didn't know this boy and certainly didn't need the burden of caring for another child. But they couldn't leave a traumatized child alone among the remains of every person he'd ever loved. No one knows what became of that child.

Eventually, Nne, Angela, and the kids reached a tiny village deep in the woods, far away from any towns or cities that were the prime targets for the raids. My grandmother knew some people there and they were allowed to shelter in relative safety until the war was over. Miraculously, they all made it through in one piece. The family reunited back in Nimo, where they remained until the first wave of Nigerian immigrants arrived in America and other parts of the world in the late 1970s.

Although the war has been over for more than fifty years now, the scars haven't entirely faded. The three main tribes of Nigeria are still divided by different languages, customs, attitudes, demeanors, and rituals. Some of the same conflicts that started the Biafra War continue to cause problems in Nigeria today. Although Nigerian expatriates in the diaspora gravitate toward each other, we are highly aware of which tribe we come from, and we prefer to marry and befriend those in our own.

Mom's experiences of witnessing the suffering of others and feeling powerless to help stayed with her, and inspired her dream of being a healer. She enrolled in Durham's North Carolina Central University, a historically Black college and university (HBCU), to get her bachelor's degree in nursing. When I was around five years old, I sat next to her in her classes with my coloring books. I remember being transfixed by all the glass tubes and pipettes in her chemistry class. I attended her graduation ceremony, cheering louder than anyone when she accepted her diploma. She worked so hard; nothing was ever given to her. She was my role model. I wanted to achieve like her, and for her, to pay her back for what she did for us.

The path to the first degree in our family, Mom's BSN, began in that small, humble apartment at the Lakewood housing complex, an unlikely launch pad for the academic achievements that continue to define us.

Although my mother raised me, in a way I feel like I raised her, too. I've been there for all *her* milestones. When she got her college degree. When she got her first master's degree. When she got her second master's and walked in a graduation ceremony, carrying a candle and wearing all white. Needless to say, she was there when I accepted my degrees—*all four of them* (but who's counting?)—as well as Yvo's ceremonies. Mom often said, "We are all we have," and being there for each other to celebrate our victories meant the world to me, to us.

As for her daughters' path to success in America, Mom set her sights high. It wasn't subtle. When Dad left, Mom wasn't truly ostracized, but in our community, people talk. Without a father in the picture, wagging tongues started predicting our doom. Mom sat Yvo and me down at the table and said, "Girls, when you grow up, you're going to be a doctor, lawyer, or maybe an engineer. Otherwise, you're not accomplished."

"Yes, Mommy," we replied.

"So what do you want to be when you grow up?" she asked, eyeing us expectantly.

Yvo said, "I want to be a doctor!"

I said, "I want to be a lawyer!"

"You are my daughters, and you will be a doctor and a lawyer. Let's pray on it."

She took out her ever-ready rosary—she was Roman Catholic—and we got on our knees and prayed to God that we would have the strength and courage to follow our mother's dreams.

The script was written for us, and we replayed the scene over and over.

"Good! And how will you become a doctor or a lawyer?" she asked.

"By going to school and getting an education."

Our job was to chase success. Nothing else was acceptable. I never questioned, I just tried to live up to my mom's demands. She knew what was best for me.

Once, I came home from preschool and said, "When I grow up, I want to be a clown!"

Mom laughed as any parent would, then she got dead serious. "You will *not* be a clown," she said. "You will be a doctor or a lawyer. Maybe an engineer."

"Yes, Mommy," I said.

"Say it."

"I will be a doctor, lawyer, or engineer," I replied.

"Good," she said, sounding almost relieved.

Nigerians believe in the "power of the tongue." As the saying goes, "As a man thinketh, so shall he become." Nigerian parents tell their children what to do. They put their children on the narrow path—become a doctor-lawyer-engineer, get married, have kids—and don't even speak of another one. It's a deep form of manifesting. They speak life into us.

Susan was taught to emphasize education from her father, Albert. Unlike most of the residents of Nimo who spoke only Igbo, he could speak the language of many Nigerian tribes. His education and intelligence got him far. He was a high-ranking captain in the Nigerian police force.

Albert wanted all his kids to get an education—*especially* the women. During that era, a woman's highest expectation was to get married and bear children. So his pushing his daughters to go to college was revolutionary. Aunt Winifred was the first woman of Nimo to get a bachelor's degree.

It might have been unusual for Albert to push for women's education in Nigeria back then. But for the first wave of Nigerian immigrants who came to America, attaining an education was the whole point. As soon as government incentive programs made it easier for them to pursue degrees outside the homeland, Nigerians came to the United States in droves. In 1978, the year my mother first arrived in California, there were only twenty-five thousand Nigerian-born immigrants in the US. By 2018, that number had grown to over four hundred thousand.[*] During those forty years, Nigerians in America have been kicking ass.

Nigerian Americans have a higher level of educational achievement than any other racial or ethnic group in the US.[†] More than 61 percent of Nigerian Americans twenty-five and older have a bachelor's degree or higher (twice the rate of the US general population), and 29 percent have graduate degrees, compared to 11 percent of the rest of the country. I know what you may be thinking: *Here goes Wendy bragging about her degrees again!* No, not at all. There is an old saying that you can't know where you're going unless you know where you come from. Well, this, my friends, is where I come from.

As of 2013, one-quarter of Black Harvard Business School students are Nigerian.[‡] Only 5 percent of US doctors are Black; 77 percent of them are Nigerian.

Then there are the economics that surround being Nigerian in America: contrary to what many might believe for a Black immigrant population, the Nigerian poverty rate is lower than the national rate. The median annual household income of Nigerian Americans is about 11 percent higher than the US average. Thirty-five percent of Nigerian American households earn at least ninety thousand dollars per year.

Why are the numbers so good? Because *every* Nigerian immigrant of Mom's generation demanded that their children rack up advanced degrees. One master's was okay. Two MAs were better. But an MD, JD, and/or a PhD was better still. Mom wasn't unique in pushing for our academic

---

[*] "Nigerian Diaspora in the United States." Migration Policy Institute, 2015.
[†] "Detailed Look at Sub-Sahara African and Caribbean Ancestry." United States Census Bureau, 2017.
[‡] Chua, Amy; Rubenfeld, Jeb. *The Triple Package: How Three Unlikely Traits Explain the Rise and Fall of Cultural Groups in America.* Penguin, 2014.

achievement, but her relentlessness had an edge to it. It was about more than just family pride and financial security. For Mom, our success would be her redemption.

Although Mom was accepted in the Nigerian community, and the Igbo community, which was a small world inside a small world, plenty of people were still talking about her behind her back and predicting that her decision to split from Edwin would be a disaster for all of us. Mom knew just how bad it was thanks to her favorite younger brother Hyke (sounds like "bike"). He kept her in the loop about what people were saying.

In the family order of Mom and her eight siblings, Mom was number six, and Hyke was number eight. The two had a fierce bond. After Edwin left, Hyke became a bigger presence in our lives. To my eyes, he was a man's man. Over six feet tall with a sturdy build, and a slightly crooked grin that made you smile back, he had a confident, masculine energy that made you feel safe. Women picked up on it, and he could always find someone to take him in. Between girlfriends, he lived with us.

According to family lore I picked up by listening to the adults talk around the kitchen table and at parties (Nigerians have only two topics of conversation, family history and politics), Mom was a tomboy and she cut up as much as her three younger brothers in Nimo. When they stole my grandfather Albert's car, for example, Mom was the one steering the car while the brothers pushed it out of the family compound, a cluster of small houses with a square border wall around them.

Uncle Hyke had a habit of breaking Albert's strict rules. One rule was to always be inside the compound walls by a certain time each night. At the appointed hour, Albert locked the entry gate. If anyone didn't make it home in time, they would have to find someplace else to sleep. Hyke's logic was, if he came home past curfew, he'd just scale the gate. One night he tried it. My grandfather shot him in the back with a bow and arrow.

Nigerians parents do not play when it comes to their kid obeying their rules. Their word is law, and if a child breaks that law, he or she will face consequences. Albert loved all his children, but he was a force to be reckoned with. As a police captain, he was determined not to let any of his kids turn into the kind of people he spent his career arresting. He was also an excellent marksman and knew where to aim the arrow to avoid causing any serious damage. Hyke learned his lesson. He never crossed Albert again.

Albert's wife, Angela, didn't go easy on her kids, either. All of five foot five, she would climb onto a table so she could give a good punch to her six-foot-two sons. Once, when Mom was around seven, Angela gave her and all the kids the equivalent of a quarter to spend at a big, annual food bazaar. Mom ran through the bustling market and got in line at her favorite food seller's table. When it was her turn, my mother dropped her money into a box on the table and reached to take a plate of food. The food seller started yelling at her. "What are you doing?" she said.

"I put the money in the box," replied Mom.

"You're supposed to put it in my hand!"

It seemed like a minor procedural squabble. She was just a hungry, excited kid. But the lady was pissed, and she yelled loud enough for Angela to hear. Instead of taking her daughter's side and telling the food seller to calm down, Angela beat the heck out of her daughter, in front of everyone there.

"Mommy, I didn't do anything!" Mom protested. "I put the money in the box! She's yelling over nothing!"

"You shouldn't have done anything in the first place to make her yell," Angela replied.

The incident had a lifelong impact on my mother. She vowed that if she ever had daughters of her own, she'd never yell at them in front of a stranger or take someone's side against them, even if they were 100 percent in the wrong. Mom lived up to that childhood vow. She never yelled at my sister or me in public nor took someone else's side over ours.

Growing up, I received the occasional spanking, but I never got slapped in public or shot with an arrow. Luckily.

During my early childhood, I would never have broken the rules. I stayed on the narrow path Mom set me on, because I knew how important it was to her that my sister and I lived up to her expectations.

At all those parties at our house, the adults talked openly in front of me, and my big ears took it all in. No one was as candid with Mom about local gossip as Hyke. Once, I overheard him tell her, "Edwin's people are saying you're going to go crawling back to him. They say the girls are going to get pregnant and drop out of school at fourteen. They're all waiting for you to fail."

Her response was, "Let them talk." She was determined to pull off a miracle and prove everyone all wrong.

As a parent, I have read articles in American magazines about how you can help a child find their passion and figure out what they want to do in life. In Nigerian culture, the parent decides, and the child obeys. If a child is rebellious, Nigerian parents will either beat it out of them or refuse to talk to them until they fall in line.

My grandparents certainly kept my mother in line, using strict tactics. And it followed that I was raised not to challenge or contradict my mother about anything, including her prediction that we would be successful. I can't tell you how many times I heard people say to her, "You can't raise two girls on your own." She never gave into their dire predictions, and reinforced her expectations of us by simply saying, "My daughters, you *will* be successful."

Like Mom, I expect my kids to do what I say. I expect them to be successful. But I want them to define their own paths for themselves. Like Mom, I expect the kids to be respectful of their elders. But unlike my mother (and grandmother), I encourage them to set their own boundaries. For example, I don't force my kids to give an auntie or uncle (what we call any older person) a hug if they don't want to. They should always be polite, but saying hello is enough. It might seem like a small thing to let my kids determine the level of affection they choose to give. But independent thinking starts with making small choices. Today they have autonomy about whom to hug. Tomorrow they'll have autonomy over their careers and marriages (within reason).

Mom was old-school about children being unequivocally obedient. She didn't grant us any autonomy. Our success on the narrow path was so important to her. Since she was all we had, it was important to us. My biggest fear in life was letting her down. Just the thought of it gave me a horrible feeling in my stomach.

No matter what, I would become the girl, and the woman, and the lawyer she expected, demanded, me to be.

THREE

Welcome to the Good Life

*T*he Christmas I turned six, Santa Claus knocked on our door. The *real* Santa, with a beard and everything. He gave my sister a life-size Black doll that looked just like her. He gave me . . . honestly, I can't remember. I was just blown away with happiness that Santa Claus came to our own apartment to see us.

And if that wasn't enough, Santa said, "There's another special surprise for you girls."

Yvo and I were beyond excited. What could possibly be better than this? Santa left and we begged Mom to tell us about the surprise.

She grinned. "Pack your bags, we're going to Disneyland!"

We *freaked out*, screaming, running in circles. It was the best news I had ever heard.

The same day, we drove to the airport and flew to Los Angeles. It would have been faster and easier to just drive to Disney World in Orlando, Florida, from North Carolina. But the longer journey to glamorous California felt extra special. We did it all. We went on all the rides. We visited the Walk of Fame on Hollywood Boulevard and found the stars for our favorites, like Michael Jackson and Elizabeth Taylor. Even though Susan lived in a Nigerian bubble, she appreciated some American culture, and went out of her way to expose us to it.

How on earth did she make that happen while raising two little kids all on her own? I don't know. But it was the. Best. Christmas. Ever. The whole time, I remember feeling *rich*. I kept thinking, *What? This is* my *life?* Just as Mom gave us love, a home, food, family, goals, she gave us the precious feeling of wealth.

We were always well dressed and well groomed. Appearances mattered to Mom. Her style inspiration came from the one sister who still lived in Nigeria, Cordelia, number three in the birth order. Mom spoke of her with affection and reverence. She was my favorite "character" when the family gathered and told their stories. Everyone adored her. She was the most beautiful sister (Mom being the second). From a young age, she was groomed to marry well and elevate the family's status.

She achieved that objective by marrying a captain in the military. In Nigeria, the military runs the country. So her husband was the status equivalent of, say, the chief of staff for a US senator. She married him for the accolades, and although his military side was with the opposition (his side of the military fought against the Igbos during the Biafran war), she loved him and obeyed him. Along with rank and power, he had wealth and everything that went with it: influence, chauffeurs to drive his big German cars, cooks, and a big house on a protected military base. A humble girl from Nimo, Cordelia was swept up into a luxurious fairy-tale life, like Cinderella or Princess Diana.

When Susan was nine — several years after the war — Cordelia invited her to come live with her and her rich husband at the military base. Angela had no problem letting her daughter go. It wasn't unusual to send children away from home if they could have a better life somewhere else. Angela had her hands full with the three mischievous sons. Susan spent all her time with her brothers and she might become more feminine if she lived with Cordelia. Plus, Susan would get to enjoy Cordelia's cushy life, get a great education, and stay safe on the military base.

Susan idolized Cordelia. When the two of them went to the market, they got dressed up in chic, pricey outfits with layer upon layer of gold jewelry. The chauffeur drove them in a spotless Mercedes with a military escort, blinking lights, sirens, the whole deal. A presidential motorcade just to go shopping. For a nine-year-old, it was thrilling. Cordelia was more affectionate, loving, and attentive than Angela, and Susan appreciated that. She stayed with her beloved sister for seven happy years until she finished school.

Clearly, Cordelia was Mom's everything, and if my mother loved her, then I did, too, even if I was too young to remember meeting her. "She never wore the same outfit twice and dressed up even if she didn't leave the house," Mom would say whenever the conversation turned toward her at family parties. "Cordelia got her hair done every single day, and she would wear it down when driving around in her Mercedes to show off." I thought of Cordelia as our family's very own princess. "All her clothes were custom-made of only the finest fabrics. What you put on your body is as important as what you put into it, Wen. Remember that." I grew to fantasize about Cordelia's fairy-tale existence, and how she embodied the good life.

As a people, Nigerians tend to be extra. This is never more evident than in how we dress. The majority of Nigerians wear custom-made clothes. In Nigeria, tailors bill over $8 billion in sales each year and are a highly respected class of society. The Nigerian clothing industry generates $19 billion annually. That's a lot of *aso ebis* (traditional Nigerian garb)!

The bolder the colors, the better. Unpredictable combinations and patterns and embellishments? Bring it on. Whenever I see a Western woman in a chunky, coral, or beaded statement necklace, I wonder if she realizes the look originated in West Africa. Nigerians practically invented layering statement necklaces. It's not just about flash, though. Dressing well is about pride. Mom always said, "If you look shabby, people will assume you are a shabby person. If you look put together, they'll assume that you respect yourself and that they should respect you."

Mom didn't have Cordelia's money, but she still managed to be super fashionable, whether she wore traditional Nigerian attire or her usual Western clothing. Her style can be over-the-top. Her *geles*—intricately folded head ties—really stand out in their vibrant green, yellow, and orange. If you walked into a party full of women in geles and spotted the biggest and brightest one from clear across the room, it would be my mother's.

It's popular among Nigerians to "dress to match." We love color-themed parties and nights out. A group of friends will wear the same color gele when out together so people can see how united they are. On every holiday, my whole family color coordinates. This past Mother's Day, we all wore pink. On the Fourth of July, we all wore red, white, and blue. When we go overseas, our swimsuits match one another so I can spot my kids in the pool. Eddie and I are always conscious about how our outfits look side by side, and we always dress in complementary colors—I'm not sure why we do this, it's just our thing. The attention paid to color and coordination isn't just to avoid clashing in photos. It's so we look polished and harmonious as a family.

Just as Cordelia dressed Mom, and Mom dressed me, I make sure my kids are stylish and neat. Mom always said, "You can't look like a million bucks when your kids look dirty." You don't want cleanliness to prevent kids from being kids, but they can still look sharp.

It's not about being designer conscious. It's about my being the parent. I was raised that the kids should always be at the same level as the parents. If I dress in Chanel, my kids can have some high-end pieces, too.

As kids, we always had the nicest clothes, the freshest sneakers. My hair was always done. Mom bought us the most amazing birthday gifts. When I was nine or ten, she gave me a brand-new shiny hot pink twelve-speed mountain bike with white and black trim. Receiving that gift was the first time I cried tears of joy. Back then, I wasn't wondering whether Mom was saving or being responsible with her income. I only knew that I wanted for nothing. However, that doesn't mean Mom spoiled us. She made sure that we understood that the good life was conditional. We received nice things from her when we upheld our end of the bargain by meeting her unwavering expectations. And if we didn't clear her high bar, we were denied the things we loved and wanted the most.

For instance, I *loved* getting my braids done. Mom knew that all too well. One day when I was six, Mom sat me down when I came back from a morning at catechism school and said, "Did you learn your prayers?"

"Yes, Mommy," I said. (Not exactly true. I tended to drift into day-dreaming and had only a fuzzy memory of the lines.)

"Recite the Lord's Prayer," she requested.

The Lord's Prayer is only five awkward-sounding sentences. I should have been able to recite it, but I'd completely forgotten everything but the amen at the end. After I made a couple of weak attempts to fumble through it, Mom had had enough.

She said, "Wen, you are not going to get your hair done until you memorize the Lord's Prayer word for word."

I *loved* getting my hair done. I *needed* to get my hair done. So this was a huge blow. I gave her some pushback like, "Are you kidding me?"

She was not kidding. "Now you have to memorize the Hail Mary, too. Word for word."

I had the two prayers on a piece of paper, just eight sentences (and two amens) total, but the language was weird, and it didn't flow off the tongue. I stayed up all night, though, studying to get it right.

Mom quizzed me every morning for three days until—miracle of miracles—I finally got both prayers right. True to her word, Mom took me to get my hair done that very afternoon, and what a relief and joy that was. Nowadays, parents might take away a kid's phone or toy, some precious object they value, to punish them or get them to do something. My mother knew what was important to me—she had instilled the value of looking good early on. So she didn't need to take away a toy to get me in line. She withheld my braids.

The importance of having nice things and getting our braids done wasn't only about being extra or presenting well to the judgmental Nigerian community or meeting her expectations. It had to do with Mom's particular brand of manifesting. She only spoke of aspirations, not fears. She dressed and lived for the life she wanted. She didn't save and scrimp like someone who expected to be poor forever. She believed that by living well, we would make the good life happen.

I'm on board with this Nigerian style of parenting. Kamrynn just started school, and every three weeks, a stylist comes to the house and braids her hair. Just like I have a stylist, so does she. I am role modeling and teaching that appearances matter.

Still, possessing all the clothes and glamour of the good life doesn't really protect you from bad outcomes. This was proven to us on what I think of as one of the saddest days of Mom's life. It started like a typical day at home. Mariah Carey was playing on the stereo. I was playing on the floor of the living room. Mom casually answered the phone and listened to the speaker on the other end. While I watched, her face froze. Then she let out a shriek that drowned out the music. I'd never heard her make that sound before or since.

"It's Cordelia," she said flatly. "She's gone."

I was speechless. It was terrifying to see my mother, who didn't seem to be afraid of anything, suddenly crumble. I didn't know what to do. Thinking of that moment still pains me today.

Cordelia's fairy-tale life hadn't lasted forever. She and her husband had five children and they'd been content (if not happy). But sometime before Mom and Edwin split, Cordelia left her husband. She was the first person in our family to get a divorce, and it was a big blow to Mom. The fairy tale she'd dreamed of for herself was shattered. It had the effect of, say, Barack Obama and Michelle breaking up, as in, "If they can't make it, love is dead." When Cordelia got divorced, Susan was determined that it wouldn't happen to her because of the shame it brought to the family. Angela could only take so much.

Cordelia was the one who taught Mom to forget about what people said. So when it came time for her to decide to stay in her marriage or leave it, she had Cordelia's example to guide her.

And then, a few years later, we got that call. Cordelia was gone. Yvo, then nine, had the presence of mind to ask Mom, "What happened to her?"

While tears ran down her face, Mom told us what she'd learned.

One day, out of the blue, Cordelia felt a strange pain in her gut. She went to the hospital, and the doctors tested her for everything they could think of to figure out the cause of her pain. It wasn't cancer. It wasn't a bowel obstruction. They still didn't know what was wrong with her when she suddenly passed away in her hospital bed two days after being admitted.

"None of it makes sense," said Mom. "A perfectly healthy woman in her thirties gets a stomachache and is dead within forty-eight hours? How could this happen?"

The mysterious circumstances of Cordelia's death made the loss even worse for Mom. More bad news came from Nigeria about her funeral. Per Igbo tradition, the pallbearers carried her casket to the grave site and buried it. The moment that was completed, clouds gathered and the heavens opened. Everyone scattered until the rain stopped, but when they came back, no one remembered which exact plot was Cordelia's. They knew the area, but they couldn't say for sure where she was buried. Not having a place to go to mourn Cordelia devastated the family.

As a young girl, what struck me about the story of Cordelia was how a woman with so much beauty and elegance could just be wiped out. She had all the finer things, but happiness was fleeting. She had wealth, but it didn't keep her safe. The way she passed away hardened Mom. You could have it all, but life wasn't fair. Terrible things happened regardless of whether you followed the rules or broke them. Out of one side of her mouth, Mom told us to marry good Igbo men who would provide for us, and out of the other side, she taught us to be independent women who didn't count on a man for our survival or stability.

The story of Cordelia continues to inspire me to this day. She and Mom are the faces on my Mount Rushmore of women, for their grace, elegance, love of fashion, and no-bullshit attitudes. My own no-nonsense attitude comes from them. I don't know if I love that quality in them because that's who I am, or if they made me this way.

Mom's love of the finer things never dimmed. She aspired to live the good life throughout my childhood, as much as the next Nigerian (meaning, a lot). But she reminded us often after Cordelia passed away, "When you are six feet under, you don't take your handbags or your credit cards. But you will take your education. No one and nothing can take what you've learned."

Even in the face of tragic loss, Mom reinforced her core message to us. By getting advance degrees, we would be protected, we would be safe. A degree is better proof of success than any external sign, like designer clothing and expensive cars. For some cultures, material acquisition might be evidence of one's success. To a Nigerian immigrant, nothing is as admired as the letters "MD" and "PhD" after your name. Cordelia didn't have that safety net, but Mom was determined that Yvo and I would.

FOUR

Us Against the World

When I was seven, we moved from the Lakewood apartment to a second-floor unit in a big white apartment building with black railings so Mom could be closer to work. She had gotten a nursing job at a hospital with a demanding and unpredictable schedule. Some weeks, she worked from 7 a.m. to 7 p.m., which was okay. Sometimes, it was 7 p.m. to 7 a.m., which was rough. I remember Mom coming home from an overnight shift and just collapsing on the bed. If she was really lucky, she'd get the 3 to 11 p.m. shift, which allowed her to see us off to school and pick us up. She didn't intend to do shift work forever. Mom always had her eye on the prize: a director job in hospital administration, where she'd work a traditional nine-to-five schedule and make more money. But until then, she had to work long, crazy hours, sometimes overnight, while we were left alone until morning.

Yvo and I were latchkey kids. Mom was usually around for breakfast, and then she'd see us off to the school bus. In the afternoons, my sister and I would take the bus to our stop, go straight to the apartment, open the door, lock it behind us, and call Mom to say we were safely inside. Yvo, then ten, was in charge of me until Mom got home. She warmed up our dinner, served it, and made sure I ate. She would sit me down and oversee my homework.

After homework, we watched TV. In a way, TV raised us. Our concepts of life toggled between our mother's world and what we saw on television. It gave us a window into how other people lived. When I was growing up, we had *The Fresh Prince of Bel-Air*, *A Different World*, and *Martin*. On all those shows, the father/husband was dark skinned, and the wife/mother was always light skinned. You never saw a family on TV where the mother/wife had dark skin.

Subconsciously, my brain picked up the sitcom message that to be loved and have a family one day, women had to have light skin. Men would only choose a partner who could dilute the skin color in the next generation. It was the same story on music videos on MTV and BET, too. Black female performers didn't get a lot of airplay, and those who were there at all tended to be of a lighter hue. The girls playing the love interests in the videos were always fair skinned or racially ambiguous. Dark-hued girls, like me, were all but invisible. Whenever Yvo and I saw a dark-skinned girl on TV, we *loved* it. The NBC series *In the House* with LL Cool J and Debbie Allen was a favorite of ours because of Maia Campbell. I thought she was the most beautiful girl on earth.

We also logged hours watching medical and legal dramas like *ER* and *Law & Order*, necessary viewing to prepare us for our future careers. I saw myself in the young lawyer characters and said, "I'm going to be like them one day."

When it was time for bed, Yvo would tuck me in and tell me bedtime stories. Yvo's stories weren't from books. She created a universe that was full of everything we wished we had, like a big white house with a picket fence, a mom and a dad who loved each other, a dog, fancy schools. The main characters were cheerleaders and star athletes who drove expensive cars, had tons of friends, and played out minidramas at restaurants and concerts and basketball games.

"Time for sleep," my sister said when my eyes started to shut.

"No, Yvo. Keep going," I begged.

"Okay, Wen. Just a few minutes more."

It wasn't just that Yvo was a gifted storyteller. I could *see* her words, like she was inserting the images in my mind. We did everything together. We were all that each other had in the tiny world of our apartment. It's no wonder we were (and still are) mentally connected. As two little kids who spent so much time without adults, our survival depended on our closeness and togetherness. By telling those Sweet Valley High for Black people stories, we created a vision of a better life. In so doing, we manifested our futures. In fact, everything we talked about in those stories, we eventually got in our adulthoods: fancy schools, nice cars, big houses. We mapped out our lives as children and realized them as adults.

If Mom was my first mother, and Yvo was my second mother (she spent more waking hours with me than Mom did), Hyke was like a surrogate dad, although I can't imagine a real father being as loose with the rules as he was.

I caught chicken pox and had to stay home from school. Mom had to work, so she called Uncle Hyke to babysit. I remember sitting down at the table for breakfast, and he put a steak on a plate in front of me. I asked, "Steak for breakfast?"

"Why not?" he said.

I was supposed to stay in bed, but Hyke said, "Let's go drive around." We got into his car and went all over town, visiting various places where he had some things going on. Wherever we went, people greeted him like visiting royalty. I felt special just being seen with him.

Soon after, Hyke opened a huge convenience store in Garner, North Carolina, between an ice cream store and a barbershop. When Mom had to work, Hyke brought us to hang out at the store. I was literally a kid in a candy store, allowed to take whatever I wanted—beef jerky, Cheetos—right off the shelf and eat it. Or he'd take us next door for ice cream.

"What looks good? Order whatever you want," he said.

"I want a banana split sundae with hot fudge," I said. The works. I think Yvo got the same. Hyke spent thirty dollars and didn't blink.

We sat down at the shop to dig in. I ate some of it, but I kept thinking about an episode of some show on Nickelodeon when the kids had an ice cream fight. I thought it'd be funny to reenact it, right there, right then. So I took a handful of ice cream from my dish and threw it at Yvo's face. She proceeded to dump her sundae on my head. Immediately, I burst into tears. Ice cream fights weren't as hilarious as they looked on TV. The ice cream was sticky, cold, and made a mess of my hair. Yvo started crying her eyes out, too. Mom was going to be furious.

Hyke sized up the situation in an instant. "Come on," he said. "Let's go next door."

With both of us still crying, he took us to the barbershop. After slamming a hundred-dollar bill on the counter, he said to the owner, "Fix them up." We got our hair washed at the men's barbershop, and Mom never found out what happened.

That was Hyke, spoiling us and making sure we were all fixed up. He was amazing, a counterview I yearned for. He wasn't as demanding as Mom, but he wasn't my friend, either. He was a father figure you could have fun with. I always felt safe with him.

One day, Hyke brought us to his girlfriend's house to hang out until Mom got home. We were young and bored, and resented having to stay at this place all afternoon. Not to mention, my sister and I did not like this girlfriend. She had a beautiful garden in her front yard. We took it upon ourselves to trash it. We pulled up the flowers, kicked the dirt around, threw the border rocks. It wasn't a nice thing to do, but we were kids. I felt some guilt about doing it. But not too much.

That night, once we were back home, Hyke called to talk to Mom. My sister and I knew what it was about and waited in fear for the hammer to come down.

Mom gestured us over to her and asked, "Did you girls mess up that woman's garden?"

We said no.

We could hear the girlfriend's voice through the phone, yelling, "I know they did it! No one else was here!" Uh-oh. Stomach drop. Now we were going to get in trouble.

But Hyke said, "They said they didn't do it, so they didn't do it." That ended the discussion. His unquestioning loyalty stuck with me. He knew we were guilty, but he wasn't going to take anyone else's side over ours. He always had our backs, good, bad, and indifferent. Needless to say, his relationship with that girlfriend didn't last long.

I don't know if Mom knew we were lying (Hyke did, and he laughed about it with us years later). If she did know the truth, she wouldn't have sided with a stranger over us in public. In private she would have disciplined us by withholding something we cared about or grounding us. That is how I'm raising my kids. Embarrassment is not part of the discipline package.

Once, Yvo and a girl named Jenna exchanged some words on the bus ride home. Jenna's boyfriend, Damian, a kid way too tall for his age, decided to meddle in their business. He told Yvo if she said something to his girlfriend again, he would clock her. The bus fell silent and suddenly everyone was watching. At our stop, it seemed like every single kid filed off the bus. A crowd formed, surrounding Yvo and Damian, chanting, "Fight . . . fight . . . fight." In a flash, Damian punched Yvo in the nose and broke it. With blood streaming down my sister's face, we ran home, opened the door, and locked it behind us. I was only seven, but I knew first aid from Mom. I did my best to patch her up with gauze and surgical tape. I remember feeling so helpless. Yvo had always protected me, and in that moment, I hadn't been able to protect her.

When Mom walked into the house, she saw Yvo's face and exploded. "Who did this?" she demanded.

We told her the story.

She stormed over to Damian's apartment complex and demanded to speak to his parents. Mom would not allow anyone to hurt her children. Damian's parents apologized, but that wasn't nearly enough for Mom. She decided to press charges. I don't recall how that played out exactly, but I do know that neither Damian nor anyone else in that apartment complex ever messed with Yvo or me again.

Even though Yvo and I had each other's back, and Hyke pitched in, we were often left completely alone without an adult to supervise or protect us. One night when Mom had the night shift, we heard a ruckus right outside our apartment door around 9 p.m. My sister looked through the peephole to check it out.

"Let me see!" I said, crowding up behind her.

She pushed me back. "No, Wen."

"Come on! I want to see," I insisted.

It sounded like two people were having an argument, a man yelling. It was kind of scary, but exciting, too.

Yvo kept shoving me away from the door, but I held my ground. I just *had* to know what was happening.

Then we heard a big boom. Yvo was still blocking me, her eyes still glued to the peephole.

"What's going on?" I asked. My question was punctuated by another loud bang, but this time on our front door. Someone was pounding to get in.

Yvo acted quickly and pulled me away from the door, dragging me behind her into another room. She grabbed the phone and called 911, telling the dispatcher, "We heard gunfire," and then she hung up and immediately called Mom. "Mommy, you need to come home right now," she said. Her tone was level, but there was a hitch in her voice I'd never heard before. She was frightened, and that made me terrified.

We sat on the couch, Yvo holding on to me. She refused to tell me what she saw. By this time, I was petrified and holding on to her just as tight. A few minutes later, we heard sirens and the police arrived on the street outside. Shortly after that, Mom came home and told us to go straight to bed. As if I could sleep!

The next day, when I left the apartment for school, I saw yellow police tape on the neighbor's door directly across from our apartment. I'd figured out the loud argument was between him and his girlfriend. I only learned the gory details by spying on Mom and Uncle Hyke after school when she told him what happened.

"The fight had started when our neighbor's girlfriend wouldn't let him into their apartment," Mom told Hyke. "Yvo heard him yelling, 'I'm going to kill myself!' over and over. Then he took a gun out of his pocket and shot himself in the left side of his chest. He had enough strength to stumble over to our door and banged on it for help. Yvo saw it all through the peephole! She saw him shoot himself. The police found his body on the stairs right outside. We have got to get out of this building."

My sister heard it all, but she pushed me away so I couldn't see and hear the worst of it. She took that trauma for me, and she never told me anything about it.

I'd seen our neighbor earlier that day. He was an average white guy with brown hair. He looked normal, in jeans and a white T-shirt. It was incredible to me that a man I'd seen walking down the street just hours earlier was now gone. Forever. In the aftermath, it gnawed at me. In times of quiet, my young mind circled back to it again and again. I suppose everyone has an experience that introduces them to the harshness of dying. This broke through my consciousness, and it grew into a deep-seated fear of death.

But Yvo had tried to block me from the violence, to keep me in the dark about painful realities. She would play that role for me for my entire life. *Keep Wen safe. Keep Wen happy.* Yvo was like a mini-Mom, imitating the attitude and behavior of our fearless leader. The two of them seemed to have an unspoken agreement to work together to spoil and shield me, to paint a picture of safety and security.

Yvo's nightly stories, I realize now, were part of it. She spun her plots about pretty rich girls whose biggest problem was not getting the right boy to notice her. I always accepted the truth my mom and sister gave me. I believed we *were* rich and safe. But the truth was, we were not rich, and we were not always safe. But we had Uncle Hyke. We had one another. We had our family's unfailing loyalty. Fierce loyalty isn't so much a Nigerian thing as it is a Susan thing. She brought it out in people.

As immigrants, we were vulnerable in ways that I hadn't yet understood (but I would soon enough). But no matter what dangers came knocking on our door, I knew that Mom, Yvo, and Hyke would do whatever they could in their power to keep me safe.

FIVE

The Nigerian Bubble

While we lived in the Lakewood apartment, I was attending Pearsontown Elementary School. I learned to read earlier than any of my classmates, and when I was in second grade, we were assigned little books to read. The teachers would give us a week to finish them. I'd be done in a day.

I always volunteered to read aloud when no one else did. Week after week, I went to the front of the room. One of those times, I was reading a book about baking, showing off my skills, when I stopped abruptly.

"Go on, Wendy," said the teacher, a white woman.

I stared at the next word—"flour"—with increasing anxiety. It wasn't that I didn't know what it meant. I didn't know how to *pronounce* it. Nigeria is a British commonwealth country, and it's official language is English. However, we don't say the words exactly the same way as Americans (or Brits). Americans say "flower" and Nigerians say "floor." In that moment, I forgot which pronunciation was right for the classroom versus at home.

I rolled the dice and restarted the sentence. "Mix a cup of sugar with a cup of floor . . ."

My classmates burst out laughing at me. One burly white boy turned to his blond-haired friend and said, "She's so stupid."

The blond kid replied, "African booty scratcher."

"Yeah, go back to Nigeria," said the first kid.

Everyone laughed, none louder than the African American kids. After what felt like an eternity, the teacher hushed the room and I continued reading, barely getting the words out until I could return to my seat.

I was embarrassed and humiliated, of course. But more than anything else, it was a reminder of what my mother often told us at home: "You're not American." In that moment, I realized she was right.

I came to the US so young I had no recollection of my native land. I was raised in a Western environment. But to the American kids, white and Black alike, I was different. They seemed to be waiting for me to mess up so they could place me outside the circle. The flour incident might sound minor, but I remember it as nothing less than brutal. Whether you're a first gen—raised in America by immigrant parents— or not, every kid wants to fit in. I loved my Nigerian culture at home, but at school, I wanted to be just like everyone else. My mispronunciation of "flour" was another opportunity for my classmates to remind me, "No, you're not one of us. You're different. You don't fit in."

When I unpacked my lunch box at school, kids would say, "What is that *smell*?" It didn't smell bad, just different. But anything other than a peanut butter and jelly sandwich was weird to them. For kids, weird is confusing, and therefore threatening. In the words of the great poet (and rapper) Nasir Jones, "People hate what they don't understand, fear what they can't conquer." I often relate to these lyrics from Nas, especially when I think of my first-gen status, as a child and now.

If any of those American kids came over to my house for a playdate, they would have been overwhelmed with weird. Immigrant homes are like outposts of the nations our parents came from. On the kitchen counter, they would have seen the spices and ingredients from the African market, or if they opened the fridge they might have found goat meat marinating. They would have heard Igbo spoken. If they peeked into our closets, their eyes would pop when they saw the vibrant traditional garb, made for us by Nigerian tailors, that we wore to special occasions at the Nigerian Catholic church, weddings, or traditional ceremonies.

First gens like me know the customs for a country that we might never have visited, and we are taught the traditions of another place, and possibly another time. And those traditions are strictly enforced by our immigrant parents. First gens struggle to define their cultural identity, when in reality, both identities have coalesced to form a new one, an identity only understood by other first gens. We are in essence our own ethnic group.

Listening in on Mom and her siblings talk at all those gatherings was how I learned to speak Igbo. In contrast, my children are not constantly exposed to the language or the stories about the old country like I was. My second-generation children know they're Nigerian, but they aren't steeped in Nigerian culture. When we talk about people and politics (Nigerians' only two topics of conversation), we talk about their American friends and American lives. Eddie and I had a frank conversation recently with our sons about Black Lives Matter and what it means to be a Black man in America. My son Karter made me cry when he said that he hoped to be a unifying figure like Martin Luther King Jr. He dreams of being a great American.

My children don't feel different from their classmates, because they've been raised as Americans. But the overarching experience of being first gen is of fighting against being different while being inherently different. It's loving your culture and being afraid to show it. I adored my mother's food, and come lunchtime, I wanted to eat it. But was a container of spicy, smoky jollof rice worth the bullying? I never would have dared to ask Mom to pack me a "normal" lunch, though. Rejecting her food would have been the greatest insult I could have made.

Mom tended to wear Western clothing, which saved me a lot of torment at school. I had a Nigerian friend whose mom always wore the most beautiful traditional clothing. My friend cried while telling me, "Why can't my mom just wear jeans and a T-shirt?"

Our parents tell us we are not American, even if we were born here and have lived here for our entire lives. Our parents reinforce our between-two-worlds status by keeping us separate. Since we lived in a Nigerian bubble growing up, news about US mass shootings, drug use, and crime seemed to beam in from another planet. "Can you believe how Americans live?" Mom and her siblings would say, as if we didn't live in America ourselves. Elders in the community, including my mother, looked down on what she identified as American behaviors—like a perceived lack of discipline and drive. One of Mom's refrains growing up was, "We can live in America, but don't act like Americans." The message was to stay in our culture, to know that you're a Nigerian and to act like one, no matter what. Put family first. Make no excuses. Stay out of trouble.

I tried my best to avoid being singled out, but I wasn't always successful. The same year as the flour incident, I and two other Black students were kept outside the building as a form of punishment over a minor infraction. One of the others was a boy named Michael, who had brand-new red-and-black Air Jordan 11s. After waiting outside for a long time, Michael told the teacher's assistant who was monitoring us, "I have to go to the bathroom."

The TA, a young white woman with long, black hair, said, "No. You're going to stay right here."

He repeated, "I *really* have to go." You could tell he was serious; his eyes were turning yellow. But she wouldn't allow it.

A minute later, it was too late. "Oh shit," he said.

Michael was wearing jean shorts, and I could see the pee trickling down his leg, right into those fresh, new Jordans. Even though he'd repeatedly said he needed the bathroom, the TA ignored him, which seemed intentionally cruel.

The next day, I asked Michael if he'd told his mother what happened. "Yeah, I did," he said.

"Well, what did she say?"

"She said, 'Next time, listen to the teacher and you won't get punished.'"

His mother took the white woman's side, even though she'd created a humiliating experience that no seven-year-old child deserved.

I told my mother the whole Michael pee story, and when I got to the part about his mom not defending him, she said, "Typical."

It was understandable: living within systemic oppression can wear you down. Still, it had tragic consequences.

Not too long after the pee incident, the same TA kept me outside for some other perceived failure of mine to do exactly what she said. It was a chilly day, and I didn't have a jacket. Shivering, I asked, "Can I please go inside?"

She put her finger in my face and said with surprising anger, "You're not moving an inch. So get used to it." I remember feeling confused and embarrassed, and *cold*. I didn't know what I'd done to make her so furious.

When I got home, I told my mom about it. Let me tell you, there was smoke in the city the next day.

Mom knew how to communicate effectively, and she jumped at the opportunity to do so. (My love for public speaking comes from her.) So she marched into the school for a meeting with the all-white administrative board. "I don't care what my daughter did," she said. "You do not keep a child outside in the cold, put your finger in her face, and speak to her with anger."

The day after that showdown, I approached that TA. "Are we coloring today?" I asked.

"I cannot talk to you unless another teacher is present," she said quietly. Then she ran to find her colleague to answer my question about crayons. I connected the dots: my mother had put the fear of God in her. The TA never spoke to me again unless another teacher was there as a witness.

This isn't an example of helicopter or snowplow parenting. My mother wasn't doing my homework, hovering protectively, or removing obstacles I needed to learn to get around on my own. She was *defending* me, and showing me that I didn't have to fight my battles alone. No matter what,

Mom made sure I knew that she had my back. By knowing her worth, Mom taught me to believe in mine, too. If someone did you wrong, you had the right to confront them and demand accountability. I don't think of myself as a confrontational person. But you can push me only so far before I push back (as fans of *The Real Housewives of Potomac* already know).

Mom saw herself as different from American parents. This was not unique among Nigerian immigrants. Eddie, a first gen, told me a story about the day his family went to Sears to take a portrait one year. The family ahead of them in line was a Black couple with two little kids. Eddie's Nigerian father went on a rant, saying, "Look at them, Black Americans. All they do is have children out of wedlock. They're not married. They don't have jobs." He didn't know these people. He just made crazy assumptions based on nothing. The hate in his voice stuck with Eddie. His dad had contempt for a random couple he'd never met based on his own prejudice. He was hardly alone in holding these biases. A lot of Nigerians of that generation felt the same way.

The tight, insular Nigerian community had created a reinforcing feedback loop. Even though people in my mom's generation have been here since the seventies, they don't have any American friends. I wish Mom hadn't been so discriminatory about my friendships, because it did close off my social pool. But when I was young, I was happy to just be with Mom and Yvo anyway.

The irony for Mom, at least, was that the first American she met when she originally immigrated to the US was an incredible friend to her. If she were to judge all Americans by his standard, she should have adored and trusted them.

The story of Susan's journey was another legendary tale told around the kitchen table growing up. In 1978, my seventeen-year-old mother was encouraged to come to America by her parents with the vague plan of visiting her oldest brother, Fred (the firstborn son in the family), who lived in San Francisco. Maybe she would apply to colleges, and stay on in

California to get a bachelor's degree. She didn't have the money for a plane ticket, but she finagled a free flight from Lagos to JFK Airport in New York City from a Yoruba man—a pilot for Nigerian Airways, she'd been seeing (chastely). From there, she would take a domestic flight from New York to San Francisco and meet Fred at the airport. Fred had already been living in California for several years and knew his way around, which was a good thing, since Susan knew *nothing* about American life.

The flight to New York was uneventful. Susan's pilot friend escorted her to the crew lounge to hang out before her connecting flight to California, then rushed off to prepare for his next route. Using a pay phone—this was decades before cell phones and pagers—Susan called the number she had for Fred. When a voice on the other end came on, she started talking. But it wasn't an actual person. The answering machine had picked up and instructed her to "Leave a message at the beep!"

Susan didn't even know answering machines existed, and it took a second for her to realize the voice was a recording . . . and that it belonged to an American woman. Did Susan have the right number? What if she couldn't reach Fred? What if she landed in San Francisco and he wasn't there to greet her? She tried the number again and again during her six-hour layover. No one answered.

As she became increasingly freaked-out and paced back and forth by the pay phone, a white man in his midthirties standing near her asked, "Is anything the matter? You seem upset."

Mom was tall, shapely, and beautiful (as she says of herself, "I was attractive to all creation"), so her guard went up when this random man began acting interested in her. But after six hours of frustration and anxiety, she needed to vent. "I can't get in touch with my brother," she explained, "and he's the only person I know in America."

The man introduced himself as Philip King. They boarded the plane and continued to talk for the duration of the flight. When they landed,

Phil helped her call the number again, but there was still no answer. He said, "Look, it's your first day in the US. Let's go to my house where you can use my phone and call anyone you want." He told Susan how he had been to Nigeria and was familiar with Nigerian culture. Phil then told Susan, "I want to help you because there are people in Nigeria who have helped me."

Lord, help me, she thought. *This is the only human I know here.* Her only choices were to park herself in the airport and run through dime after dime calling that number, trying to reach Fred, or to go with this seemingly kind stranger who offered her a phone and a place to shower and rest.

"Philip King, I am a child of God, and my father is a police captain," she said. "He taught me police tactics for how to defend myself. Don't fool around with me." She didn't mention that she also had a can of mace in her purse and would not hesitate to use it.

"I just want to help you," he said.

She decided to trust him, got into his car, and rode with him to his five-bedroom town house in Sausalito. Locking the bathroom door securely, she took a shower, ready to use her fists to fight off Phil if it came to that. It didn't. They went out to eat, and he introduced her to Mexican food. After dinner, they drove around his neighborhood and he pointed out the supermarket, the post office, and the shops and schools, while giving her a casual explanation of American life. Back at his town house, he gave her the full tour, including the flower garden in the backyard, and a lengthy tutorial on the answering machine, a black box with two cassette tapes. Now that she had Phil's call-back number for Fred, she left it on his machine.

With no reason to believe otherwise, Susan decided that Phil was okay. All signs pointed to his not being a creep or a murderer. Going by his kindness and generosity, and appearing in her life at exactly the right moment, Susan saw Phil as an angel sent from God to help her. Rosary in hand, she prayed that God would see her through this bumpy arrival and slept deeply on a king-size bed in the luxurious guest room, with the door firmly locked. (He might be an angel, but he was still a man. True to his word, Phil didn't make any stupid moves.)

By the time Fred got her message, twenty-four hours had passed since Susan's arrival in California, and he was going out of his mind with worry, convinced something terrible had happened to his baby sister. Apparently, he'd gone to the airport to get her, but somehow they'd missed each other, and he'd been searching for her ever since.

Fred rushed to Sausalito to pick her up, and she moved in with him and his girlfriend, a woman named Karen, in San Francisco. (It was okay for him to live with a woman, because there's a Nigerian double standard for men and women.) Karen, by the way, was crazy. Even though Fred told her that Susan was his youngest sister—their age difference was sixteen years—Karen had convinced herself that Susan was actually Fred's Nigerian wife. After a week of unbearable tension in the house— dirty looks, unguarded hostility—Karen threw a fit at 4 a.m. and screamed, "I want her out of here! Now!"

Fred was too embarrassed to tell Susan that Karen thought she was his wife, so she was confused as hell by the outburst. But it was clear that Karen was unhinged and that Susan had to leave before the woman got aggressive. Fred helped her pack and took her to a cheap hotel, basically four cinder block walls and a questionable bed, in the Tenderloin, a famously gritty downtown neighborhood.

Fred was more upset than Susan was about being kicked out. He cried and said, "I'm leaving that crazy woman! I'm going to stay here with you."

But Susan didn't want Fred to uproot his life because of her. "Don't worry, I'll figure something out," she said. Mom was just a kid, brand-new to America. Fred was a thirty-three-year-old man with friends and experience. *And yet she was comforting him!* And he left her there. Now she was stranded, on her own, in a dump. I liked my uncle the few times I met him, but when Mom told me this story, I couldn't help thinking, *Damn, Fred. Man up.*

The next day, Susan met her first transexual woman by the hotel pay phone. She was learning new things by the minute in California! Then she got back in touch with her rescuing angel, Phil King, her only other friend there. "I've been abandoned by my brother and I have no idea what I'm going to do!" she said, summing up the melodrama.

Angel Phil swooped in to save the day *again*. He picked her up at the "floozy" hotel (Mom's word) and installed her in his house for the foreseeable future. "You can stay as long as you want," he said.

Phil kept his promise and let Susan live at his house rent-free in exchange for doing his shopping, collecting his mail and newspapers, watering his plants, and turning the lights on and off when he traveled frequently for work as a businessman (Mom can't remember exactly what he did). He also set up an account for her at the local grocery, so she ate for free as well. *And* he paid her four hundred dollars a month to be his house sitter.

When Fred came to Sausalito to check on her soon after, Mom couldn't help but gloat a little. "I *told* you I'd figure it out. I've been in America for two weeks and I've got a job and I'm living in a gorgeous house. You've been here for how many years?"

This is not a love story, by the way. That's not where this is going. Phil was in Mom's life only briefly, but he made a huge impact. He saved her. He was just a good-hearted human who saw someone in need and stepped up to help. If only we all had a Phil King come into our lives at exactly the right moment.

The problem was, he was the only American Mom got to know.

Soon Fred (no longer with the crazy ex) brought Susan into the Nigerian community in San Francisco, and it became her entire social life. Within a year of her arrival, Susan caught the eye of a man named Ambrose at a Nigerian party. Smitten, Ambrose told Fred that he wanted to marry her. He recruited a friend of his named Edwin to tag along one evening on a date with Susan. "I want you to check out my future bride and let me know what you think," Ambrose said.

The evening turned into a double date, with Susan's friend Charlene, at a nightclub. Back in Nigeria, Susan never would have gone out with two men she didn't know. "I had my mace, and I would have sprayed anyone in the face if they got out of line," she always said when she told the story to us. At the club, the bouncer wouldn't let Mom in because she was clearly underage. Edwin went inside, and paid a random woman five dollars for temporary use of her ID for Susan. The ploy worked and the two couples danced all night.

When they left, Edwin gallantly gave Susan his black leather jacket to wear. It smelled great, and Mom took a closer look at Ambrose's friend and liked what she saw. They walked and talked, and she learned that he was a premed student at the University of San Francisco, and a soccer star with dreams of becoming the Nigerian Pelé. The conversation flowed easily, the whole time, and Mom was mesmerized by his cognac eyes and captivated by the scent of his jacket. She fell for Edwin that night. Poor Ambrose never had a chance.

Susan and Edwin got engaged after only a few months, and, bowing to tradition, flew back to Nigeria so the families could settle on a "bride-price"—the dowry paid from the groom to the bride's parents. The bride-price is symbolic, but if the bride is very young, pretty, and smart, it can bring wealth to her family. (Virginity was a given.) When the bride's family accepted a groom's offer, the couple was considered married. Whatever offer Edwin made, Mom's father, Albert, ultimately accepted it.

The newlyweds came back to California and hit some roadblocks. Things didn't work out for Edwin in medical school. His dream of becoming a professional soccer player didn't materialize, either. They decided to move to North Carolina, where Mom's older sisters lived. They got a US marriage license and had a "white wedding," where the bride wears a white gown at a Catholic church, in Durham. In the wedding pictures, Mom's little baby bump is plainly visible. She got pregnant with Yvo between her Nigerian and American weddings.

To pay the rent, Mom worked at McDonald's, walking a couple of miles to get there every day. When she arrived a few minutes late one day, the boss warned, "If you're late again, you're fired." She started leaving her apartment earlier and tried to pick up the pace. But as her belly grew, she just couldn't move that fast. The next time she was late, her boss fired a twenty-year-old expectant mother on the spot. His casual cruelty stuck with my mom. This was life in America? Despite the kindness of Phil King, that experience soured her impression of Americans, an opinion that still hasn't changed.

Edwin worked hard to provide for his young family. He rose through the ranks at a different fast-food restaurant until he became the manager. Only twenty-two, he was now the boss of a small business. The restaurant gave him the opportunity to achieve something, to earn a decent living. For him, being the manager of a restaurant was his piece of the American Dream.

When Yvonne was two, duty called Susan and Edwin back to Nigeria. Like all Nigerians who got their degree elsewhere, Edwin was required to return home and put in a year with the National Youth Service Corps, a government program of nation building and development. The transition back to Nigeria was rough. Susan had the financial support of her parents, but the young couple still struggled to make ends meet. They were apart for long periods while Edwin did his service.

Mom wanted a second child, but she didn't conceive as easily as she had the first time. So she prayed and fasted, asking God to give her another baby. The prayers must have worked. I was born in Nigeria in 1984. My middle name is Onyinyechukwu, shortened to Onyinye, which means "gift from God."

My first name comes from the restaurant chain my father worked at back in North Carolina: Wendy's. Just to be clear: I was not named after a hamburger joint. My father equated his success at Wendy's with achieving the American Dream, so he bestowed his second daughter with the name of the place he associated with his accomplishment.

The stories about Mom's earliest years as an immigrant are full of contradictions. She came to California to experience a new way of life, made a great American friend, but then insulated herself in a Nigerian-only social life and married a fellow immigrant very quickly. They named their child in honor of their vision of the American Dream. Mom left her husband (twice), risking her status in the Nigerian community, so she could raise her daughters in America, and repeatedly told us not to be anything like Americans.

So what was I supposed to do as a kid, desperate to fit in with Americans, when my mother and all her friends were telling us to avoid them and that they weren't good enough for us?

Yvo, the only one of us who was born on US soil, occasionally challenged their beliefs while we were kids. "Americans aren't all bad," she said.

"Don't disrespect your elders," Mom always replied.

When I was in elementary school, Mom started screening my classmates. She wouldn't let me get close with anyone on our block. She didn't trust outsiders (even though, technically, *we* were the outsiders). I just obeyed and did as she asked. I could play with the neighborhood kids to pass the time, but it was never more than that. And again, I was okay with it because I had my sister, uncle, and mother for company.

Once, I asked, "Mom, can I bring a friend home after school?" Playdates were a thing, I was aware of that. I'd seen kids go to each other's houses on TV shows.

"No. I don't know anything about her," she said. Along with being very protective of her children, Mom just didn't trust people and she was skeptical of Americans from what she'd seen in the media. She loved true crime shows like *Cops* and *America's Most Wanted*. A stream of crime and violence came in through the TV, and Mom thought it was an accurate portrayal of everyday life. "Look at what goes on this country!" she said. "You will not leave this house unless I can keep an eye on you."

In Nigeria, in the "it takes a village to raise a child" way of life, there was a sense of accountability. Nobody would hurt you because they know your grandmother, they know your uncle. It's a community. America is very insular; people don't know their neighbors. From my mother's perspective, without a sense of community, how can you trust anyone?

The idea that Mom would send me to a playdate at a classmate's house? Nope. "You'll see each other Monday through Friday," she said. "Why hang out after the bell rings?"

Shopping trips to the mall? The only time I went to the mall with my friends in high school was to drop in before heading to the library to study and wait for Mom to pick me up after her job.

Summer camp? One of my favorite Nickelodeon shows was *Salute Your Shorts*, about kids at summer camp. It was not even a question that I would ever go. Mom couldn't believe any parent would trust complete strangers in the wilderness for weeks at a time with your kids.

Sleepovers? "We don't play those games," she said. "What are you going to do at nighttime that you can't do between nine and five?"

I wasn't allowed to participate in typical American kid activities, but frankly, I didn't mind. I was content chilling at home with Yvo, watching TV shows about those activities, reading books about them, and listening to my sister's stories about them. I was immersed in American culture without really participating in it fully. We weren't hermits. People called us and invited us to gatherings. Sometimes we went to approved parties and events. I socialized with people, I just didn't think of them as my friends.

As for how I'm raising my children, I allow playdates and let them pick their own friends. After much discussion with my husband, I agreed to send the boys to day camp. I was against it at first, but Eddie convinced me. But I vowed to be open and flexible as a parent (since my mother was closed and inflexible). So we dropped them off at the camp and picked them up at four. The car rides home were full of excitedly told stories about swimming, soccer, and games.

On the first day of camp, and every day after, Mom called me to say the same thing. "You made a terrible decision. We don't do camp."

"We don't do camp," I said. "But my kids do. The boys are having a blast and that's all that really matters." But forget about sleepaway camp. Never going to happen.

And sleepover parties? Hard no. When Kamrynn turns eight or nine and her friends start throwing such parties? I don't care if she begs. No, girl. My daughter is not going to sleep at some stranger's house. I'm not hosting a sleepover party here, either. A dozen kids running around, screaming and spilling juice on my white rugs? Why would I, or anyone, invite that chaos into their home? Makes *no sense* to me.

Why have I reconsidered many of Mom's isolationist tendencies now that I'm a parent?

The reason is simple yet profound: Mom raised us in the world she was living in. I raise my children in the world they are living in.

Read that again twice!

SIX

Movin' On Up

Moving defines the immigrant experience. But it doesn't stop when immigrants arrive in a new country. To support their family in a new environment with little or no connections, they go where the work is. And that work is most likely to be low-wage odd jobs, at least at first. Once they establish themselves in a career, they can earn enough to settle down. That's the goal.

Mom's journey toward hard-won career success had many stops along the way. Her switching jobs often meant we had to move houses whenever a new and better work opportunity presented itself. I never had more than two birthdays in any one house growing up.

In the case of the apartment building where our neighbor killed himself—we *had* to change addresses. It was suddenly clear that our living situation wasn't safe. We moved into the biggest place we ever had in Durham, our first single-family home, a New England–style colonial house. It had a walk-in pantry. We each had our own bedrooms. My room was the dream of any little girl, pink and white everything. Mom's bedroom was enormous and luxe, and it had what we called the "Elizabeth Taylor" phone, a gold princess phone with a handle that you'd pick up and hold against your ear to say a breathy "Hello?" There was even a charming little bridge over a stream that you had to drive across to get to our house. It felt like we were moving up in the world.

The house was on the outskirts of Durham, which took some adjusting. We were used to living in the city proper, and this house, as nice as it was, felt isolated. It was in a white neighborhood. We were the only Black family who lived there.

Around that time, racial tensions were heating up nationwide. In October 1995, more than eight hundred thousand Black men went to a massive protest in Washington, DC, called the Million Man March. It was all over the news. In front of our mixed-race classroom, my white teacher said, "Instead of going to work to provide for their families, *these people* are marching in the streets."

The point of the march was to call national attention to the wildly disproportionate rates of unemployment and poverty between Black and white America. Even a fifth-grader can understand that racial inequality was unfair. I also understood from the teacher's comment that she resented the protesters, men who looked like my Uncle Hyke. As an adult looking back, I think her outspoken contempt for Black men was just out of pocket. As a kid, it made me deeply uncomfortable.

While I got lessons on prejudice in the classroom, Uncle Hyke, my teacher of the world, gave me an education about how to be freaking awesome. He took me to see the premiere of *Juice*, starring Tupac Shakur and Omar Epps. I was dying to see it, because I loved Tupac. At age ten, I was a bit young to go to an R-rated movie. I should have been at home asleep, not at a theater at 10 p.m. But I told Hyke that I wanted to go, and he took Yvo and me.

Uncle Hyke sometimes picked me up from school in a black Mercedes, Tupac blasting. The tinted window would roll down and he'd call, "Hey, Wen-Wen!" Sometimes he had a friend or two with him in the car. They all wore black leather and looked like they just stepped out of a rap video.

I turned to the girls I was standing with and said, "That's my ride."

Wowed by the car, the music, the men, they asked, "Who *is* that?"

Just the coolest guy on earth.

Not everyone was so thrilled to see Hyke's car pull up to school or to our new house. Our very presence in our new white neighborhood was apparently disturbing to some.

Mom, Yvo, and I were driving home after grocery shopping one day. Mom slowed down to cross that little bridge that led to our house. "Girls, don't be scared," said Mom suddenly.

I didn't know what she was talking about. Scared? Of what?

Then I looked out the car window and saw that someone had left a message for us on the gray stone walls of the bridge. I only caught a glimpse as we drove by. In black spray paint were the letters "KKK."

After we pulled into our driveway, we got out of the car and took a closer look. Along with "KKK" were the words "Monkey" and "Niggers don't belong here."

Mom repeated, "You are children of God. You have no reason to be afraid."

In response to the racist graffiti, Mom started praying on her rosary, as she did at least once a day, every day. She kept a string of rosary beads in her purse, along with a first aid kit, always prepared for any emergency. "When life gets hard, pray, but don't wait until it gets hard to do it," she often said. During every trial Mom faced, her faith carried her through. It was her not-so-secret source of strength. It happens to be mine, too.

We went inside and prayed together. It seemed to help Mom and Yvo. I said the words, but the feeling of terror didn't dissipate. I'd made the mistake of recently seeing the movie *Mississippi Burning* and learned that in the not-too-distant past in the South, Black people were killed just for having dark skin. And now we'd clearly triggered a disturbed racist in our midst. If they had no problem defacing property with hateful slurs, what else would they do? Should we brace ourselves for a burning cross in our yard?

When Uncle Hyke saw the bridge, he was *pissed*. He said, "Whoever did this is going to be sorry!"

"Nothing is going to happen to us," Mom said. "We're going to sit down and have dinner in our beautiful house." Mom didn't speak to negativity, I got it. But what about reality? Was I wrong to be scared? I didn't think so. I didn't question Mom's apparent nonchalance, though. If I had, she would have told me that I was being ridiculous or disrespectful.

"We need to wash it off, right? We can't look at it every day from now on," said Yvo.

"Should we move?" I asked.

"We are staying right here," said Mom.

Before we had a chance to research how to clean off spray paint, we woke up to a shocking surprise. In the cover of darkness, someone spray-painted over the original message. In vivid pink, purple, and yellow, they drew a giant peace sign and the words "Practice Love Not Hate." The dichotomy of the black racist words covered by a rainbow message of peace and love moved me profoundly. Some people wanted to scare us into leaving, but others wanted us to feel welcome.

"I was right," said Mom. "We're welcome here, and we're staying."

Mom had made her declaration, and we were obliged to get on board. For me, making the conscious choice to feel welcomed wasn't easy or automatic. An angry hateful person was still out there, and he or she wanted us to leave.

But not only did we stay in that house, we *celebrated* living there with holiday festivities and Sunday postchurch all-day parties as usual. Mom cooked up a storm and filled the whole neighborhood with the aromas of spicy meat curry, sweet fried plantains, stewed tomatoes, and smoked fish. She was the center of attention in the kitchen, her happy place. The bigger the house, the bigger the crowd. So many people from church and the Nigerian community came to those parties, the driveway was like a car show—and everyone seemed to have a shiny Mercedes or Lexus without a single scratch. Everyone dressed to stand out. Everything was loud: the music, the clothes, the voices.

Nigerians believe in happiness, the good life, and being joyous. If you come into a Nigerian home, especially during a party, it might seem like we're fighting, because we talk at a high volume. But we're just bois-terous, enthusiastic people. The clothes and the cars are how we show off. Yet, on the flip side, we're also very judgmental. If you repeat an out-fit you wore from a previous party and wear it to another, we will say you don't have any clothes. If you drive around in a Honda, they'll gossip about how poor you are. It's not that we're materialistic, per se. It's just that we're extra.

My uncles were the stars of those parties. They were all around six foot two, with goatees and mustaches, in jeans, bright-colored button-down shirts, gold chains, Cuban link gold bracelets, gold watches. My Uncle Ike wore a gold nugget pinkie ring. And they all smelled so good: woody and spicy. Scent is a big deal with Nigerians. You could smell my uncles for five minutes after they left the room.

My uncles would bring all their boys to those Sunday parties, filling my house with fine, young single guys. They loved Mom because she fed them and joked around with them. All the Nigerian girls had crushes on them, but the guys paid special attention to me, their pseudo-niece. Not in a romantic way, but in a big brother, little sister way. They would come over to give me a hug, saying, "Hey, Wen-Wen." The girls glared at me with pure envy.

Sundays were the best.

Our racist neighbors probably clutched their pearls seeing all those Black people who converged on our place every week, but they never sullied our bridge again. Eventually, someone from the town sandblasted the bridge clean, and I allowed myself to relax about the hidden threat in our midst.

But the threats to our safety were still out there.

One night, I woke up at 2 a.m. and wandered into Mom's room. She hadn't come home yet, which was strange. She had enough seniority by then not to have to work the late shifts anymore . . . so where was she?

I went into Yvo's room, woke her up, and asked, "Where's Mom?"

"She's okay," she told me. "Just go to sleep."

I did as I was told, went back to bed, and fell asleep. I woke up the next day and went into the kitchen, expecting to find Mom there as always. No sign of her. I checked her bedroom again and saw the unslept-in bed. Now I panicked.

"Yvo!" I yelled. "She's still not here. Where is she?"

"She's fine. She'll be back soon," she said. Nothing in her expression told me that she was lying.

"Why are you so calm?"

"I'll make breakfast," she said. "What can I get you?"

An hour later, Mom arrived with Uncle Hyke. He had to help her walk from the car into the house. Her arm was in a cast and a sling, her face badly bruised. Bandages covered deep gashes on her forehead and lip. (To this day, you can still see the scar above her lip.) I ran to her, both relieved she was back and horrified by her state. Yvo, I noticed, was taken aback by how she looked, but she didn't seem surprised. Whatever Mom had been through, Yvo, then fourteen, knew, and she had kept it from me. I was eleven. At what point were my mom and my second mother going to stop treating me like a baby?

"What happened?" I asked.

Uncle Hyke looked more upset than Mom did. His cheeks were wet, as if he'd been crying. As protective as he was, he still wore his heart on his sleeve.

"I'm fine, Wen. Don't be scared," said Mom.

Mom and Hyke sat down at the kitchen table to talk, while I listened just outside the room. "I'm going to kill him," Hyke told her. The words landed heavily, like a punch. I was sure he meant it.

"Forget it," said Mom. "It's out of our hands."

By listening to Mom's conversations on the phone over the next day, I figured out the gist of what happened: Mom had gone out for drinks at a hotel bar with the man she'd been seeing. (I knew she was dating, but she never brought anyone home.) She tried to break up with him, and in response, he hit her across the face with a bottle and broke her arm. The bartender called an ambulance, and she was rushed to Duke University Hospital, where she got patched up. She spent the night there with Hyke at her side.

"When did you know?" I asked Yvo that afternoon. I rarely felt anything but love for my sister, but I was done with being kept out of the loop.

"The EMS guy called here when Mom was in the ambulance," she admitted. He told her that Mom had been violently attacked and was being rushed to the hospital. Yvo held that in all night and all morning.

"Why didn't you tell me?" I asked.

"I didn't want you to get upset."

"I deserve to know what's going on here!" I said. I felt like the odd girl out. They were doing what they thought would shield me from fear and pain, but not knowing the truth—and being lied to—was hurtful, too.

I'm sure Mom had her moments of processing the violent assault and opened up to her siblings or friends about the trauma, but I never heard it. I never saw her tears. She hid her vulnerability from me, thinking it would spare me pain. Why? From her mother, she learned never to let them see you sweat. Mom had always put on a brave face, no matter what. She was the stylish charmer at the stove, cooking for the crowd, the extroverted center of attention. If she needed solace, she prayed. Her pain wasn't public.

It created a disconnect in my young brain between what I could plainly see in front of me and what they told me to believe. I *knew* going to the ER after a bad date was not normal, but when I showed appropriate concern, Mom said, "Don't worry, Wen."

A week later, we made our annual trip to the Bronx to "summer" in New York City. We had started this tradition a few years before, after my aunts Ekwy and Nkiru moved north. (Nkiru was single; Ekwy was married and would have one son.) During the school year, being latchkey kids was okay. But once school let out, Yvo and I couldn't be alone all day, every day, while Mom worked crazy hours. The solution was for us to spend June to August each year with my aunts in their apartment on East 217th Street between Bronxwood and Barnes Avenues. Saying we summered in New York sounded pretentious as hell. When Mom described it like that to other people, she was nurturing an illusion about our lifestyle. She could convince anyone (including me) that we were doing great. Part of that was having a "home" in the city. It wasn't like we were chilling in the Hamptons. But those months in the Bronx each year felt like a luxury to me.

As soon as we arrived, the girls from the block would come by to say, "Hey, girl, hey." They became our summer "cousins." Most of them were the children of African, Jamaican, or Trinidadian immigrants. We all had nothing to do all summer but hang out for eight to ten hours a day before our mothers would yell for us to come home for dinner with their thick accents. We didn't divide into African and Caribbean cliques. We were all Black first gens and had a common bond as foreigners. I really looked forward to seeing those girls each year, not only during the hot months, but whenever we came to New York for holidays, weddings, or baby showers.

I have so many memories of classic New York moments in the Bronx: Trying (and sucking at) double Dutch. Opening the fire hydrant and running through the waterspout, screaming and laughing. I'd ask for a few dollars and walk to the bodega on the corner, where I developed a devotion to Sour Patch Kids. When we'd hear the Mister Softee song, all the neighborhood kids ran to the ice cream truck. We sat on the stoop of my aunts' building for hours, eating our snacks, drinking Capri Sun, and just hanging out.

In New York, I felt like a different person. I had freedom. For one thing, my aunts were more hands-off than Mom. Nkiru didn't have kids and I felt she had no parenting skills, so she didn't ask questions like, "Where are you going?," "Where have you been?," and "Who were you with?" Unlike in Durham, we could come and go, and hang out with whomever we wanted. Ekwy's son was much younger than we were—

a toddler when we first started going—and she was busy with him and inexperienced in raising preteens. For another, you weren't dependent on a car in the Bronx. People lived so close together you could hang out on a stoop and chitchat with passersby all day long. One guy was the DJ of the block, with music pouring out of his window. We didn't like his taste, but we loved the vibe.

I even loved the eight-hour drive from Durham to the Bronx in Mom's white Toyota Camry, which had gold detail, tinted black windows, and a tan leather interior. Her rosary hung on the rearview mirror, swinging back and forth to the beat of Luther Vandross, Anita Baker, Whitney Houston. During those captive hours in the car, we bonded over a shared love of music. We sang along and danced in our seats to countless songs. It was heaven.

Not only did I love going to the Bronx with Mom, I loved being there with her as well. She didn't stay long after driving up, just a few days before she had to return to her nursing job in North Carolina. But when she was in New York, she reveled in the big-city vibe. One of my favorite photos of Mom hangs on the wall of my office. She was sitting at the shiny black bar with gold trim at my Aunt Ekwy's house in the Bronx, wearing black leather pants, strappy, open-toed gold stiletto heels, a beige silk shirt, a gold Versace belt with the Medusa logo buckle, a thick, gold herringbone bow, hands embellished with gold rings, and candy-apple-red lipstick. Her big, fat roller curls and French manicure were fresh and perfect. She could have strutted right off the pages of a magazine, but this was her everyday hangout look in New York.

Much of my personality comes from those summers. When people meet me, they often say, "You don't give me North Carolina, you give me New York." That's because the Bronx raised me. I could not have cherished our time there more. My love for southern food and my sense of hospitality come from North Carolina. But my attitude, demeanor, mentality, and love for Caribbean food come from New York City.

After Mom's assault, I didn't know if we were still going to go to

New York. How could she do the drive with her arm in a cast? But on the date, as planned, we loaded our suitcases into the car and piled in. Mom drove the whole eight hours with the use of only her left hand. I remember watching her in amazement during that drive. I thought she was the toughest person on earth.

We arrived at my aunts' home, and of course they wanted to know about the cast on Mom's arm. Mom gave Yvo and me some money and sent us on an errand to buy something at the bodega, an obvious ploy to get rid of us. I rushed along, wanting to get there and back so I could hear what they all said.

We caught the tail end of it. One of my aunts said, "Look at you, Susan. You have two daughters, and this is what you do? Let's see if they ever do anything with their lives. Let's see if they ever get married." A girl's marriageability to a quality Nigerian husband largely depended on her family background. My aunts looked at Mom and saw her as a liability for us.

"My daughters will marry well, and they'll get their degrees," Mom countered. Her voice sounded shaky, though. Usually it was full of confidence and certainty.

Over the past several years, I'd heard them needle Mom for choosing to stay single. And now they criticized her for dating? You couldn't win with the aunts. It sounded petty and bitchy to my ears, but if I'd stepped in to defend Mom, I would have been swatted down for disrespecting my elders. The sisters loved hard, but they cut deep.

Mom was supposed to stay for a few days, but she wound up leaving in the morning. She drove back to Durham alone, lived in the bridge house alone, recovered from her injuries alone, and continued working long hours to fulfill her responsibility as a Nigerian parent to provide for us. One of my aunts, the most critical of Mom as a parent, never even had kids. If she walked a mile in Mom's shoes, she might have changed her tune.

But I knew all Mom did. Even at eleven, I understood that Mom lived for us and that she was the strongest, most capable woman in the world. There were forces that tried to stop her from moving up in the world. Our racist neighbors tried to scare us away. Instead, she showed them we weren't afraid and weren't going anywhere. When she was attacked by that horrible man, she could have crumbled in self-pity. But she didn't give into the negativity and kept her promise to give us another summer in the city. Even her own sisters seemed to try to bring her down, but she refused to listen. Nothing could stop her upward trajectory.

This was only more clear to us when we came home from the Bronx that summer and Mom surprised us one day by announcing a short road trip.

"Girls, we're taking a drive," she said.

"Where?" I asked.

"Danville, Virginia."

"Never heard of it."

Danville was deep country. Durham is not exactly a buzzing metropolis, so for me to call Danville "the sticks" meant it was a real backwater. After an hour's drive, we pulled up to a yellow ranch house next to a big cornfield.

Before Mom could explain, a large (white) family—three generations—came out of the house to greet us and invited us inside. We were introduced to about a dozen people. The oldest man, around seventy, said, "My whole family wanted to meet you, Susan, to give you a great meal and to thank you for saving my life."

What?

They prepared classic southern food—collard greens, black-eyed peas, fried chicken—which I loved (but could have benefited from more seasoning). While we ate, the old man told us the minute-by-minute story of what happened to him during his recent stint at Mom's hospital as an in-patient in the cardiac unit. In short, he was admitted with a heart condition. Mom was his nurse. She came to see him every day, even on her days off, to check on him, going above and beyond for him.

She didn't have to, but she did, just because he was her patient, and he was in bad shape.

One day, his heart gave out. Mom was there, and she started performing CPR on him. He wasn't responding and his heart monitor flatlined. The other nurses in the room said, "Let's call it," meaning they needed to record the time of death for the report.

But Mom refused to stop. She kept on giving him chest compressions, and after a minute or two, the heart monitor started blipping again. He came back to the land of the living.

"I would not be here today," he said of Mom's lifesaving efforts, and if the other nurses had had their way. "You, Susan, are my daughter now."

This thank-you dinner wasn't a one-time thing. The family called and wrote to Mom for years.

I knew my mom was a dedicated cardiac nurse, and that she went to the hospital sometimes when she didn't have to, a fact that I resented fully. But I had no idea that she routinely saved lives and affected people so profoundly.

If I was impressed by Mom before this dinner, I was in awe of her now. I wanted to be just like her, a woman who wouldn't let obstacles stop her on her path toward success.

SEVEN

Love, Nigerian Style

For every parent-teacher conference or school event, Mom showed up in chic skirts, dresses, or suits, not a hair out of place, trailing her signature scent. She cut through the throngs of casual moms, standing out like a peacock among pigeons.

Kids would ask, "Is that your mom?"

"It sure is," I replied.

"Where's your dad?"

If I'd said, "He's in Nigeria," that would only open the door to their saying something like, "Why don't you go back to Africa, too?"

Mom was such a force of nature that she was enough for two parents, but I still felt the lack. I never discussed those feelings with Mom. She wouldn't have liked hearing it or approved of my giving voice to them.

I was proud of the fact that Mom saw parts of herself in me—confidence, intelligence, love of food and music—but we had important differences, too. I am far more demonstrably emotional and vulnerable than she. Nowadays, I wonder what our relationship would be if Mom knew I was not as tough as she was. Showing any kind of weakness was not her style, or how Nigerian parents raised their kids.

I had to assume she knew that I missed Edwin. It wasn't like my father fell off the edge of the earth. We kept in touch with him by phone. Edwin's brother, Uncle Mike (yes, I had uncles named Mike, Hyke, and

Ike), lived in the Durham area, and he would turn up at the random Sunday postchurch dinners at our place. I harbored a secret wish that my father would one day just show up at our door. As month after month, and year after year, went by, that hope dimmed.

When I was eleven, one night at dinnertime, Mom said, "Get dressed! Your dad is here! We have to get in the car to go see him."

I screamed with elation. Yvo and I rushed to put on our very best clothes and make sure our hair was perfect. I remember laughing as we scrambled into the car, bouncing on the seats with excitement. It felt like Christmas in September; after all this time, I was going to see my father again. Would he recognize me? Would I recognize him? Was he here to stay? All the questions and anticipation made me dizzy.

We pulled into a Pizza Hut parking lot. As soon as the car stopped, Yvo and I ran into the restaurant. A few families were sitting in the booths, but otherwise, the place was empty. Dad was nowhere in sight.

"Surprise!" Mom said.

I didn't get it. "Where's Dad?" I asked.

"He's not here. The surprise is that we're having pizza for dinner."

Pizza was a rare treat, and I would have been thrilled about it . . . if the setup for getting us in the car hadn't been an emotional bait and switch.

We walked to the counter to order. Mom asked, "What do you guys want?"

I'd lost my appetite. "I'm not hungry," I said.

"What's the matter?" asked Mom.

I just shook my head. If I said one word, I might start crying, and that was not acceptable. Mom sighed and said, "I was just joking." The implication: *Don't be so sensitive. Get over it. What's wrong with you?*

How could she think going to Pizza Hut would make me as happy as seeing my father after seven years without him? She didn't understand my heart, my pain, at all. Why would she? We never talked about it, not after that man killed himself outside our door; not after the teacher humiliated me; not after she played a cruel "joke" about seeing my father. If she didn't know how I felt—and didn't seem to want to know—what kind of relationship was this?

As close as Mom and I were, there was a wall between us.

The irony is that Mom didn't know the wall was there. I knew that the level of intimacy between us wasn't what I longed for it to be. It wasn't close to what I saw in American families on TV, and in real life. When an America kid was sad or had a problem, the parents asked, "Are you okay? How can I help? Tell me what's wrong." They would talk it out, hug, and say, "I love you." If a first-gen Nigerian had a problem, their immigrant parents didn't notice, or if they did, didn't ask.

You could live in a Nigerian household for a year and never hear anyone say, "How do you feel?" Feelings are messy, embarrassing, and a sign of weakness. Emotions are just not discussed openly; in fact, conversations about feelings are discouraged between parent and child. Why? Emotions are a distraction from schoolwork and other pursuits of excellence.

In an emotionally closed relationship, you can spend tons of time with your parents, obey and respect them, but never open up about what was truly in your heart. It's not a Nigerian parent's job to tend to their child's emotional well-being. They are not their kids' therapist. They tell their children what to do, and the children march forward on the path that their parents put them on.

In a traditional Nigerian home, the interpersonal tone between parents and kids is formal and detached. My mother, breaking from tradition, is a hugger. She says "I love you" at the end of every phone call. Hearing us, a lot of Nigerian people think we were weird. Eddie's parents never said "I love you" to him, and they showed no affection at all. When he came into my life and saw how my mom hugged and kissed us, he said, "I didn't know I was missing something."

So I got the hugs, but I didn't get the intimacy I longed for. Ironically,

Mom understood how it felt to long for that connection and not get it. While my grandmother Angela was staying in our house on an extended visit from Nigeria, Mom and one of her sisters got into a disagreement on the phone. I can't remember what it was about, but I do recall how upset and frustrated Mom was. It was one of the few times I had seen her cry.

While they argued on speakerphone, Mom paused at one point, turned to Angela, and said, "Please. Mama. You know she's wrong. Say she's wrong."

Angela, stone-faced, said, "I'm not speaking."

Mom begged Angela for a modicum of support, and Angela refused to give it to her. For all I know, Angela agreed with Mom. She just wasn't going to take sides or reveal how she truly felt. Nigerian parenting can be bloodless. If Mom was upset, that wasn't Angela's problem. I empathized with Mom's frustration. I felt the same longing for emotional support from Mom and was always shut down or dismissed with a terse "Everything's fine," "Don't worry," or "I was just joking."

The emotional detachment might strike Westerners as unloving. But it's not that Nigerian parents don't love their children. And it's not like Nigerian children think their parents hate them. The huge distinction is that Nigerian parents are not there to hold your hand and make it better. Their job is to push, hard. The child's job is to meet their sky-high expectations. And when the children are grown, the parents get to say, "It was worth it, right? You're a doctor. You're married. I instilled my values in you, and you ended up being successful."

My mom never lets my sister and me forget that she was hard on us for a reason. "You grew up with a single immigrant mother. You could've been a statistic. You could've had a different life. But because I raised you to be strong, no matter what our circumstances were, you grew up to be successful. You would not be doctors if it weren't for me," she still tells us frequently.

Many first gens just smile when our parents take credit for our accomplishments, because the potential verbal lashing that will ensue for discrediting them is far worse than taking a ding to our own egos.

WHEN I WAS starting seventh grade, Mom made a big announcement. "Girls, I've been offered a great job in Pittsfield, Massachusetts." It was a major step up for her, from nursing to working as a hospital administrator.

I thought, *Massachusetts? Who the hell would want to go there?* The farthest north our family had ever been was New York. Massachusetts seemed like a remote ice-covered planet. The opportunity was too good to turn down, though, with significantly more money and stable hours.

"So we're moving to Massachusetts?" I asked.

"Well, I am," said Mom. "You are going to stay here."

"Wait," I said, astonished. "You're leaving us?" Life without Mom was unthinkable. Were we to stay in our current house by ourselves? Would Hyke live with us full time? Who would cook dinner?

"I'm going up alone to see if the job works out," she explained. "I'm not taking Yvo out of private school unless I have to."

My sister had always been an excellent student. She'd been kicking ass at a ritzy private school, Sweet Valley High–esque, a match in setting for those bedtime stories she told me when I was little. It had been her dream to go there. Yvo was one of three Black girls, at the top of her class, and she had a lucrative scholarship. Graduating from there would help her get into a great college and a great medical school, which to my mom was the entire point of Yvo's life.

So I understood why she had to stay. "But I can come with you," I said to Mom.

"No. You will stay here with your sister," she replied. End of discussion. "The two of you will live with Aunt Winifred at her house until I get settled in Pittsfield, and then I will come back and get you."

I was twelve, one year older than Mom was when Angela sent her away, never to live with her parents again. The thought of never living with Mom again terrified me. I bit back tears and tried to appear brave. Inside, I was a wreck.

Aunt Winifred, Yvo, and I went to see Mom off at the airport. In those days, you could walk someone all the way to the gate to say goodbye. As soon as Mom disappeared onto the jet bridge to board the plane, I broke down. As I had watched her walk farther and farther away, I felt abandoned. It was a devastating blow, triggering the pain I had felt at the loss of my father. And now Mom was leaving us behind, too. She was all I had, and now she was gone. I crumpled to the floor at the gate.

Logically, I understood she was taking an opportunity to better our lives, and until she knew how it was going to pan out, it didn't make sense for her to disrupt our lives and schooling for an opportunity that might not work out. I also believed we'd be reunited as soon as possible, but that didn't change how I felt then. I didn't want her to go and I was devastated when she did.

My sobbing on the floor at the airport—such an emotional outburst in public—was excruciatingly embarrassing for Winifred. She waited about five seconds and said, "That's enough, Wen. Come on, let's go." She didn't say, "It'll be okay." She didn't offer me a hug. That was never going to happen.

Of my six US-based aunts and uncles, I utterly adored and respected Winifred as our family historian and an accomplished, brilliant woman, the first from our village to go to college, the first to get a PhD. Aunt Winifred was an educator who worked with kids and adults with mental disabilities. But like most Nigerians of her generation, compassion wasn't a personal strength of hers.

She was one of the first people in my family to buy a house—the house we'd now be living in on Wedgewood Lane. I was amazed by the size of it. White with burgundy shutters, it was as large as our house by the little bridge, yet with only one person living in it. As a child, I thought, *It's a mansion*. Truth be told, I went back there about three years ago and was a bit surprised to see the house with an adult's perspective; it was nowhere near as huge as I remembered.

Winifred's lifestyle impressed us, too. She drove a new teal E350 Mercedes Benz with a cream interior. Part of the welcome package with the purchase of a Mercedes back then was a classical music CD, and when we drove in that car, my sister and I would play that CD with the windows down and put our pinkies up because that meant we were officially rich.

Still, it wasn't all peaches and cream on Wedgewood Lane: along with the car and the house came Winifred herself. She wasn't really a substitute for a mother figure. With no children of her own, it was tough for her to relate to us. I thought she treated us more like free laborers than her nieces.

Of course, we'd always done chores. Nigerian girls had to learn to cook and keep house. Every Saturday, Mom, Yvo, and I cleaned our entire house together, top to bottom. But Aunt Winifred put us to *work*. Yvo and I were enlisted to do serious deep-cleaning jobs.

Once, Winifred handed me a pair of rubber gloves and said, "Come with me." She brought me to her kitchen and opened the oven. "I want you to take out the oven racks and clean them."

The racks were black from years of spills that had turned into carbonized gunk. They'd probably never been scrubbed before. "How do I do that?" I asked.

"Cleaning supplies are under the sink," she said, and left me to my work.

We were raised to respect our elders and wouldn't have dared object. I removed the oven racks and labored over them for hours. It was just one of many, many chores she had us do around her house.

No offense to Winifred, but we hated living there. It wasn't only having to do dirty jobs. It was the quiet. Unlike Mom's house, there was no music at Winifred's. No crowds of guests arriving for Sunday dinners. No delicious vanilla perfume. No comforting cooking aromas. And all that scrubbing destroyed my nails.

Despite the free housekeeping, Winifred seemed to dislike us living with her as much as we disliked it. Whenever Mom called, Winifred would tell her, "Susan, your daughters aren't respectful enough. They're not obedient enough. They make too much noise."

When I got on the phone with Mom, our conversations were frustrating. "No, Mom, I am respectful. I am obedient. I'm as quiet as I can be." I would have loved to tell her that I shook with silent crying at night from missing her or that I was mad at her for leaving us behind.

Mom got sick of listening to the complaints, so during winter break in December, she drove down to North Carolina from Massachusetts— a ten-hour drive—to get my sister and me. When Mom first arrived, I ran down to her and wrapped her in a tight hug. She hugged me back, and said, "I love you," as always. There was no discussion about how it felt to see her again. She was here, and that was what mattered.

The next day, we loaded up all our stuff in the car and the three of us drove to Pittsfield to live with her. It was the best day of my life. So far.

EIGHT

The Strongest Shape in Nature

The Pittsfield house was a charming brown brick colonial with white columns. Once a single-family home, it'd been converted into an apartment building with three units. Our apartment had two bedrooms, a living room, and a balcony with faux turf. Mom's room was right off the living room. Its glass double doors were aesthetically beautiful but provided no privacy. When we had a guest in the living room, Mom had to change her clothes in the bathroom. It felt cramped after Winifred's house, but we were together again, and that was all I cared about. Mom's scent filled the rooms and made the apartment feel like home.

We'd barely unpacked when Mom said, "Girls, your father and I have been talking, and we are going to try again. The three of us are going to Nigeria to see him."

Emotional whiplash. Yvo and I hadn't lived with Mom for six months. We hadn't seen our father for eight years. And now we were all going to fly across the world to see the father whose absence had loomed so large in my life. Why didn't she tell us about this development sooner? What did it all mean? It was too much to process for an almost thirteen-year-old. Of course, I was excited to see my father again, but I barely knew him. I didn't know what to expect. I didn't understand what caused Mom's heart to soften toward him after she'd fled from him when I was three, and then sent him packing when I was four.

I would have asked her to explain her change of heart—and the truth about why their marriage had been such a roller coaster—but, you know, we don't do that.

Yvo and I had our theories that we discussed in our room late at night. "She was probably just lonely by herself up here," she said.

"If she was lonely, she could have talked to us," I said. She did call, every day.

"It's not the same." Yvo was sixteen. She hadn't dated at all because Mom forbade it, but at that age, she understood more about the forces that drew men and women together. The fact was, after all this time separated by an ocean, my parents hadn't gotten divorced. Mom's forays into dating had been disastrous. In her thirty-six years, she'd had only one love in her life. She was just too young to give up on romance, and, as they say, first love dies hard.

But love didn't erase history, and theirs was complicated. In Mom's telling, the dark period of their relationship started not long after my birth and came to a head when she fled Nigeria in the middle of the night with her daughters in pajamas. What went wrong between them? Mom didn't tell us about it. Their first attempt at a reconciliation—when Edwin returned to North Carolina and lived with us on Fargo Street— fizzled after one year when God called him back to Nigeria. Why didn't Mom go with him? As she always said, "I wanted to give you girls a better life. I'd seen both sides and thought you'd have more opportunities in America."

I'd learned from chatter at family parties that a major conflict between them was religion. When I was a newborn, Edwin had become a pastor in a Nigerian church called Body of Christ, a Christian fundamentalist group with its own worship practices. Mom, a strict Roman Catholic, wasn't happy about that. Neither was my grandmother, Angela, the most devout Catholic I'd ever met. "Marriage," as Angela said, "should be bonded in common faith. How can a husband and a wife pray to a different God?" Angela told Yvo and me explicitly that an acceptable husband for us had to be Catholic first, Igbo second, and a doctor-lawyer-engineer third. But Catholic was the top priority. Was Edwin's conversion to a different religion the reason we left Nigeria in the middle of the night? I was sure it played a part, but perhaps it wasn't the whole story.

I hoped that our trip to Nigeria would bring more clarity about my parents' relationship, and uncover the core mystery of my life: Why aren't we all together?

Arriving in Nigeria for the first time since I was a toddler felt like a homecoming. Although my memories were faint and few, it triggered something deep in my soul. The food smells were just like those at home in Mom's kitchen. The music on the radio and on the streets was a mix of highlife and traditional sounds, which I'd always been drawn to.

First we went to Nimo, Anambra State, to visit with my mom's parents. The next day, we drove for two hours to my paternal grandfather's compound in Obazu, Mbieri, for the meeting with Edwin. Hoping to make a good impression, I agonized about what to wear, and ultimately decided on a simple and classic outfit of a crisp white shirt and denim pants. On the drive, I imagined what the outcome could be. If all went well, it was possible my parents might get back together. Did that mean we'd all live in Massachusetts? Would we move to Nigeria? It was a lot to take in, on top of everything else we'd been through in the past year. My mind spun.

We arrived at the compound and a man was waiting. We exited the car, and my father was standing right in front of me. I'd seen many pictures, but they didn't do him justice. He was as handsome as Mom always said, with the deepest chocolate-colored skin (like mine), low-cut dark hair, and those orange-tinged cognac eyes. Anyone seeing the two of us together would know we shared DNA. It was a weird feeling to look at a virtual stranger and recognize myself. He was dressed in a white shirt and jeans—like father, like daughter.

I had no idea what to say. Edwin and I gave each other an awkward hug. He smelled good, a woody musk scent mixed with baby powder. He hugged Yvo and Mom. We were invited into a small house and sat down at the table for tea. The four of us stared at one another, my father's gaze jumping from me to Yvo to Mom and back.

"How was the flight?" he asked.

I said, "It was fine, thanks for asking."

"Any trouble finding the compound?" he asked.

"Not at all, thanks," said Yvo.

"And the traffic?"

"As bad as always," said Mom.

Mom watched us interact with Edwin, her eyes and body language telling us to be decorous and polite, good Nigerian girls who were respectful and deferential to our elders.

After a few minutes more of small talk, Edwin said, "God brought you back to me."

Yvo and I glanced at each other. Were we supposed to agree?

"God wants us to get together," he said.

None of us knew how to respond, so Edwin continued in this vein . . . for a good half hour. It was no longer a conversation. We sat and listened to Pastor Edwin deliver a sermon. It triggered a memory of being a small child at my father's church, starting to cry in the middle of his sermon, and Mom rushing me out of the room. The longer Edwin went on, the more passionate he became.

I looked with concern at Yvo, who seemed as confused and disturbed as I was. Mom smiled patiently, like she didn't want to give Edwin the impression that he was alienating us.

With Edwin in this state, there wasn't much we could do or say. We left after only an hour at his family's compound. On the drive back to Angela and Albert's compound, I remember feeling disappointed more than anything. We'd come a long way to get to know our father. I hoped to make some new memories to add to the few I had of him, to bond with the man whose sudden departure had left a gaping hole in my heart and life. But Edwin was still as mysterious to me as he was before our meeting.

We spent some quality time with Mom's family: Angela and Albert, whom I knew from their visits to America; Fred, Mom's oldest brother; and my great-grandmother Nne, the family matriarch. She was ninety-nine, and her immense life force was still palpable. She hadn't lost an inch of her six-foot-two height. She was so tall, she slept on a custom-made bed.

Mom spoke openly with her dad about the possibility of renewing her vows with Edwin. He was her first love, her one and only true love.

"Don't do it, Susan. He's crazy," I heard Albert tell his daughter. "He speaks in tongues!"

Angela was also dead set against my parents reuniting. Mom and Angela had whispered discussions about it, but I heard enough to get the gist. Angela knew Edwin would insist on our living in Nigeria and joining his ministry. "Your daughters are still at risk. They'll be married off as teenagers or worse," said Angela. "Nothing has changed since you left him the first time."

As a twelve-year-old first gen raised in America, I didn't fully appreciate the physical dangers and cultural limitations of being a girl in Nigeria. Women had to play the roles of wife and mother and have no expectations for themselves. If Mom were to be a conservative pastor's wife, Yvo and I had to be the pastor's daughters. This would mean a lifetime of subservience. In Edwin's fundamentalist community, Mom would have to abide by her husband's rules. Yvo and I would have to do the same. Women who dared to step outside those bounds would be ostracized or punished.

Susan wanted us to have full lives, to get a quality education, become doctors or lawyers. You'd think those considerations, *and* the display we'd witnessed of Edwin's religiosity, *and* Albert and Angela's strong objections, would have been enough for my mother to end the relationship once and for all.

"I still love him," said Mom to Angela.

"Are you getting back together?" I asked Mom.

"We'll see what happens," she replied.

My feeling at the time, with the information I had, was, *If Mom sees potential in her marriage, then so do I.* I missed having a father.

"I do not approve of this," said Angela.

She was one to talk. As legend had it, there was a family tradition of parents disapproving of marriages, including Angela's, and a lot of drama around contested unions.

Some sixty years earlier, when Angela was just a baby and Albert was a teenager, Angela's mother, Nne, and Albert's mother, Ifekewsi, joked that one day their children would marry. When Angela was twelve and Albert was twenty-five (right before he left the village to fight in World War II), his parents offered a bride-price to her parents. It was accepted by Nne's husband, a calm, sweet man. By shaking hands on the bride-price, the deal was sealed and effectively Angela and Albert were married.

But they didn't start living together yet. Nne sent Angela away to a training school, where young girls were taught how to be subservient wives, as was the custom. Albert went off to Burma and other parts of the world as a soldier. He survived the war and returned to the village a few years later, ready for his life to begin with Angela, but he discovered that his bride was nowhere to be found.

"Where's my wife?" Albert asked her mother, Nne.

Nne had some explaining to do, for sure. Nne and Ifekewsi had been friendly when their children were young. But in the years since, Nne had grown to despise Ifekewsi. Nne didn't care much for Albert, either. So she was never truly on board with the arrangement. While Albert was off fighting, Nne secretly took Angela out of wife-training school and married her off to someone else.

Albert was not going to just walk away. He took Nne to court, saying, "You can't marry my wife to another person, no matter how much you hate me and my family. We had a deal!"

Nigerian culture was stacked against Nne. At some point during the war years, Nne's husband had passed away. Even though Nne was a powerful person, as a woman, she had limited rights under the law. The court ruled in favor of Albert, because a mother couldn't give away her daughter in marriage. Only the father could. Since Angela's father had passed away, he was in no position to reverse his early decision to give Angela to Albert. The Nne-approved marriage to the other guy was invalidated, and Albert claimed his fifteen-year-old bride.

In their wedding pictures, Angela looks sad, and Albert is beaming with joy.

Nne lost that battle, but she made it clear to Ifekewsi that she wasn't done fighting.

When Angela was a newlywed, she left the gate to Albert's family compound open by mistake. Leaving the gate open meant that anyone could just walk right in. It wasn't that big a deal, but Ifekewsi yelled at Angela about it and made her cry.

When Nne heard about the incident, she was furious. She started saving up ashes from her fires. On Oye, the market day when the entire village came out to shop, Nne put the ashes in a bucket, went to the market, and waited for Ifekewsi to show up. As soon as she appeared, Nne ran over, threw the ashes at her and then beat her with the bucket.

"If you make my daughter cry, this is what happens to you," she said. Nne didn't play when it came to her own. If anyone hurt her daughter, they would get a beating.

Resigned to reality, Nne turned her attention toward keeping Angela and Albert's marriage together. It wasn't exactly harmonious, especially in the beginning. Having nine children would be rough on any young mother. Culturally, divorce was just not an option. It would dishonor both the families. Angela didn't have the strength to fight for herself and her own interests in the marriage, so it fell on Nne to keep Albert, and his nagging mother, in line. Nne repeatedly told her daughter, "Keep your head up, no matter what people say or what your husband does." She carried the weight of her daughter's troubled marriage—and the family's reputation—on her back.

My understanding of my grandparents' marriage was that both Angela and Albert were good people, products of their time and culture, in difficult circumstances. In their later years, when I knew them, they lived separate lives for the most part. But they were at peace with their marriage. In short, they did as best they could.

Mom came from a generation where divorce was still scandalous, but it was done. Cordelia had done it. Susan had left my father. Now she stood at a crossroads: renew her vows to the man she loved, even though there were conflicts between them about major issues, or divorce and bring shame to the family. Mom didn't seem different to me around Edwin, but he would demand changes that would dim her light. She'd have to go from independence and leather pants to subservience and long skirts.

She could not make up her mind. Mom, Yvo, and I stayed in Nigeria for two weeks, without a resolution about what was going to happen with Susan and Edwin.

WE RETURNED TO Pittsfield, which was still completely foreign to me. Massachusetts was nothing like North Carolina. For starters, there was a foot of snow on the ground, and the air was dry and pine scented like a car air freshener. People talked differently, saying "uh-yup" instead of "yes," and "guys" instead of "y'all." I'd never had a heavy parka before and had to get used to wearing big ugly boots. Walking around the town, you'd see nothing but white faces in every direction, partially obscured by furry hats with ear flaps and the upturned corduroy collars of mustard Carhartt barn coats. I'd never seen so much plaid flannel in my life.

The immigrant story is characterized by constant movement for work, as well as continual searching for a community that will love and accept you, where you'll do well and fit in. Massachusetts didn't seem like it was going to be such a place.

Mom enrolled us in private Catholic schools. Yvo transitioned seamlessly, but then again, she did everything brilliantly. At my new school, I was the *only* Black girl, not just in my grade, but in the entire building. I felt like I didn't belong, not just because of my race and first-gen status, but because all my classmates had known one another forever. I'd had that in Durham, where I'd been in the same school system for most of my life. Now I was an outsider.

I studied my new environment and asked myself, "What makes a kid popular in Massachusetts?" The code wasn't hard to crack. It helped to be pretty (check), have cool clothes (check), and be good at something, like sports. Well, Nigerians aren't *good* at anything. We're great! And, at five foot nine, I happened to be great at basketball. I'd been a star player in North Carolina and became a superstar in Massachusetts. Even though I was the new girl, I became well liked within the first few months.

At the end of the day, a middle schooler needed only one quality to lift herself into the social stratosphere: confidence. I've always been overly confident—as I said, Nigerians are prideful, maybe to a fault. When people sensed that you believed in yourself, they gravitated toward you, whether you wanted their attention or not.

Bowing to Mom's demands, I pushed hard in class. To achieve excellence, I drove myself hard on the basketball court. When we had games, I was a high scorer, often shooting the winning basket. In victory, the other girls clamored around me.

We spilled into the locker room, celebrating our win. "You were amazing out there, Wendy," one girl said.

"We couldn't have done it without you," said another. True that.

"Can I touch your hair?" asked a third, a persistent redhead. (I can't tell you how many people tried to touch my hair in Pittsfield, but at least they were polite.)

With a smile, I said, "Maybe another time."

"Okay, sure," she replied. "Hey, you never said if you're coming to the party at my house tonight. It's just pizza and MTV. The whole team will be there. I'd really love it if you could come."

I said, "I'm so sorry, I already have other plans."

Unfailingly courteous, my Pittsfield teammates wouldn't dare ask what my "other plans" were—watching BET at home with Yvo. I'd just spent hours with these girls, all day at school and all afternoon at the game. Why did they want to hang out together at night, too? When school and practice were over, I went home.

"Okay, sure," said the redhead. "Call me if you change your mind."

My blackness and Nigerian-ness made me stand out in a positive way in Pittsfield. Unlike North Carolina, no one told me to "go back to Africa." I'd made a big cosmetic change between Winifred's house and Pittsfield that probably worked in my favor. Before, I always wore glasses. In Massachusetts, I started wearing contact lenses for the first time. I chose colored contacts that were a vibrant shade of blue, an homage to one of my favorite artists at the time, Lil' Kim. In her video *Crush on You*, she had piercing blue eyes, and I told myself, "I want to look like her." The contacts were expensive, around three hundred dollars, with a kaleidoscope of cobalt and azure lines and swirls around the black pupil. They looked real, even up close. Everyone assumed my irises were really that color, and I did not correct them.

The girls on the team were fascinated by the effect of blue eyes and dark skin. "You're so exotic," one always said. If I'd lost the contacts and shown up at school with my glasses and brown eyes, they would have been shocked. I suspect the contacts made me more palatable to them as well. They couldn't relate to my chocolate skin, but we all had the bluest eyes.

For an entire year, I had everyone fooled. The lenses were a kind of transparent shield that allowed me to see them, but they couldn't see me . . . a perfect metaphor for those superficial friendships. How could they be anything but superficial? The idea of telling these New Englanders about the racism we'd endured, the violence we'd seen, the culture we came from, was unthinkable.

My mom always said, "The only friends you have here are me and your sister. We're all we have." Her meaning was, no matter how close you get with people outside the family, you can't trust them like family. When your best friends are your mom and your sister, the bar is so high that anyone else who comes into your life is expendable.

To this day, I don't have a lot of girlfriends. I don't need them, because I have my mom and my sister. Maybe my mother, sister, and I are too dependent on one another. But if you're going to depend on someone, let it be your family. My family comes first, and that will never change.

Some might wonder if having such a small, tight, closed circle is suffocating or lonely. I find it fulfilling. I'm blessed by it. My great-grandmother Nne told her daughter Angela, who told her daughter Susan, who told me, "Having one good friend you can trust is better than having ten untrustworthy friends." Sure, my relationship with Mom wasn't as intimate as I wanted it to be, but Yvo and I understood each other as only best friends and sisters could. That's not to say my family relationships were perfect, or perfectly healthy, but there was no question that we would always show up for each other. The trust and loyalty were absolute.

As to the question of whether Edwin was going to join our tight family unit, it remained open. While Yvo and I were just starting our new lives in Pittsfield, Mom and Edwin talked on the phone daily. He kept up the pressure on Mom to give their marriage another try.

Soon after New Year's Day 1997, Mom put Uncle Hyke in charge of us in Pittsfield and returned to Nigeria to our father to renew their vows. She wouldn't agree to it until Edwin promised to do it in a Catholic church. As for her motivation to take this step, it was likely a combination of love, loneliness, and the stigma of divorce in the Nigerian community. She also probably hoped that she'd also get some financial help from Edwin, after supporting us on her own for so long. Yvo and I had no idea what to make of this development, or what it would mean for us.

Mom assured us, "You will stay here. We're not going to live in Nigeria."

My grandfather was strongly opposed. I didn't hear the conversations between Susan and her father, but Hyke revealed that Albert doubted Edwin's sincerity about giving Susan the freedom to make her own decisions about parenting and her career.

Mom returned to us a few weeks later, a newly remarried woman, and my parents resumed their marriage by phone. Her end of those conversations was kind of quiet. Mom just held the phone and nodded a lot. It wasn't normal for her not to be talkative and boisterous. When I got on the phone with Edwin, we made small talk for two or three minutes, and then he'd ask to put Susan back on. Their reconciliation didn't really change any practical aspect of my life. Still, I was glad that my parents were back together, and happy for her that she believed it would work out.

"He wants us to live in Nigeria. He says it's God's will," she told Hyke one night while cooking dinner for us all. Hyke was staying on at our place for most of that year. I was in the kitchen, too, listening. Shooting me a glance, she added, "Don't worry. It's not going to happen."

"Is he going to come here?" I asked. Yvo and I both hoped he would. Maybe if he were here he would act more like the joyful, sweet man I remembered him to be.

"I don't know," she said.

As I found out later, Albert and Angela reported to Susan that Edwin was becoming more unhinged in his fervent religiousness. What ultimately ruined any shot of their third attempt at marriage was Edwin's habit of asking Mom to send him money. I would overhear her tell him that she couldn't afford to send him anything. Asking for money wasn't that unusual. All Nigerians ask Americans for money. They think we're all rich. But in this case, it was audacious of my father to ask Mom for cash when he'd never contributed a penny to our upbringing. He never asked her how she'd paid for her own college education, or even our private school tuition. He only cared about how her career success could benefit him, while also expecting her, as his wife, to give it up and move back to Nigeria to struggle alongside him.

After a year of disappointment and disillusionment, Mom had had enough. "Girls, I've decided to get a divorce," she announced at dinner one night, dropping the bomb casually, like she might say she'd decided to change her hairstyle.

At this point, I was numb. Part of me knew that the reconciliation was never going to work, and I'd grieved this dream for so long already it wasn't that hard to finally let it go.

Albert was only too happy to use his influence in the Nigerian government to help Susan get a divorce. Edwin had no idea what was happening until he received the papers. But he didn't contest it, much to our family's surprise and relief. He said the divorce, too, was God's will.

A few years after my parents divorced, my father married again. He and his wife had five children together. When I learned about his second family, I felt jealous of the half siblings I've never even met. Over the years, some of my half siblings have tried to reach out to me, but I'm not interested in connecting. Yvo and our dad's oldest Nigerian daughter speak occasionally. I just can't do it. I don't want to hear her stories about growing up with Edwin and having that special relationship.

The end of my parents' marriage was, for me, the end of my relationship with my father. Over the years, he called every few months. Our conversations at first were just small talk, but they've gotten a bit more in depth lately. I know Yvo and he speak more often, but they had enough time together during her first seven years of life to form a real relationship. I envy my sister for those years, and her memories of my father from early childhood. I have so few, and no foundation to build an adult relationship upon. Unlike Mom—but very much like a first gen—

I don't feel the need to put on a brave spin for every bad situation. It doesn't make sense to pretend that I'm interested when I'm not, and that my bitterness doesn't exist.

The definitive end of my parents' marriage reinforced the sense that, for Mom, Yvo, and me, all we had was one another. The strongest shape in nature is a triangle. With our sturdy base, the three of us provided one another tremendous support. We were the Eiffel Tower, the pyramids of Giza, built to withstand any challenge. I didn't need friends, because I had my family. No matter where we were—and even if we were apart— we always had one another.

NINE

Change Is My Normal

Our lives were always in flux because we frequently changed apartments, schools, and for Mom, jobs. But as for the way we lived inside our homes, in our family, things stayed very much the same. Mom was the overlord, Yvo was her second, and I was the baby of the family.

Still, Mom's career was changing for the better. With every new position, she had more responsibility and earned more money. Not a fortune, but a decent income. Yvo was always ascending to the top of her class at whichever school she attended. I was a rising star on the basketball court. As individuals, we were each progressing along the narrow path toward success. Some things would never change, like the goals Mom put before us, and the bonds within our family of three. Mom was more committed than ever to her Nigerian traditions and her identity as a single woman. After the divorce, I didn't think she'd even consider dating again.

And then, when I (and she) least expected it, my mother met someone.

In June, we drove from Pittsfield to the Bronx for our summer in the city. My aunts, I'm sure, had a lot to say about Mom's choice to renew her vows with Edwin and then, within a year, get a divorce. I was spared that tension, preferring to spend much of my time outside, hanging with my friends.

One night, the entire family went to a party at a community center banquet hall. It was a typical Nigerian party, multiple generations of people crammed into the space, music thumping, luxury cars circling in search of parking, heat, sweat, smiling faces, gold jewelry, loud voices, and, of course, plenty of food and drink.

Our crew squeezed into the crowded hall. In the crush of people, the sound of one man's laughter rose above the rest. It was hearty, genuine, uninhibited, the kind of laugh that makes you start laughing, too. I found the source, a middle-aged man with a caramel complexion and a meticulously kept beard. He wore a black suit, and had on gold-rimmed glasses and a gold chain. For someone who laughed as boisterously as he did, I was surprised to notice that he was missing a tooth in the back of his mouth. I thought, *Why are you laughing so wide with that missing tooth?*

His gaze turned in our direction and zeroed in on Mom. He pushed his way through the crowd, straight over to us, and said to her, "You're beautiful."

She must have liked what she saw, too. From that night on, Mom and the Laughing Man, Darlington Okuzu, were in a relationship.

My mom's new boyfriend was the cleanest guy I've ever known, second only to my husband. You would *never* see a lose thread or stain on Darlington's immaculate dapper suits—always white linen in summer—nor a speck of food in his white teeth, or a smudge on his alligator shoes. He had pairs in every color—green, red, orange, and brown—to match any outfit. They were a stylish couple.

It was a bit odd to see Mom in a relationship after all that time of her being perpetually single. I approved of Darlington for her, although I didn't know him well at first, but I was a bit surprised that being in a relationship didn't soften her edges. At home, Mom was just as authoritative and independent as always. Maybe she was wary of being influenced by a man after all the back and forth with my father. Or she was thickly settled in her ways by thirty-seven. A new man wasn't going to change her or her priority: to raise her daughters to be the best. The same pressure on us—become a doctor or lawyer, marry a Catholic Igbo, have beautiful children—didn't let up. Our achievement would be her redemption, and we knew that if we failed her, we would be invalidating her entire life.

The more things change . . .

When Mom got a new job offer to be the director of nursing at a hospital in New York City, she jumped on it. It was another major move up, more money and a big title. We'd be closer to her sisters in the Bronx, and to Darlington, who lived in New Jersey.

We packed up again and left Massachusetts after a year with barely a goodbye, and moved to Coram, Long Island, into a three-bedroom, one-level, single-family home. What it lacked in height it made up in width. We had a fenced-in backyard and lots of space for us all.

I would be the new girl *again* in eighth grade. Because of my never-let-them-see-you-sweat Nigerian upbringing and our immigrant experience of habitually starting over, I'd learned to override my fears by then. Plus, I had evidence that I could be successful and do well—socially and academically—in a new school system. It stood to reason that I could do it again, even better this time. I was comfortable with being uncomfortable. New-girl status was my "normal."

Over the years, as I've moved through life, I've noticed that people often get stuck because they fear change. They might be miserable in a marriage or job, but they don't leave because it's familiar. Familiar misery seems safer to them than venturing into the unknown. But for me, change *was* familiar. As a result, I can adapt to any new environment quickly. Joining the cast of *The Real Housewives of Potomac* (RHOP) in season five was like leaping onto a speeding train. A lot of people would have been pulverized by the preexisting conflicts, constant arguing, and backstabbing among the cast, but I was just fine. And why would it be otherwise? I've been making such leaps since preadolescence, and I always stick the landing. On my first day at a new school, I just told myself, "No big deal. They're just people." No anxiety. No self-doubt. High confidence plus low expectations is a formula that has worked for me in pretty much every situation.

In New York, Yvo and I attended Stony Brook Preparatory, a private school. Private school was expensive enough for one child, let alone two! Luckily, we received financial aid. Our classmates were the sons and daughters of diplomats and lawyers, and their parents had no problem paying the exorbitant tuition out of pocket. Meanwhile, Mom enrolled at the Long Island University Post to get her master's degree in nursing.

Mom knew that education was crucial for success. Over the years, having applied and interviewed for many jobs, and just by living in a country that glorified and rewarded alumni of schools like Harvard and Yale, Mom had learned that not all education was equal. There appeared to be a clear dividing line between the haves and the have-nots, and that line was a *quality* education at a prestigious institution. So she put us in a school with the children of millionaires. Being among the elite completely changed who I was as a person. I always had confidence. At Stony Brook, I developed aspirations.

One of my goals was to be more independent. Change was normal, but Mom's rules were set in cement. After years of conditioning, Mom's dream for me to become a lawyer became my own. My prime directive was to make her proud, absolutely. But I wanted to make *some* decisions for myself. Like most teens (first gen or otherwise), I became a bit rebellious.

I wasn't the only one. Yvo began pushing back against Mom's fixed rules, too. Nigerians don't believe in dating. We believe in marriage. My American classmates cycled through a boyfriend a week. As first gens, relationships were off the table. "You will marry, and you will marry well, a Catholic, Igbo professional," Mom had instructed us since birth. In the meantime, my mother didn't have time to vet a parade of suitors. She only wanted to meet our husbands. If we weren't going to marry a boy, why bother wasting time with him when we could be studying or pursuing another opportunity to excel?

When Yvo was sixteen, she met a neighborhood guy, a slim Dominican with melted dark chocolate eyes and a champagne Lexus ES 350, and dared to date him. She knew he was a bit older, but he was really into her, and she was flattered. (We later found out that he was twenty-two and married with kids!)

He asked her out and she told him, "I can only go if my sister comes along."

I was my sister's eighth-grade wing woman and enjoyed each adventure.

When she knew Mom wasn't going to be home, Yvo planned for her date to pick us up in the Lexus—and he had a friend with him. It was a double date? I was almost fourteen. The guy smiled eagerly at me. I think I shook his hand and got into the car.

We drove a few blocks to the movie theater by our house. We were about to get out of the car to buy tickets when we saw my mom through the windshield, tearing around the corner, heading straight for us. A gust of wind lifted her hair in a swirl, her black trench coat flapping behind her. Like a female Shaft, she strode toward us with steely determination and murder in her eyes.

She knocked on the car window and said, "Girls, get out of there, right now."

"It was Yvo's idea!" I protested as she dragged me out of the car. "She made me come along." (Yes, I've had bratty moments.) Our punishment was to be sequestered in our home for over a month and the utter despair of knowing how disappointed Mom was with us. Of course, all communication with Mr. Rico Suave was discontinued.

I have no idea how Mom knew where we were or what we were doing. Maybe someone in the neighborhood saw us and tipped her off? Whenever we tried to sneak around, she always busted us. "You can't fool me," she'd say. "I know *everything* you're doing." We kept trying to get around her, though. We thought we were so smart, but she was smarter.

Another traditional rule of Mom's that I wanted to change: I desperately wanted to get a tattoo and to double pierce my ears. But Mom believed that a potential Catholic-Igbo-professional husband might consider body decoration as a sign of waywardness and would reject us. All my favorite rap artists had tats and wore multiple earrings, and I wanted to look like them. I begged her to let me get a tiny tattoo or to double pierce my ears, but she said no. "Only after your wedding."

Since it was my body, I thought it was my choice what to do with it. So one afternoon, I went into my room and numbed my ears with ice for a couple of minutes. Then I took a post earring—with a blunt tip—and double pierced my lobes myself. A nurse's daughter, I knew to soak the earring in alcohol and to swab the hole. I fastened the earrings and considered the job done. I thought that if I wore the studs in only the new holes (leaving my original holes empty) at home, Mom wouldn't notice. I'd bring a second pair of earrings to school and put them in once I got there.

The plan worked . . . until it didn't. One evening, Mom and I were in the kitchen before she left for work. The space was tight, and as I tried to squeeze by her, she did a double take, and then started squinting at the side of my head. *Oh shit*. On reflex, I pulled my hair down to cover my ear, but it was too late.

She said, "Did you pierce your ears?"

"No!" I said. I tried backing away from her, but she grabbed me by the ear and pulled me closer so she could get a better look.

"Yes, you did!"

She removed my earrings and popped me, too, which she did rarely. Mom's preferred punishment style was to make us feel the crushing weight of her disapproval, and to ground us. I definitely got grounded for the double piercing and would miss a big school dance that I was really looking forward to. Along with feeling powerless and humiliated, I was just so angry. She expected so much of us, but she didn't give us the freedom to make small choices for ourselves. If I had no self-determination, I'd be the baby of the family forever.

The more things stayed the same . . .

My grandmother Angela was living with us at the time. (Angela made frequent, extended trips to visit her seven children in America; so did Albert, but they never traveled together.) As Mom ranted at me and I stood there crying, Angela didn't say a word. After Mom stormed out of the house to go to work, Angela silently went to the kitchen counter and took out some ingredients. She cut some plantain, drizzled thick, red palm oil into a ceramic dish, and salted it. She then sliced a hot habanero pepper into the ceramic bowl. The room filled with heady aroma and the sound of sizzling oil. She asked me to sit down and put a plate of her simple, soul-satisfying food in front of me. She rubbed the top of my head and said in Igbo, "*Oga di mma*." Loosely translated to English, it means, "It's going to be okay." I sniffed back my tears, ate, and felt better. Food and my grandmother's love calmed me down.

In that one exchange, Angela showed me more affection and comfort than she'd ever given to my mother. Just the acknowledgment that I was sad helped me feel better (a lesson in child raising I took to heart and have used with my own children). It was one of my favorite memories of my grandmother. Whenever I'm feeling down and I need to hit the reset button on my mood, I cut some plantains, drizzle salted palm oil, and tell myself, "It's going to be okay."

The night of the dance, while my friends were having fun, I cried hot teenage tears in my pillow, cursing the fact that I had a mother who was so strict and so stuck in her traditional beliefs. Not half as strict and stuck as my father would have been, of course. But I had only one parent and her word was law, so all my frustration and anger were focused on her. I was Nigerian, but I lived in America. American girls could double pierce their ears without worrying about a future marriage suitor rejecting them. It seemed *so unfair*! The downside of being a first gen: we lived with our feet planted in two worlds. One world was ruled by the traditions of our ancestral country and present on a daily basis in our homes. The other world conformed to the traditions of the new world, which we witnessed whenever we left home. One represented a fixed point of view, and one represented change. I was Nigerian in some ways but American in others. There was no changing Mom's mind when it was made up, and her rigidity kept me stuck in between.

Mom's inflexibility didn't often make sense to me. One rule she had was: "If I can't buy you something, you don't need it." I wasn't allowed to borrow anything from anyone. To her credit, Mom did give us nearly everything we wanted. If Jay-Z rapped about a two-way pager in a song, that Christmas I'd find one under the tree. When kids at school started to get cell phones, Mom bought one for me for my birthday. Because Mom made sure we had the latest gadgets or newest sneakers, I was convinced we were well-off. She wasn't spoiling us; she kept us in style because of Nigerian pride. No child of hers wouldn't have what the other kids had. No one would judge us or gossip that we were poor.

So she was right, I didn't "need" to borrow things from people. But there were still times when borrowing was the simplest, best option. For example, I had this really cute outfit of dark blue Parasuco jeans with a matching white baby tee, and I *needed* the perfect sneakers to go with it. I had a great collection of sneakers: red, green, black. I was not hurting for colorful footwear. But for this outfit, only white sneakers with baby blue stripes would do. A girlfriend of mine lived across the street, and she had a pair of Pumas with the perfect color scheme. I knew Mom would be mad if I borrowed them, but I did anyway.

I rocked my outfit at school, but when I came home, Mom noticed the sneakers right away. "What sneakers are those?" she asked.

"You bought me these," I told her, trying not to blink.

"No, I didn't," she said.

"Yes, you did."

She said, "Okay. When I look in your closet tomorrow, I better find these sneakers."

My friend wanted them back that evening, so they weren't going to be in my closet the next day. I tried to pull a fast one by drawing a Puma stripe with a blue Magic Marker on a brand-new pair of Reebok Classics. It didn't come close to fooling Mom. I thought I'd be in big trouble, but Mom never brought it up again, apart from making an "I told you so" face and sounds when she noticed my Reeboks with the awkward stripes that looked terrible. If I hadn't borrowed the sneakers to wear for one day, I would have had fresh Reeboks to wear on many days. But now I had neither. Mom must have thought my learning the lesson the hard way was punishment enough. I never borrowed anything from anyone again.

When Mom caught me doing something we weren't supposed to be doing, I'd get a very specific kind of feeling—a "busted" stomach drop and a sense of panic about how she was going to react, and the terror of disappointing her. She had a sixth sense for any violation of the rules; it was uncanny. As a kid, I had no idea how she did it. Now that I'm a mom, I get it. I can always sense when something is off. Recently, my son seemed strangely hesitant to go to bed. I asked, "What did you watch?" I just knew that he'd seen something online or on TV that he wasn't supposed to and got scared. Mothers can tune into their kids' frequency, and if something's not right, they can feel it. Mom knew me so well that the subtlest shift in my body language—like trying to hide my pierced ears with my hair or shuffling with borrowed sneakers—was like waving a red flag.

It was understood that as long as we lived under her roof, Mom ruled with an iron fist. But that wouldn't be the case forever. Some changes were inevitable. When I was fifteen, Yvo left home to be a freshman at Duke University. I missed her terribly, of course, and begged to visit her at college as soon as possible. Before long, I was allowed to travel to Durham (Winifred was there to keep an eye on me) and spend a night with Yvo in her dorm room.

It was like opening a door to another world, one full of basketball stars. In Durham, where I grew up, college basketball is life. Duke's Blue Devils were a top NCAA team each year. Yvo and I were walking back to her dorm after a campus tour, and I noticed a big black Lincoln Navigator with Alaska plates pull up outside Bassett Hall. I thought, *Alaska? Who's here from Alaska?* And then a six foot-nine giant stepped out of the car.

"Oh my God!" I said, grabbing Yvo's arm. "That's Carlos Boozer." The future NBA All-Star was a student at Duke at the time. He was on a poster in my room at home.

She said, "Jason Williams and Dante Jones live in my dorm."

My mind? *Blown.*

Dorm life seemed like a free-for-all. People came and went; at all hours they were in and out of one another's rooms. They all seemed happy, smart, and so grown-up. A spontaneous party broke out in a room on Yvo's floor, and suddenly music was blasting and people were dancing in the hallway. I had no idea that college was a nonstop party. I'd thought it was all about hard work.

Drugs and alcohol didn't tempt me, or Yvo, because of the way we were raised. Going back to the "power of the tongue" manifesting style, Nigerian parents don't tell their kids what *not* to do. Mom's belief was, if you speak in the negative, you give power to it. So Mom didn't sit us down and say, "Don't do drugs." It was simply understood to be unacceptable in no uncertain terms. Nigerians of Mom's generation thought that people who did drugs were criminals. I knew my high school classmates were smoking weed every weekend. Since I didn't hang out or go to parties, I wasn't exposed to or put in a situation where I'd have to "just say no."

As for alcohol, the Nigerian style is to slowly savor the beverage of choice—my uncles' loved Hennessy cognac at parties—for the flavor and the little sparkle it gives you. Nigerians don't chug beers to get wasted. It's not a celebration anymore if people get drunk and sloppy and break things. When I was fourteen or so, Mom said, "If you're going to drink, drink here." I never really took her up on it. Once in a while, I would have a sip of wine or beer if she offered. Being given permission to drink demystified alcohol for me. I didn't think of it as a big deal. Looking around at the kids in Yvo's dorm and from what she told me, they seemed to be running wild in college because they had sudden access to alcohol. As soon as they were away from their sheltered lives, they said, "Another round! Keep it coming!" and proceeded to vomit in the bushes. Because Mom gave us permission to try alcohol, we never felt tempted to abuse it. Even now, I hardly drink.

What amazed me about college life was the freedom to make your own choices. Every person there could do whatever they wanted, whenever, with whomever, without anyone coming down on them.

"Is it always like this?" I asked Yvo.

"Pretty much," she said, grinning. "You have to go to class and do the work. But, yeah, no one tells you what to do, what to eat, who you can talk to, when to go to bed. It's great."

That one night at Duke opened my eyes. College was a ticket to real change, a new me that wasn't hemmed in by my mother's rules and traditions. For Yvo, going by how happy she seemed, it was transformative. She grew up fast as my second mother and was always under pressure to take care of me (on top of pleasing Mom and getting straight As). Going to college relieved her of parental responsibility for the first time. Leaving home for most people is when they think of themselves as grownups. For my sister, it was her chance to finally be a kid.

What would this change of life be like for me? I couldn't wait to find out.

TEN

Failure Is Not an Option

During our first year in Long Island, Darlington visited us every weekend. He was a welcome presence, with that contagious laugh. An Igbo immigrant of Mom's generation, he came to America at eighteen to study politics at Rutgers University in New Brunswick, New Jersey. He graduated and earned a good living in sales.

We bonded over our obsessive fandom of the New York Knicks. Our favorite players were the scrappy fighters of the era like John Starks. When I went through a *Godfather* fan phase, he sat down with me on our black leather couch and told me all he knew about the crime families of New York City—the only Black man I knew who could name all five. Darlington was a gifted storyteller with an eye for detail and kept me parked on the couch with him for hours. Did a teenage girl need to know about the sordid, violent history of John Gotti's rise to power? Probably not. But Darlington told me about it anyway. More than anyone in my life, he fostered my love of learning about how the world works. If Uncle Hyke was my professor of the streets, Darlington was my walking Wikipedia, book smart *and* street-smart. I could ask him about any car on the highway during our long drives, and he'd say, "That's a 2000 Cadillac DeVille," or "Ford Mustang, 2007." His mind was a steel trap.

The day after I turned fifteen, after they'd been dating for two years, Mom and Darlington got married. Apart from being annoyed that their wedding dimmed my birthday spotlight, I was thrilled for Mom. The wedding was large and over-the-top, reflective of their personalities. All of Mom's bridesmaids wore tuxedo shorts, white-collared shirts, fishtail tuxedo jackets, black cummerbunds, blue bow ties, black top hats, and carried white canes. Yes, you absolutely read that right! Why on earth did Mom think that her bridesmaids—including me—would want to wear this? Almost twenty years later, and I still don't know. But that was Mom, always marching to the beat of her own drum and living her best life in the way she knew how.

It's unusual for a child to be the bridesmaid at her own mother's wedding, but our family was not typical. Just as I'd attended all her graduation ceremonies, I cheered for Mom as she legally joined forces with a good man. Darlington moved into our house in Coram. And just like that, I had two parents.

Life in a two-parent household was not all kumbaya. The marriage wasn't perfect. A disparity became apparent between them. Mom was committed and focused on her career goals. She knew what she wanted to achieve and had a plan to do it. Darlington didn't have her focus, or her drive. She had a long-term career; he had a series of short-term sales jobs. He must have felt like he paled in comparison to Mom's achievement. This dynamic might be difficult for any man who equated masculinity with income or purchasing power. It was especially hard for a Nigerian, since our culture puts the man first. The man is supposed to be the dominant presence in a marriage and household. The woman is supposed to be subservient. But in our household, Mom made the money and the decisions. She had left Edwin three times so she didn't have to answer to a man, and she did not enter a new marriage to be told what to do. It wasn't that Darlington expressly wanted control over Mom. I don't believe he did. But culture runs deep. Even if he had modern American ideas about gender equality, Mom's success still shined a light on his lack of direction and dissatisfaction with his own career in comparison. I think he felt eclipsed by the sun that is my mother. I could relate.

He succeeded in other ways, becoming a leader in the Nigerian community. We went to his ancestral village for his chieftaincy ceremony, basically a coronation for a high-ranking person. The ceremony itself involves saying some vows and performing traditional rites like picking a chieftain name. I got to wear traditional garb and a beaded headdress. Hundreds of people came out to honor Darlington, and even more showed up at the party afterward for the music, dancing, food, and drink.

Susan and Darlington could have loved each other better. She didn't know how to bend—which I knew all too well as her daughter—and he wasn't built to teach her how to do it. Mom was as stubborn and demanding a wife as she was a mother. If he didn't meet her standards about something—from taking out the garbage to being her companion—she let him know. As an observer of their interactions, I often felt sorry for how hard she was on him. I empathized, because she was just as hard on me.

During our three years on Long Island, we went to Manhattan every Christmas to see the spectacular giant tree all lit up, the rows of golden trumpeting angel statues, and the ice-skaters at Rockefeller Center. One year, Mom and Darlington wore matching all-leather black outfits, circa 1980s Eddie Murphy. It was a great day, very festive: mittens, scarves, hot chocolate, and french fries at a diner.

On the way home, we parked in front of a bodega in the Bronx to pick up something or other. A song by the artist Joe came on the radio, and Darlington turned it up as loud as he could. He grabbed Mom's hand and said, "Let's dance." He coaxed her out of the car and the two of them danced in the middle of the street in their matching outfits, the streetlights framing them like in a movie. I watched them from the back seat, feeling warmed by the sight in the cold air. They looked so cute and happy.

If it were me, I would have been dazzled by the spontaneous gesture. It would have bought any partner of mine a week of my not starting any arguments. For her, the romantic moment passed as quickly as it came.

They got back into the car and we headed home. Darlington didn't signal a turn, and Mom said, "You didn't put on your blinker. You should have signaled."

Darlington's shoulders slumped. I rolled my eyes, thinking, *Lady, come on. Give it a rest.*

She is never happy, I said to myself. *Nothing makes her happy.*

I knew that standing up for Darlington would put my own feet to the fire (it did), but I went ahead with it anyway. That moment marked a turning point for me. I'd always had blind faith that her way was best. I was starting to realize the inherent contradiction of my mother. She expected perfection from her children and her husband, but she was far from perfect herself.

I prayed that Darlington, like me, could find a way to get through to her. And maybe, just maybe, she'd back off a tiny bit when we didn't live up to her expectations.

BEING SO CLOSE to New York City, I asked Mom to take me to some casting calls for teen modeling jobs. She took me to an audition here and there, but they were one-offs. We didn't invest the time or effort needed to make an impact. "Be a lawyer first, then you can be a model," she always said. Every conversation about my interests ended with the comment, "Be a lawyer first."

Basketball was an approved and encouraged extracurricular activity because it kept me occupied in the afternoons when she was at work or grad school, and I was great at it. If I sucked, I would have been forced to drop that, too.

The Nigerian rule is, "Be the best. Being less than the best is an excuse." With natural ability and if you push yourself, you *can* be the National Spelling Bee champion, the top NBA draft pick, or a valedictorian. We were trained to believe that nothing, I mean *nothing*, was out of our reach. Nigerian first gens internalized that. It's actually an incredibly powerful and consequential framework.

American kids are taught to try their best and to do things for the fun of it. Nigerian kids are taught to be the best and that fun is irrelevant. Our culture shuns mediocrity. It sounds harsh, but when you are trained that excellence is the baseline, you can achieve amazing things. Recently, I read an article about a Black girl graduating high school with scholarships to every Ivy League college. I said to myself, "I bet she's Nigerian." She was. I read a story about a Black ten-year-old chess prodigy who was beating professional adults. I said, "I bet he's Nigerian, too." Again, he was. How did those kids succeed? They had natural gifts, of course. But they must have worked their asses off. Working as hard as possible is a responsibility drilled into us by our parents. Failure to be the best resulted in sharp criticism, such as one of Mom's favorite comments, "Did someone *else* get an A?" I was raised that failure was not an option.

And yet, failure could happen. It did happen to me.

My first year at Stony Brook, the elite prep school, came to an end and the summer began. Now that we were New Yorkers ourselves, we didn't "summer" in the Bronx. I was old enough to take care of myself anyway. I waited anxiously for the mail every afternoon to receive my grades for the year, sorting through the pile of catalogs and bills for an envelope with the school letterhead. The one day that Mom got to the mail pile before I did, the letter arrived.

She said, "Your grades are here," and held up the envelope.

She opened it and held it out of reach as I tried to grab it, laughing. When she finally read my report card, she stopped laughing. "Explain this, Wen," she said.

I took the paper and scanned my grades. They were okay. The most important number on the page was my cumulative GPA. The second I saw it, my throat instantly dried up. *Shit.*

It was a 2.9. To keep my financial aid, I had to score a minimum GPA of 3.0. I was one decimal point below where I needed to be. There was no way Mom could pay the full tuition to keep me there. My breathing became shallow. I had the urge to run out of the kitchen, out of the house, and as far as my legs could carry me.

"How did this happen?" she asked. "It wasn't easy to get you into that school. Now what are you going to do? You'll have no choice but to go to public school."

When Mom envisioned a life for her kids, she saw us among the best and being surrounded by the best. Public school was nowhere near her ideal for us. In public school, the kids weren't the children of millionaires like the kids at Stony Brook. The point of going to private school wasn't to make friends with the rich kids. It was to observe them, and ultimately become one myself.

"How did this happen?" she repeated.

I just shook my head. Anything I said would sound like an excuse, and Nigerian parents did not tolerate excuses. The only explanation Mom would accept was full accountability and solutions to fix it. I might've stammered a bit, but I was too ashamed and scared to speak.

Not cutting it at an elite school was humbling; failing to meet Mom's "be the best" expectations was devastating. If a sinkhole opened up in our front yard, I would have gladly jumped into it. Greatness was the baseline expectation, and I didn't live up to it.

Parents in other cultures might instill in their kids the belief that they can do anything or become the president one day. I'd seen evidence of that on American TV. In sitcoms, though, if a kid doesn't succeed, the parents often comfort them and gently encourage them to try again, with supportive "let's figure out what happened" dialogue mixed in. Nigerian parents skip the comforting and encouragement parts completely, and go straight into demanding accountability. A Nigerian child knows that the penalty for failure is being a disappointment to the parents. Their approval is the sun, air, water, food. Failing them feels like dying inside. This emotional imperative is the main reason failing happens so rarely for Nigerian first gens.

When I emerged from my room a few hours after the life-changing report card arrived, I was ready to throw myself at Mom's feet and beg for mercy. I'd do anything to make her forgive me. She hadn't even been that hard on me. The voice in my head was much harsher than she'd been.

I found her (where else?) in the kitchen. Much to my surprise and utter relief, Mom didn't dwell on it. While chopping okra, she said, "You will get back on track and you will succeed."

In her mind, my becoming a lawyer was already a foregone conclusion. This hiccup didn't matter. Mom was using the "power of the tongue" to manifest my success by speaking about its inevitability.

"I'm so sorry this happened," I said.

"It's a bump on your way to being a lawyer," she said.

"Yes, Mom," I said. "Can I help you make dinner?"

She just shook her head and told me that dinner would be ready in an hour. As usual, Mom never let me stand at her side, shoulder to shoulder, while she cooked. She was the mother; she prepared the food. I was the child; I ate the food and did what she said. That was how it always was; that was how it always was going to be.

I would have agreed to sit in the corner day and night, as long as she didn't yell at me, compare me to my superstar sister, or tell me about all the sacrifices she made so I could become a lawyer in America. That would have been like twisting the knife.

The thing was, I *had* studied and done the work, but I could have pushed harder. I had no one but myself to blame, and it killed me.

"You will work harder," she said.

"I will. It won't happen again. I promise."

Bottom line: true failure was giving up. Yes, I had been kicked out of an elite school, but my life plan—lawyer, marriage, kids—hadn't changed. On the narrow path that we walked, of course we'd hit some obstacles.

Obstacles weren't deterrents, though. Nigerian immigrants aren't intimidated or thrown by roadblocks, because overcoming them was just what you had to do to reach your goals. First gens grew up listening to our parents' stories of survival, their tales of hitting obstacles and navigating around them. Compared with what Mom went through to educate herself and make a life for us, my struggles were puny. I had to turn this setback into a victory. Doing that would be a truer measure of my "be the best, no excuses" capability.

What Mom didn't know, and I was not about to tell her, was that there was another aspect to changing schools that deeply affected me. I had a secret boyfriend at Stony Brook, and I didn't want to go to a different school than he did, because it was the only time I got to spend with him.

Kevin was a year older, tall, dark-skinned like me, with sleepy, sexy eyes and full lips that were always turned up at the corners. He resembled the rapper Loon and was very much a ladies' man as a result. He was smart, kind, an all-around good kid from a good family. Mom had met Kevin at a school event. She liked him and approved of his pedigree—he came from a good family—so she allowed me to have a friendship with him. But he would never be an approved potential husband because he wasn't Nigerian.

"Can Kevin and I go to the movies?" I asked early on in our "friendship."

"No," said Mom.

"Can we hang out after school?"

"No."

"Can we go to the diner for lunch?"

"No," she said. "You can see him at school, but you can never ever be alone with him."

As far as Mom knew, we hadn't even kissed. Eventually, Kevin was permitted to come to our house, but only if Mom was there. By controlling the environment and our relationship, she thought she could control us. Her fears were justified. I was only a few years younger than Mom was when she married Edwin. If I'd told her how I truly felt about Kevin, Mom would have locked me in my room and thrown away the key.

As luck would have it, Kevin had to leave Stony Brook, too—why, I don't recall. Based on our addresses, Kevin and I were zoned for different public schools. I begged Mom to figure out a way to send me to the one he was zoned for. She wound up paying $350 a semester for me to go to that school outside our district.

Mom didn't do it so I could spend more time with Kevin. The extra-fee public high school was better than the one in our zone. She also wanted to separate me from the girls in our neighborhood (Mom predicted trouble ahead if I got too close to them). At my new school, which was overwhelmingly Dominican and white, I stuck out as one of the only Black students. I didn't care, though.

The day before the start of ninth grade, I got my nails done for the first time. Mom took me to a salon and said I could get acrylic tips in the classic French manicure style. I dressed it up by polishing the nails baby blue and adding an airbrushed tiny yellow Tweety bird to each one. The manicure cost eighty-five dollars, which seemed like a lot. Mom was making more money than ever before, so she could afford the splurge. My nails were an investment in my confidence. She knew how shaken I'd been by my failure at Stony Brook. This was her way of setting me up for success this time, by making sure I walked into a new school feeling like the coolest kid there. You can't put a price on that!

I was on my own path to redemption now. My victory would be keeping my head down, doing the work, raising my GPA so I'd qualify for an elite college. Our success stories had always been intertwined. The only thing that mattered to me was redeeming myself in my mother's eyes. The very thought of letting her down again . . . I did not speak it or let my mind go there. Failure was not an option.

It'd help me to have some stability. Change was my normal, but even

I reached my limit. I was starting over at the fourth new school in as many years. Mom seemed to like her job in Manhattan. I counted on our staying on Long Island until it was time for me to go to college. We were settled in for the long haul, I believed.

Once again, I was wrong about that.

ELEVEN

The Crowded House

When I was sixteen, Mom got a new, better job offer at a hospital in Maryland. She was excited about it. "It's more money and we'll be closer to Yvo at Duke."

"Works for me," I said. Kevin was headed to Howard University in Washington, DC, so I'd actually be closer to him.

When we arrived in Baltimore, we did what we always did: locate the Nigerian community in the area and learn who was who. One of the first families we met was the Osefos, a husband and wife and their five kids, three girls and two boys. Their oldest son, Edward (affectionately known as Cho by his family), was five months older than I was. We first met at a Nigerian cookout at another family's house. I thought he was terrifically handsome (and still do). He had on khaki shorts and a collared polo shirt. He was tall, with close-cropped dark hair, yummy chocolate skin, cognac eyes that reminded me of Edwin's, a smile to light up the room, and an easy confidence. His eyes seemed to follow me around the party, so apparently the appreciation was mutual.

I was the new girl in town and enjoyed being the fresh face. I heard some ask each other, "Who is *she*?" Eddie was just one of many. Even if I were open to dating—which I wasn't, because of Kevin—Mom would never have allowed it. I had to focus on my studies at my new school and start thinking about college.

A boy came up to me at the cookout and said, "Eddie likes you. Do you like him?"

"I can't date him," I said. "He doesn't have a car." It was a joke, a harmless way to send the message *not now, maybe never.*

He kept tabs on me anyway. A month or so later, he came to my house to pick up some food containers. Cecilia, Eddie's mom, did catering on the side. My mom, being the life of the party, had recently held an event for which Cecilia cooked jollof rice. I found her plastic cooler and held it out for him to take. Eddie was acting weird, like he wanted to say something to me, and finally, he blurted, "I've heard you're dating Steve," referring to some random guy I barely knew.

I was *not dating*, and I didn't like it that people were talking about me behind my back.

Just to mess with him, I said, "Yeah, I am seeing him. Steve's the best."

Eddie snatched the cooler out of my hands and stormed off with it, like, *You broke my heart, now gimme my Tupperware!* After that, we saw each other at Nigerian parties, but we were just friends.

Cecilia *loved* me at first. She joked around with Mom, saying, "One day, your daughter will marry my son Eddie." It was a funny echo of Angela and Albert's mothers joking about their kids getting married one day . . . and look at how that worked out.

Just like Nne and Ifekewsi, the friendship between Susan and Cecilia ended before it really began. Susan had a lot of practice at coming into a new Nigerian community and charming everyone with the natural force of her personality. She casts a bright light wherever she goes, and people are drawn to it. When she talks, they listen. What she says, goes. Mom's instant rise in status and leadership among Baltimore's Igbo community was welcomed and wonderful for everyone . . . except Cecilia. Mom overshadowed her. Their doyenne vs. doyenne drama intensified as time went by. I think Eddie's mom felt threatened by mine, and she drew a line between her family and friends, and Susan's people.

While Mom established herself in Baltimore by going to parties, church, events—even founding a Nigerian women's support organization—Darlington struggled to restart his life. He wasn't as used to moving as Mom. Mom thrived in the newness of it all. He'd spent his whole life in the New Jersey area, and our move to Maryland was like tearing up his roots. When we lived in New York, he was fit and happy, with a job and tons of old, close friends. When we moved to Maryland, he tried to find work as a salesman, but nothing materialized. As for making local friends, he missed his old ones too much, and couldn't get up the energy to forge new ones. His torn-out roots were too damaged to take hold in the new ground.

As the months went by, it became apparent that Darlington had lost his spark, and we saw less of his gap-toothed smile. His booming laugh that made him so fun to be around was quieted. He had no energy and got out of breath easily. Mom, a cardiac nurse, recognized the signs, and it turned out she was right. Not only was he in bad shape emotionally, he was in the early stages of heart disease.

I missed the Darlington I'd first met back in the Bronx. But he loved my mother so much he would have followed her to the ends of the earth, even if it made him miserable.

As for my adjustment, I dusted off my New Girl playbook at the Towson Catholic High School in a suburb of Baltimore. I was laser focused on my grades and on not disappointing Mom again. But sometimes, I slipped and acted a bit rebellious at school. One day, I was sitting in the back of science class with two other Black girls. The science teacher, a quirky white man, said to us, "Okay, I want you guys to sit in the front of the class."

"I don't want to. I'm staying back here," I said. Granted, my response was a bit spicy.

"No. Come and sit in the front," insisted the Mad Scientist.

"No, I'm staying in the back."

"Go figure," he said. "Who would have thought that the Black girls would want to sit in the back of the class."

He was referencing Rosa Parks, the civil rights activist who in 1955 told a Montgomery, Alabama, bus driver that she would not go to the back of the bus to the colored people section, and instead plopped herself down in front in the whites-only area.

The science teacher's implication was that the three of us were self-segregating by sitting in the back of the classroom. It was a lame attempt at a joke, meant to shame us into changing seats. He must have known, as all teachers do, that sitting in the front of the classroom is like being under a microscope. He wanted to keep a close eye on us, perhaps because we were Black. Or maybe just because he liked to break up friend groups to avoid distractions. Whatever his reasons, by making that "back of the class" comment, he brought race into it. By emphasizing our blackness, he gave the other students permission to view us as second-class citizens. For nearly all our years in New England and New York, I hadn't had to deal with racist comments from teachers. This incident was an unwelcome reminder that we were back in the South, and would have to face the prejudice that came with it.

That night, all three of us told our parents what happened. Collectively, the families requested a meeting with the principal to discuss it. When Mom got home from that gathering, I asked, "How'd it go?"

She said, "I'm the only parent who stood up for my daughter. I don't know if it's because the other students are on financial aid, and their parents didn't want to bite the hand that feeds them. But they just sat there and let the principal railroad them and blow smoke up their ass."

Mom would not let anyone railroad her. "I was the one who said no, what happened was racist," she continued. "And I need an apology from that teacher. I need to know that my daughter will not be discriminated against." She was a warrior for me, but also for the other parents who didn't have the courage or will to defend their kids. If a teacher singled out three Black girls and called attention to their race in a snide way in front of their white peers, he needed to apologize. It seemed obvious.

It was the same old song, just a new verse. Every time something could have gone wrong in my life, my mom set things right. And one day, I would pay her back for all of it.

NIGERIANS DON'T PLACE a high value on emotional support. Financial support, however, is another matter. Our culture has clear guidelines that are only heightened through the immigrant lens. Our parents gave up so much of their financial wants to ensure we attended college, went to graduate school, and had every chance for success. Once we achieve it by becoming a professional, there is also the expectation that we pay back our parents for all their hard work in raising us. It's almost like the concept of the "angel investor" in business. Our parents believe in our dreams and therefore they financially invest in us, but once we make it, they get the financial rewards.

One pragmatic example: it's common for aging parents to move in with their adult children. In the old days, the integration of multigenerational houses started much earlier, when the senior generation were in their forties and fifties. Nowadays, parents move in with their adult children later, but it's still the way things are done. In Western society, many adult children consider their obligation met by putting their aging parents in a nursing home. Nigerians don't believe in nursing homes or assisted living. Culturally, the way our parents took care of us when we were children is how we are expected to take care of our parents in their old age.

The transactional nature of "I took care of you, and now you take care of me" adds another layer to the emotionally detached tone of Nigerian parenting. Why should there be hand-holding, emotional wellness checks, and affection? Parenting isn't personal, it's just business. The upside is that since Nigerian kids know they'll be financially responsible for their parents one day, they are extra motivated to become successful to ensure they'll have the resources they'll need for themselves, their children, *and* their aging parents. The downside is feeling crushed by the weight of that responsibility. It's a lot of pressure, but pressure makes diamonds.

When my grandparents Angela and Albert were in their final years, they lived with their daughters for extended periods. Angela usually stayed with Winifred. Mom took in Albert. Not only did she house him, she assumed the financial burden of his health care and basic needs.

With my adult perspective, I can only imagine the pressure Mom was under. She had one child at Duke, another at a private high school. And her ailing father required a full-time daytime nurse when Mom was at work. She handled all these expenses, along with running a house and doing most of the shopping, cooking, and cleaning. Of course, I had my chores. But my job was to do well in school so I'd get into a good college, and then law school, etc.

I loved my grandfather Albert, but the house did feel a bit crowded while he was living with us in Baltimore. I'd grown up with only three of us—and sometimes Hyke—in our homes. Now it was Mom, Darlington, Albert, the nurse, Yvo when she came home from Duke, me, and sometimes Hyke. As a teenager, I craved privacy. I rarely got it.

One time Kevin took the train from Howard University to our house to visit me. The two of us were parked on the couch in our living room because I'd twisted my ankle during a basketball game and had to wear a medical boot on my leg. Mom had left for an hour to run some errands. On her way out, she said, "My father and the nurse are here. So you won't be alone."

Message received, Mom. But as soon as the door closed behind her, Kevin and I started making out. The nurse was nowhere in sight, and Albert was downstairs. We thought we were safe. We thought that if we were by the front door, we'd hear Mom come back and be able to stop and rearrange our clothes in time. In hindsight, this made no sense. We just wanted to make out and would bend logic to our will.

As you might expect, we were not paying as close attention to the subtle sounds of Mom walking up to the door as we should have been.

When she opened it, she got a sight no mother should ever see. She stood there in shock for about two seconds while Kevin and I pulled apart and covered up.

She looked at Kevin and said, "Get out."

"Mom, this isn't what it—"

"Get dressed and get out."

The nurse drove Kevin to the train station. And then Mom and I were alone in the living room.

She glared at me with a sickening combination of fury and disapproval. I can't say I blamed her. Kevin and I had been going at it in the living room, in the middle of the day, with my grandfather and his nurse downstairs. Not too smart! She must have suspected that we'd been intimate; we'd been together for two years by then. For most Americans, guarding your virginity was not considered proof of a girl's moral superiority. In Nigeria, and certainly in my mother's time, girls did not have sex before marriage.

"I did not sacrifice my marriage and work this hard so you would get pregnant in high school," she said coldly.

It was her worst fear, the thing that her sisters, ex-husband, and the gossips in the community warned was going to happen if she chose to raise her daughters on her own.

I was furious she'd sent Kevin packing. Didn't I have the right to privacy? I yelled back, "This is why I can't wait to go to college!"

To her credit, she didn't kill me on the spot. All she wanted was for me to get out of her sight. She sent me to my room and grounded my ass for a few weeks.

Kevin and I were always *very* careful. Things happen, though, and just one slip could have changed my life forever. If I'd gotten pregnant in high school or college, I would probably not be Dr. Wendy today. Now that I have a daughter of my own, I completely understand why Mom discouraged boyfriends. The thought of any of my kids being sexually active as teenagers scares the crap out of me. I have already decided that

I won't let Kamrynn have a boyfriend in high school. I will probably let my sons have girlfriends, though. I confess that I do buy into the double standard to some extent because of cultural biases. Nigerian girls will grow up to be the caretakers of their aging parents, not the boys. (One day I would be expected to preside over a crowded house of my own, with my own husband and kids, as well as Mom and Darlington when they were elderly.) Since the parents' future care depends on their daughters' sense of responsibility, girls are not given any leeway for bad behavior. Nigerian boys are cut a lot of slack. Since so much is riding on Nigerian girls, they wind up becoming amazing women. (The boys? Not always.) The double standard and extra pressures that are gender based are not fair. But I'd rather wind up amazing than not. I suppose I have that good old gender bias to thank for that.

Mom's strictness about dating and my being alone with Kevin were protective of both of us. She was guarding her redemption as well as my future. Being chaste would keep me on the narrow path, so she didn't care if blocking me from seeing him felt intrusive and humiliating for me. I had some resentment about that.

When I was a senior in high school, Mom, then forty, had an announcement. "I'm expecting," she said casually at dinner one night. Darlington was forty-four, and about to be a new father. This development seemed to lift his spirits somewhat, and for that, I was happy. But otherwise, I wasn't thrilled by Mom's late-in-life pregnancy. I'd always been the baby of the family. But now there was going to be a little sister or brother. What did that mean for my place in the family structure? Would this baby get a better, different version of my mom, like my father's second family had a better, different version of him? I felt a bit jealous of this tiny person who hadn't been born yet.

As the months of her pregnancy passed, I began to feel anxious about the baby's arrival. Our house was already crowded. The new baby would cry all night and fill diapers. Would Mom breastfeed in public, where my friends could see? I would do whatever was asked of me to help, but I was busy with basketball and applying to college. When I was accepted to Temple University in Philadelphia in the spring of my senior year, I was thrilled and relieved that the process was over. Mom was satisfied by my choice, and if she wasn't, she was too distracted by the pregnancy and the demands of her life. I immediately started counting the days until I could leave home, go to college, and experience a taste of the freedom I'd glimpsed a few years earlier during that weekend trip to visit Yvo at Duke. But until that day came, I'd just have to endure.

It was no fun to be a teenager with a pregnant mother. I was the captain of the girls' basketball team. (Fun fact: the captain of the boys' team at the time was Carmelo Anthony, now a ten-time NBA All-Star for the Portland Trail Brazers.) Mom—and her huge belly—came to my games to cheer me on from the stands, which was great. Except on the sidelines, my teammates would point her out and say, "Wendy's mom has *sex* . . ." Like I needed the reminder. I hated that.

When Mom's due date approached, Yvo was home for the summer from college. Yvo and I wound up racing to the hospital when Mom went into labor. We arrived only a few minutes after my new brother, Jordan, was delivered by C-section. A son for Mom, at last. We got to hold him soon after. Instant love! All my anxiety about losing my place fell by the wayside. I mean, he cried a lot as a baby, and that did make the house feel even smaller. Aside from that, Jordan was and is a blessing in our family's life.

I believe Jordan's arrival made my stepfather happier than he'd been in a while. As a father, Darlington seemed excited, and nervous. He had no experience with any aspect of parenting. Meanwhile, Susan was the mother of all mothers. Once again, he was overshadowed by her. It's not like he was trying to be Mary Poppins, though. But at least he was present, which is more than I could say for my father.

Traditionally, Nigerian fathers aren't very involved in their babies' upbringing. My mother had zero expectations for Edwin as a caregiver—feeding, bathing, changing diapers was women's work. Nigerian men: If your wife has a baby, she needs your help and support, so take a month off from work and be there. Don't say, "She's on maternity leave, so we're covered." My attitude was, if my career is going to be put on hold because I had a child, then my spouse's career is, too, and we're going to do this together. Eddie took paternity leave when we had children, so he got to know them and how to care for them right alongside me.

I might've felt displaced by my baby brother if he'd been born a year earlier. But his arrival came while I was planning my departure. The freedom I'd longed for was almost here. In college, I would be able to spend time with a boyfriend without fear of him being kicked out of the house. I could eat whatever I wanted, stay up all night. I would make big and small decisions for myself that Mom would never even know about.

For the first time, my life would feel like my own, even if Mom's voice and her list of expectations played like a loop in my head. The two of us had made eight moves across four states over the past fourteen years. Finally, I was going to make a move all on my own.

TWELVE

The Learning Curve

After Mom graduated high school at age sixteen (which is normal in Nigeria), she took some advanced-level courses, hoping to go to college, like her sister Winifred. Unfortunately, she just barely missed the cutoff score on the state's "challenge" testing and wasn't allowed to enroll.

But that was okay. Angela had other plans for her youngest daughter. She wanted Susan to become a nun. So Mom went to a convent and worked as hard as she could at her religious studies to make her mom happy.

One morning, the principal of the convent interrupted the students' prayer session and said, "If you hear your name, come to my office." She read off her list. Susan's name was on it. Mom and a bunch of others filed down the convent halls and crowded into the principal's small, dreary office, which had only a wooden cross on the gray walls.

The principal, a dour woman, said to the group, "I called your names because you girls have no calling from God. You are not going to be nuns."

Knowing my mom and her nonconformist spirit, this was a very accurate assessment.

Susan was kicked out of the convent. She started crying, knowing (and fearing) how disappointed her mother would be about this shocking turn of events. "What did I do wrong?" she asked.

"It's not anything you did," said the principal. "God didn't call you."

"Then let God tell me I'm not called himself!"

Her back talk might have been borderline blasphemous, which the principal considered proof that she'd been right to get rid of her. Through her tears, Susan noticed that only the girls who looked and smelled good had been expelled. God didn't call the pretty ones?

As predicted, Angela was upset and (kiss of death) *disappointed*. Albert was so angry he put on his military uniform, showed up at the convent, and stormed the principal's office. "Who made you God to decide what God wants?" he demanded of the small, old woman.

It didn't matter what he said or how angry he was. She'd made her decision and it was final.

College and the convent were off the table for Susan. Now what? Angela pushed Mom to go visit her older brother Fred in San Francisco. It was a newly popular choice for young Nigerians to go to America for an education, and the government encouraged it. The hope was that they would later return with the knowledge they'd acquired to develop their own country. Instead, what occurred was the "brain drain" of a generation of talented Nigerians coming to the US to get their degrees and not returning home. They decided to stay for a better life and to raise their children here.

At seventeen, never having been outside her own country, my mother set off for the United States by herself with one small suitcase, her brother's phone number on a slip of paper, and her rosary, with the intention of going to college. Her education had to be delayed because she met my father, fell in love and got married, and had a child by twenty.

Mom missed out on a carefree, unencumbered college experience, and she wanted us to have what she didn't. In addition, for every child of Nigerian immigrants, college was a given. You couldn't become a doctor or lawyer without a bachelor's degree. A lot of my friends were happy to collect their high school diploma and go right into the workforce. But in our house, the question wasn't *whether* to go to college, it was, "Which college are you going to go to?"

Mom didn't give us the option of not going to college because if she'd spoken of divergent paths, it might have given life to them. Eddie and I are also raising our kids by the Nigerian cultural concept of manifesting or speaking things into existence. We don't say, "If you get married," or, "If you go to college." We talk about going to their future weddings and basking in their future success. Nigerians manifest so much, if someone jokingly says, "I'm dying," every person in the room will make the sign of the cross and say, "It's never going to happen. Amen."

So college was an "already written," and Temple University in Philadelphia was an excellent choice for me. Going there was the fifth-best decision I've ever made in my life. That number is not to be taken lightly, because the first four items on that list are marrying Eddie and having my three children.

When I left for college, I took a lot more than one small suitcase and a rosary. My mom and Darlington drove me to Philadelphia with my ten suitcases, a colorful rug, a microwave we bought at Target—and lots and lots of food. I had containers of yam powder, spices, egusi seeds, rice, dried plantains, a bottle of red palm oil, and plenty of other Nigerian ingredients from the African market, which I probably wouldn't be able to cook in a dorm room. I had to use the space under my bed to store it all.

While Mom and Darlington unpacked my things and began helping to arrange my room, I cradled Jordan in my arms. My brother was only two months old, and now that he was here, it pained me that I wouldn't get to see his first steps and his other baby milestones. When I passed him back to my mother, it felt like I was handing her a new life, in more ways than one.

She had a husband now, a good man who wouldn't leave her. She had a son, which was considered a triumph in the Nigerian community. Her career was stable, so they wouldn't have to move from state to state like we did. Jordan would grow up with the deep roots I often wished I'd had. Most important, he would have a father in the house. As the only child at home, he'd receive tons of care and attention. His childhood wouldn't look anything like mine. I was torn between envy and relief for him.

With the unpacking done, Mom, Darlington, and I hugged it out, cried a bit, and they left me alone in my dorm room. As soon as the door closed, the mist cleared from my eyes. I was on my own for the first time, and I could do *whatever* I wanted.

Total freedom was a big adjustment. I had a fabulous time, but my grades weren't that hot at first. Compared to my sister, who was freaking Doogie Howser, I was barely cutting it. Mom just assumed I'd get straight As (I'd bounced back after the Stony Brook debacle and got excellent grades in high school), so she didn't nag me. She said, "I know you're going to do what you're supposed to do."

Yet by my logic, I was a college freshman. What I was supposed to do was go to parties, meet people, dance, drink (occasionally), stay up way too late having intense conversations and listening to music. So I did.

That lasted all of a year, until Yvo saw my freshman grades. Like a good second mother, Yvo pushed me to get my act together. "You need to shape up," she told me. "Stop partying and do your work." I did improve my grades over the next three years . . . but I didn't stop having fun. I coasted into a solid GPA, grades good enough to get me into grad school. Still, looking back, I fear college was a missed opportunity. I had some incredible professors and I wish I'd been more attentive to their lectures. Then again, when else in life are you surrounded by thousands of other people your own age who are all after the same thing? I reveled in it.

Growing up, Yvo always talked about becoming a member of Alpha Kappa Alpha Sorority, Inc., the first Greek letter Black sorority with alumnae like Vice President Kamala Harris, Toni Morrison, Phylicia Rashad, Althea Gibson, Maya Angelou, and countless "first Black female" chemists, doctors, poets, politicians, professors, you name it. Yvo wanted to be a part of that stellar sisterhood. However, when she got to Duke, AKA was on hiatus because two pledges at California State University had drowned in a tragic hazing accident. By the time I got to Temple, the sorority was reinstated and allowed to recruit new members.

I went through the selection process and was the only woman in my class to be invited to join the sorority. It was a very big deal, and I gleefully accepted. They gave me forms to fill out, and I noticed that there were dues and fees that amounted to five hundred dollars.

I called Mom and said, "Great news! I was selected to become an AKA!"

She'd been as heartbroken for Yvo as I had about her not being able to pledge, and was just as excited for me that I got in. "I'm so happy for you!" she said.

"I need to give them a check for five hundred dollars."

After a pause, she said, "I don't have it."

"What?"

"I don't have it."

In that moment, a spell was broken. *Mom doesn't have five hundred dollars?* I realized our family was not as rich as I once thought. Not impoverished. We always had nice clothes and loads of good food on the table. Mom gave us birthday gifts and threw parties. She paid our tuition at private schools. But all that had been carefully budgeted, and I had been shielded from any stretching my mom may have had to do to make it happen. I knew Mom worked hard and did her best to make ends meet. But I also believed in the safe and comfortable existence she presented to me. Now, when I needed a chunk of cash that was unplanned for and outside the budget, Mom couldn't come up with it. Darlington couldn't help. No one had any money saved for a rainy day.

I called Yvo and said, "Can you believe Mom has no savings?"

She sighed and said, "Wen, yeah. I believe it. This is our financial situation."

Of course, Yvo knew all about it. Mom didn't shelter *her* from reality, but they both hid it from me. They allowed me to live in the bubble of *Everything is fine! I can have all the sneakers I want!* Yvo and I lived in the same room (some of the time), ate the same food, but we were living in two different realities. While she knew we teetered on a financial edge, I was always asking for more stuff. It was just another burden she carried so I could travel light.

Learning this now at age eighteen, I felt like a fool. Why did the two people I was closest to in the world underestimate me? Why did they just assume I couldn't handle the truth?

Well, I had to handle it now, or I wouldn't be able to join AKA. Hearing my plight, my roommate, a girl I knew from high school, said, "I can lend you the money."

"Thank God!" I paid her back ASAP with what I earned working two jobs.

Once my eyes were open, the truth was only too obvious. I'd seen plenty of "haves" growing up, like the millionaires' kids at Stony Brook Prep and rich families on TV. I knew we weren't *rich* rich. But I had believed we were middle-class, that we'd always have plenty. With a new perspective, I looked back and realized we did without some basic middle-class things, like a babysitter when Mom worked the late shift, tutors, or trips to places other than Nigeria. As a single working mother raising two kids and with her own grad school tuition to pay, Mom must have spent every penny of her income keeping us well fed and clothed. Somehow she deluded me into feeling like a pampered princess.

Mom was over forty with a baby and still living paycheck to paycheck. I couldn't count on her for extras anymore. If I wanted something outside the budget, I would simply have to get it myself.

What's more, I was in the midst of a novel experience that I couldn't share with Mom or Yvo. The AKA process was rough. I can't go into detail about what I experienced, but anyone made in AKA knows what I'm talking about. Since Mom and Yvo didn't know—and I couldn't divulge—what I was struggling with, they couldn't hold me up as they had always done before. The best they could do was to say, "Hang in there."

Being the first in my family to do *anything* was a pivotal moment for me. I was used to following them and relying on their wisdom borne of prior experience. This time, I led the way. (In fact, Yvo would later join the sorority in grad school, and she would turn to me for support. And Mom joined after Yvo.) I was starting to see myself as more than a little sister or a mommy's girl. I was an individual and I could define myself apart from my family, which was both thrilling and terrifying.

It might seem odd that a person like me, someone who does not have many nonfamily friendships, would want to join a sorority. My intent was to have a complete college experience, and that included community, which for me meant Greek life. Still, several of my sorority sisters said over the years that I seemed closed off.

It's true. I wasn't vulnerable with them. My "sisters" were all very tight with one another, but I couldn't let anyone get too close to me. Just like in high school, I watched the gossiping and backstabbing that went on, and I made sure that no one really knew my business. If anyone called me out on my aloofness, I would just shrug and say, "I'm a private person," while thinking, *If you had half a chance, you would talk about me on the street. I'm not taking that risk.*

My love of privacy might come from my being around older Nigerians whose favorite pastime was to gossip about their friends. Mom on the phone, or at the table with her siblings, or at Nigerian parties, talking and talking about other people, what they were doing, what their kids were up to, with all the appropriate facial expressions and sound effects. Nigerians only talk about politics and people. I knew more about how my aunt's friend's son's failed dentistry practice was doing than I knew about my own mother's favorite books or films.

By closing myself off to my sorority sisters, I was preventing them from talking about me behind my back. To this day, I still have a hard time making new friendships and trusting people. My deepest trust and love will only go to my family.

I did feel a bit betrayed that Mom and Yvo kept me in the dark about how close to the edge we lived. But Yvo knew that I was sensitive in ways she and Mom weren't. I understood that they protected me because they thought they had to. After a year of college, I'd been exposed to harsh truths. I'd blazed trails. I didn't need their protection anymore.

During the summer between my freshman and sophomore year, Jordan turned one. We had a big party for him at Chuck E. Cheese, a place that is a bit much for anyone with working eyes and ears. I was adjusting to the bells and beeps of arcade games and the screaming of children when I spotted Eddie walking past the ball pit, wearing his signature khaki cargo shorts and smile. I was surprised to see him. An invitation had been sent to his mother and he must have seen it.

"What are you doing here?" I asked.

Why would the college-age son of my mother's frenemy come to a one-year-old's birthday party? It was either really creepy, or an excuse for him to see me. Eddie shrugged. I spent the rest of the party with him, playing Frogger and Asteroids, earning tons of tickets to trade in for crappy toys. I believe I became the proud owner of a stuffed animal rat at that party.

Eddie was attending the University of Maryland in College Park, a two-hour drive from Philadelphia, where he joined AKA's brother fraternity, Alpha Phi Alpha Fraternity Incorporated. So in a way, we became Greek siblings.

Soon after we reconnected, he sent me a message on Facebook that said, "Hey, Wendy. We're having our probate show this weekend. I would love for you to come." A probate show is when new members of the frat present themselves to upperclassmen, alums, family, and friends. It usually includes choreographed stepping and strolling, so the event isn't just a formality, it's exciting and entertaining as hell. I was flattered that he wanted me to be there to watch him present, that he was still thinking of me and wanted to get back in touch. I would have loved to be there, but I couldn't work out the logistics that weekend. I wrote back that I hoped we'd see each other soon.

I remember mentioning to Mom on the phone that Eddie and I were talking again, and she said, "He's a good boy, but you'll have plenty of time for that later. Are you working hard?"

"Yes, Mom," I said, rolling my eyes.

"I know you're making a face right now," she said. "I think I'm going to drive to Philly and see how you're doing."

Mom would make the spontaneous decision to drive the two hours from Baltimore to check up on me a few times a year. I think she just liked being in the college environment, the idea of going back to school. She was always teaching me, and the intended lesson of those visits was to remind me where I came from. Mom breezed in, looking gorgeous, bringing boxes of food, telling loud stories. Everyone would say, "Your mom is so cool! She looks like your sister." She would charm my friends and sorority sisters and I'd burst with pride. My mom was all that. She would shut it *down*, and I basked in her reflective glory.

The magic was in how she carried herself, which I was appreciating more and more as I got older. She walked with the strength of a lifetime of proving herself. She had held prominent positions as the director of nursing at several hospitals, but even more impressive than that, she was well known and respected by her colleagues and everyone else. Whenever I'd visited her at her workplaces, it seemed like every nurse, janitor, doctor, and administrator knew her and smiled at me when they realized I was Susan's daughter. My mom has left such a mark that whenever I go to an African market from New York to Virginia, the owners say, "You're Susan's daughter, right? How's she doing?"

When she came to Temple, she made her mark on my sorority sisters. Long before I joined AKA, Mom had founded a women's organization in Durham called Obiwanne ("heart of the sibling") for North Carolina–based Nigerian women to support one another as they navigated life in

America. The organization is still up and running. I've come across members who all remember Mom and praise her for what she started.

A steep part of my college learning curve was figuring out how I would follow in my mother's footsteps and leave my mark on the world. It was always on my mind. College wasn't even halfway over, but I thought constantly about the next step. I *knew* I was going to be a great lawyer. Mom had been manifesting it all along—"You will be a lawyer!"—and I did some visualizations of my own. With crystal clarity, I saw myself as a student at New York University Law School in Greenwich Village, walking under the arch in Washington Square Park, a Starbucks cup in my left hand, my Louis Vuitton briefcase in my right hand, rushing to class to learn about torts. For cash, I would be an extra on *Law & Order*. I'd be the editor of the law review journal, graduate at the top of my class, pass the bar exam on my first try, and become an important, independent lawyer who always happened to be incredibly well dressed.

My unspoken dream was to connect my work in some way to the entertainment business. But I was too chicken to consider it seriously or talk about it. So I combined my dream with Mom's and envisioned myself as an entertainment lawyer. Stars, networks, and movie studios needed attorneys, and I would be one of them. And if I happened to catch some of the spotlight for myself, well, that wouldn't be so bad, would it?

Kevin and I broke up at the beginning of my freshman year, and I'd started dating other men. I went home to Baltimore for the summer and wondered if Eddie would get in touch with me, or if he knew I was back in town.

The phone rang.

"Hey, Wen." It was Uncle Hyke.

"Hey!" I said, happy to talk to him.

"Is your mom there?" he asked. Something in his tone scared me.

"She's working. What's going on?"

"It's Mama," he said, meaning Angela. "She's gone."

Angela had been living with Winifred in Virginia for some time. She was diabetic. Her leg had been amputated and her health had been spiraling downward. The news of her death wasn't a total shock, but it was still a blow. My grandmother Angela was the first death in the family that hit me hard. I immediately started crying, and Hyke joined in.

"We have to tell your mother," he said.

She would be devastated when she heard. During Angela's extended stay in Virginia, Mom visited, but not as often as she might've liked. Whenever I asked Mom, "How's Grandma doing?," I understood from her assorted expressions and sounds that she didn't want to talk about it, but that Angela was doing badly. Their complicated mother-daughter relationship hadn't gotten any warmer over the years, and the time Mom spent growing up without Angela by her side did not help—first when Angela sent Susan to live with Cordelia, then when she sent her to the convent at sixteen, and finally when she sent her to San Francisco at seventeen.

On one of Mom's visits to Virginia, she asked Angela about that long-ago incident at the St. Patrick's Day bazaar, when Angela slapped seven-year-old Susan in public for angering the food vendor. From what I know of the conversation, Mom said to Angela, "I couldn't believe you took a stranger's side over mine. It made me so sad. Why did you do that?"

Angela shook her head, cried a little, and refused to talk about it.

It could have been Angela's chance to remove one brick from the wall between her and her daughter. I knew that would be a tall order for a Nigerian parent who, as a hard-and-fast rule, does not indulge their children's hurt feelings. And certainly never says "I'm sorry."

Now that Angela was gone, Mom would never get whatever she was looking for from her mother, some affirmation of love or an acknowledgment of the strain in their relationship. That hope died along with my grandmother.

I called Mom at work at the hospital to deliver the bad news and was told that she couldn't be reached by phone. "Please ask her to call home as soon as possible," I said.

My stepfather was at home with me that day, and he knew that my mother needed to be told immediately. If she found out we waited to tell her, she'd be furious. "I'll go down to the hospital," he said.

I stayed with the baby while Darlington found Mom at work. As soon as she saw him walking toward her with a grim expression, she said, "Oh no."

He told her and Mom burst into tears and had to be helped into the car to come home. Within hours, our entire family started arriving, from Virginia, North Carolina, New York. All the aunts, uncles, and cousins gathered at Mom's house, as they always did, in good times and bad, for every Christmas and Thanksgiving, every celebration, every birthday. Mom's house was the backdrop for our happiness. On that day, her house was the backdrop for our sorrow. All the elements were the same as a party or holiday: tons of food and drink, the delicious smells from the kitchen, the parade of cars, the crush of people. But the tone was bleak. Everyone was crying, including my uncles.

During a private moment, through her tears, Mom said to Yvo and me, "I wish I was as close with my mother as you guys are with me."

"Yes, Mom," I said.

Right there was the crux of the problem with our mother-daughter relationship. Closeness does not mean intimacy. As seen through Mom's Nigerian lens, we *were* close, much more so than she was with her own mom. I loved Mom, but the predominant emotion on my side of our relationship was fear—the fear of not measuring up. I was aware of all the truths I wasn't sharing with my mother. Maybe the wall between Mom and me was thinner than the one between Mom and Angela, but it was still there.

At that gathering to celebrate Angela's life, I learned stories about her that I hadn't heard before. I knew Angela had had a sister and one brother. But Aunt Winifred, our family historian, revealed that Nne, my great-grandmother, had had a *third* daughter, Angela's older sister. One day, the girl walked up a hill to fetch water, a trip she'd made countless times. But on that morning, she never returned. Everyone in the family suspected that she'd been kidnapped and sold into slavery. Winifred dated the kidnapping to the second decade of the twentieth century, fifty years *after* African American slaves were freed, in 1865. But the abduction and trafficking of Nigerian girls didn't end with the Emancipation Proclamation. In fact, it continues to this day.

I've always loved history and have read many books about slavery. I thought it was something removed from me, but it *had* affected our family. Ninety years ago, my family was victimized and devastated by a horrific crime. I wish I'd had the chance to talk about this tragedy with Angela and ask her how having a sister who vanished affected her life. As a scholar, I craved her perspective on the African side of the transatlantic slave trade. We don't hear much about that in the US. We usually talk about slavery from an African American perspective, the history of captured Africans and the generations of their descendants who lived in bondage in America and the Caribbean. What about the Africans who experienced unimaginable loss and heartbreak?

When Winifred told the story, it was like a puzzle piece had finally fallen into place. Trauma is passed down from one generation to the next. This one was passed from my great-grandmother Nne, a strong woman who spent a lifetime grieving the loss of her daughter; to my grandmother Angela, who lost a sister; to my mother, who was raised by a traumatized, emotionally distant mother; to me, raised by a warrior woman who tirelessly defended me but wasn't capable of intimacy. I had always felt like there was something missing in our family. The generational pain of this particular loss lived on in our cells, our blood. The wounds of this family member's long-ago disappearance ran deep.

Would I pass it down to my children, or would it fade away in my generation?

For that matter, would my future daughter tell her own daughter at my funeral, "I wish my mom and I had been closer"?

No.

I vowed to myself at Angela's funeral that I would be the kind of mother who opened up, who engaged emotionally, intimately, with my kids. I would end that form of generational suffering.

MY FINAL YEARS of college went by in a blink. College was a unique time of life when all I had to do was soak up knowledge. An education isn't limited to what you learn in the classroom, though. Throughout those four years, I learned about myself. During my childhood, I was always busy finding my footing at a new school. I hadn't had much of a chance to look inside and figure out who I was and what I wanted.

I learned about my family: the reality of our being less well-off than I thought and our painful history. I had to leave home to gain this knowledge. I learned that I didn't have to follow in the footsteps of my mother. I could, and did, blaze trails of my own, as the first member of our family to join Alpha Kappa Alpha Sorority Incorporated, for example.

As for my idolization of Mom, of how proud I was when others admired her, I realized that to some extent, I was just another one of her admirers. Despite our closeness, we weren't emotionally open with each other. As an adult, I felt I should be treated more like a friend. I wanted Mom to be straight with me, to allow me to know her truth and for her to know mine. Like Mom, I intended to leave my mark on the world. But even more, it was important for me to leave my mark on *her*, to become a person she could admire not just for her own redemption or bragging rights. I wanted to impress her personally, to hear her say, with *words*, that I'd done all right. Facial expressions and sounds alone would not be enough.

I wasn't sure what I needed to do to become someone she'd admire, but I definitely knew what she expected of me. The first step toward shifting our relationship toward equality and mutual admiration was becoming a lawyer. I would get my Nigerian daughter "success" badge. Once I had that, perhaps we could move into a new phase where we became friends.

THIRTEEN

Give It to God

After graduation from Temple, I needed a solid chunk of time to prepare for the LSAT (the standardized test for getting into law school). But first, I moved home and crammed for the GRE (the standardized test for getting into grad school), in order to get a master's degree before applying to law school.

My stepfather, Darlington, saw how stressed out I was. He knew what the penalty for failing to meet my mother's expectations felt like. He came to my rescue with food. The night before I took the GRE, Darlington offered to make his best dish for me, a boneless fish with sautéed yellow onions, red peppers, and scallions in a spicy sauce over a bed of pasta. If I could eat only one meal for the rest of my life, it'd be that. His heart issues were getting worse, and just standing at the kitchen counter to chop vegetables was exhausting for him. I said, "Please don't go to the trouble."

He took out the cutting board and frying pan anyway. It was his way of saying, "Let me do this for you because I love you and I want to make you feel better." I paid back his kindness by eating every bite, even though nerves had stolen my appetite. His cooking, and my eating his food, was how we expressed our love for each other.

His food helped me get a high score on the GRE, which helped me get accepted into a master's degree program in government at Baltimore's Johns Hopkins University. I lived at home, went to school, and studied for the LSAT. The glamorous life. Honestly, it was a lonely period for me. Most of my friends from high school had moved away, so I had only my mom, stepdad, and little brother to hang out with. I'd had a bad breakup with a college boyfriend and wasn't ready to date again. I was sick of dating, anyway. At twenty-two, I was starting to think about a future husband.

Mom noticed that I wasn't going out at all. Her solution to any problem was: "Give it to God."

"How is God going to help me get over a breakup?" I asked.

"Write down everything you want and give it to God," she said.

The solution to loneliness, per Mom, was to make an "on paper" wish list about the one person who would fill my heart with joy. I'd written so many papers in college and now at grad school. What was one more? Okay, it wasn't a dissertation-level effort. I just wrote down the qualities and traits I wanted in a husband:

Catholic.
Igbo from Anambra State.
Good-looking, six foot two.
Dresses like an adult (button-downs or polos).
Kind, ambitious.
Wants kids.

Once I'd painted a picture of this man—a husband my mother would approve of—I folded up my list and put it into my wallet. I gave it to God and waited for my man to appear.

Mom had been using such manifesting techniques for her whole life by speaking "as if," visualizing what she wanted and praying. The intensity of her prayer clarified her vision and gave it shape. Before long, it would materialize. She told Yvo from age four, "You will be a doctor." To please Mom, Yvo repeated Mom's words, and said, "I will be a doctor." Well, my sister was well on her way, in medical school and excelling, just as Mom predicted/manifested.

I used the visualization technique of manifesting about my becoming a lawyer. I fantasized about being a litigator who stood up in a courtroom and gave stirring opening and closing statements at trial. I studied the careers of my idols Thurgood Marshall and Johnny Cochran. I watched hours of *Law & Order: SVU* and visualized myself climbing the iconic Supreme Court steps at Manhattan's Foley Square. I just *knew* I was going to be the next big thing. Orating for a living felt like a natural fit, what I was born to do.

Meanwhile, that list in my wallet must have been a direct pipeline to God, because I got a phone call from Eddie unexpectedly. Apparently, he heard that I was back in Maryland and invited me to a cookout for his fraternity, Alpha Phi Alpha. I thought, *Perfect timing!* This party would be a great way to make some new friends and reconnect with Eddie, who, as he made sure to tell me, had a car now, a gold Nissan Altima.

I called up my line sister, LaShawnda, and said, "Girl, I want to go to this cookout, but I don't want to go alone. Will you come along?" I promised tons of great food and fine men. She must have been intrigued, because she came all the way from New York to go with me.

As I'd promised, the party was teeming with good-looking men. When we walked in, LaShawnda (now the godmother of my second son) said, "I'm glad I made the trip."

Eddie appeared at my side as soon as we arrived. "Can I introduce you to some people?" he asked.

"Of course," I said. The main reason I came was to see Eddie, but I played it cool, and acted like I was there to be a good AKA sister to all the APhiA brothers.

We approached a friend of his. Eddie said, "Wendy, this is Vince. He's going to be the best man in our wedding. Vince, this is Wendy. She's going to be my wife."

Vince and I both laughed. "Nice to meet you, Wendy," he said. "You just graduated from Temple, right?"

"Has Eddie been talking about me?" I asked.

Vince smiled and said, "Just a little."

Or a lot? I glanced at Eddie, who smiled confidently. Throughout the party, I was hyperaware of Eddie whenever he was near, which was most of the time. When he went off somewhere, I found myself scanning the crowd for him. A few times he caught me looking for him, and we locked eyes from across the yard, grinning cutely at each other.

After a while, my friend and I decided to leave. She went to say some goodbyes, and Eddie walked me to my car alone. It was a short walk, but we took it slow. We stopped in front of my gray Ford Mustang. He looked at me, and I looked at him. When our eyes connected, the ground shifted underneath my feet. It was a seismic moment, the air seemed electric, and the only sounds I could hear were my own heart beating and birds singing. His gaze dropped to my lips, and I swallowed hard. I just knew we were about to kiss for the first time.

We hovered there, staring at each other, feeling an immense connection and the suspense before Eddie closed the short distance between our lips. Out of nowhere, the sky opened up and rain poured down. The spell was broken, and we both started laughing. I hurried into my car and he jogged back toward the cookout. Then he stopped in the middle of the street to turn around to look at me again while the rain soaked him to the skin.

And that was it. I was a goner.

LaShawnda came running toward the car through the rain. "There you are!" she said. "Ready to go?"

"I'm starving," I said. "Let's get some dinner." How could I have gone to a cookout and ended up doing more talking than eating? Maybe Eddie made me too nervous to eat.

We drove to a restaurant and ordered some food and drinks. I could barely sit still. I was too excited by that *Notebook*-esque moment with Eddie in the rain. I told her, "Oh my God. He's perfect. I hope he—" Before I could get the words out, my phone vibrated with a text from him that said: *When am I going to see you again?*

I died and came back to life to giggle and gush about his perfection all night long. I've felt the same way about him ever since.

Eddie hits every item on my "Give it to God" list. The question is: When I wrote the list, was I fantasizing about the perfect man for me, and God brought him to me? Or was my subconscious describing Eddie himself, a man who had always been there?

Either way, writing the list helped me realize that Eddie fit my vision in every way. We started to spend more time together in Baltimore after the cookout, and I'd never felt so bonded and happy before in a relationship. I gave it to God, and I got exactly what I wanted.

"I really like him," I told Mom after we'd been dating for a month or two.

Mom said, "I like Eddie Osefo for you, Wen. But his mother!" And then she rattled off a few stories she'd heard about Cecilia, her friends, and their children.

I listened, nodded, and tried to look like I cared, but I was disappointed. I had attempted to engage her in a conversation about my hopes and desires, only to have it rerouted to gossip about people in the Nigerian community. How would we ever get to know each other when we never talked about ourselves?

Eddie and I seemed to be headed toward engagement, but I was only twenty-two and I had a lot of work to do before I took that step. Getting married before I became a lawyer might slow me down or knock me off my path. As hopelessly smitten as Eddie and I were with each other, I held back a little. I knew that as soon as I got into law school, I probably would be leaving Baltimore.

While I was writing papers and doing full-time course work in the two-year master's program at Hopkins, I studied for the LSAT, took the test (I did okay), and applied to law schools. I got accepted into Texas Southern Law School. It wasn't NYU, or another top-tier school, but I'd always wanted to live in Houston.

I got in, I texted Eddie. *I'm moving to Houston.*

At the time, Eddie was working at a "Big Four" accounting firm. He knew it wasn't the final destination for him, but he wasn't about to quit and move to Texas.

Congratulations, he texted back.

He meant it and supported my decision to go to law school. He was walking his own narrow path of parental expectations and understood why I had to do it, even if it meant leaving him.

"What now?" he asked.

Good question.

After much discussion and some tears (mine), Eddie and I agreed to "keep it light" until we were both in the same city again.

From day one, law school was challenging, much harder than under-grad or grad school. I was holding my own, though. The requirement to advance to the second year of law school was finishing year one with a cumulative GPA of 3.0.

"This is *not* going to be a replay of Stony Brook," I told myself daily.

Mom's voice was in my head: "You *will* be a lawyer."

When I reported in from Houston to Mom, I always said, "I'm doing well." Giving it to God—as well as hard work—would get me through the academic rigors of law school. If I could say "It's all good," then I would speak that into life. As the year progressed, my grades hovered close to the required average.

On Valentine's Day 2008, Eddie sent a bouquet of red and pink roses to me in Houston with a note that said, "I love you so much. I don't want to be without you." After six months of keeping it light, we agreed to restart our relationship, even though we were living in different states. Eddie was supportive, though. He didn't distract me from my studies.

My favorite course was legal writing. The professor offered extra credit for students who attended a series of lectures she curated. If I went to all of them, my grade in her class would be a 4.0—an A. That would guarantee my GPA would be high enough to qualify me for year two, so I attended every extra-credit lecture she held.

In 2008, it was impossible not to be swept up in the campaign of presidential hopeful Barack Obama. One of those extra-credit sessions was scheduled on the same evening that Obama was holding a huge rally in Houston. His primary run against the shoo-in candidate Hillary Clinton was catching fire; he'd just won against Clinton in Wisconsin, a surprise victory. I told myself, "This is historic. I refuse to miss Obama's event."

But on the other hand, attending that lecture was my insurance policy. Faced with a tough choice, about fifteen of my classmates and I signed into the lecture, and then we snuck out to go to the Obama rally.

It was an unforgettable experience to be in the packed arena, chanting "Yes we can!" with nineteen thousand of my fellow Houstonites. The energy was off the charts; it would have lifted the roof if it weren't bolted down. I was riveted by Obama's every word. He talked about how the same old leadership in government had failed us (and I knew who he meant by "us," the Black and brown people who'd filled the stands that night). He said Washington, DC, was the place where "good ideas go to die." To make a real difference in America, as he proposed, we needed new, young people to be part of the governing process and unite those across racial and ideological divides. He defined hope as the willingness of citizens like the freedom riders in the 1960s to imagine, fight for, and struggle to achieve what did not seem possible before. "There is a moment in the life of every generation," he said, "when that spirit has to come through if we are to *make our mark on history*." Change will come, he said, "when we decide to cast aside fear and doubt . . . when we are willing to reach for what we know in our gut is possible." Amen to that.

When he said, "make our mark on history," it was like Obama, a fellow first gen with African roots, spoke directly to my heart, describing the quality I admired about my mother and inspiring me to realize the vision I had for myself. In his speech, he evoked so many of the principles my Nigerian elders had been telling me all along: You *can* be the best. If you don't make excuses, if you work hard, you *will* succeed.

Obama's campaign had the "failure is not an option" intensity, a sense of destiny, which I understood all too well.

"I *will* disrupt the status quo. I *will* achieve what was once unthinkable," I told myself, sounding very much like Mom with her declarative statements.

Waving my Obama '08 sign, I screamed along with my friends and thousands of Blacks, whites, Latinos, *everyone*. It gave me a profound sense of belonging that I'd only ever felt before within our world-within-a-world-within-a-world Igbo community. My mother and her family and friends were happy to remain insulated inside it, as if they weren't living in America at all. They even isolated themselves to a degree from the larger Nigerian community of Yoruba and Hausas.

But as a first gen, I was living in America. Mom came here and sacrificed her marriage so Yvo and I could have a better life. What sacrifice would I make to give my American children (maybe with Eddie) a better life? I wouldn't limit myself to making my mark on the Igbo community. My dreams were bigger.

Obama lifted me up. I felt inspired to do better, be better. He hung around after the rally to meet and greet, and I was fortunate enough to shake his hand. I'd never met anyone before who was so built for greatness. I remember walking out of there with my classmates, elated, having experienced a high born of vision and purpose. That rally changed my life. Meeting Obama set off a spark that ignited my abiding love for politics. I wasn't questioning the validity of my lifelong goal of becoming a lawyer. But I thought maybe serving in government—with my law degree—would be more impactful than my being an entertainment lawyer.

The Obama high didn't last long, though. I was brought back down to earth when I learned that one of my classmates had seen my group of friends and me sneak out of that lecture. He didn't think it was fair for us to receive extra credit since we left, so he ratted on us.

The class received a mass email from the professor that laid out our choices: (1) admit to leaving and lose extra-credit points for that lecture, or (2) don't admit to leaving and gamble being found out, at which point our grade would drop to a C.

I chose option one. I apologized and explained my reasoning to the professor. She understood why I wanted to attend Obama's rally, but said I would have to be penalized for missing the lecture. My grade was dropped to a B-plus.

I left Houston for my summer internship at the International Center for Terrorism Studies in DC, confident that the B-plus was enough to qualify me for year two. When I arrived back east, Eddie officially asked me to be his girlfriend on June 1, 2008.

Life was good! I gave it to God, and found myself in love with Eddie, happy in my internship, and inching closer to my goals with every passing day. Mom was pleased with where my life was headed, too. Her approval meant the world to me.

And then, it all blew up.

My internship was winding down and I was set to return to Houston for my second year of law school. And then, via email, I was informed that my downgraded mark in legal writing had dropped my overall GPA from a 3.1 to a 2.9. That wasn't good enough to qualify for continuing to attend. I was not invited to return.

Because of the penalty from skipping out on *one* lecture, my future was shattered.

As I read and reread that email, the air left my lungs and my legs turned into ropes. It was a physical blow, no different from being punched in the gut. It was a replay of Stony Brook, but this time, the stakes were a thousand times higher. Having to leave law school wasn't just an obstacle on the narrow path. It was an earthquake.

Immediately, I started calling each of my professors. "Is there any way you can possibly increase my grade by a fraction? I'll do research for you for free. I'll retake tests, anything," I begged them. All I needed was one-tenth of a point. They all refused, and I can't say I blamed them.

The drumbeat of anxiety pounded in my head while I made those calls, and afterward, when I realized that there was nothing I could do to change the situation. It was like the opposite of the Obama chant "Yes we can": "No you can't! No you can't!"

What was Mom going to say? What would she do? The thought of her gossipy friends talking about my failure, saying, "I knew all along Susan's daughter was a loser," sickened me. I was queasy and hot, flushed with shame and fear. In the countless times I'd visualized my future, I had never once foreseen anything like this.

I didn't have the courage to tell Mom, not right away. I couldn't tell Yvo yet, either, because she was like my second mother. I desperately needed to talk to someone, though, so I turned to Eddie. He had just purchased his first home in Prince George's County, Maryland, and was living the life as a young homeowner, working a nine-to-five at Deloitte and making a very nice salary.

"I need you," I said when I called him.

"Anything," he replied.

He picked me up at work and took me to his house. I told him what happened, and he just held me. "It's going to be okay," he promised. He was as loving and supportive then as he is for me today. That first night, I cried myself to sleep in his arms. When I woke up, I thought it was all a nightmare, but then I realized with a sinking stomach, "No, this is my real. I'm never going to be a lawyer."

Days passed at Eddie's in a haze. I didn't know what to do. Even though I was a grown woman, practically engaged to my future husband, Mom wouldn't have approved of my staying at Eddie's unchaperoned. As far as she knew, I was preparing to return to my apartment in Houston to get organized to start my second year of law school. So now I was lying to her about two things.

I couldn't hide out at Eddie's forever. After a few weeks of avoidance, I called Mom. "I'm coming home to talk about something important," I said.

"Okay," she said.

"Yvo has to be there, too." My sister was living at home during her summer break from medical school.

"Wen, what is going on?"

"I'll be there in an hour."

I was already crying as I walked through the door to Mom's house in Maryland. My sister and I sat down on my old bed while Mom stood over us. Tearfully, I spilled the whole story, laying out the choice I'd made that resulted in the shattering of Mom's dream, and erasing the glorious vision I'd had for my future.

It was the lowest point in my life.

Yvo threw her arm over my shoulder and started bawling, too, maybe harder than I was. She felt terrible about what happened. I think she was *so* upset because she realized she couldn't lift that failure off my shoulders and carry it herself. For the first time in her life, she could not protect her little sister from life's blows. I would have to suffer them myself, and she'd have to watch. Her tears were those of frustration.

"It's going to be okay, Wen," she said, echoing Eddie's love and support. "We're going to be okay."

Mom didn't hug me. She stood in her place, dry-eyed, and said, "Don't worry, Wen. We're going to put on some really nice lipstick, spray on some perfume, and fly out to Houston. We're going to talk to one of your male professors, and they're going to give you extra points." Maybe in her day, lipstick and perfume could fix any problem. Mom's advice and solutions usually worked for me, but not this time.

"I called them already," I said. "The decision has been made, and it's not going to change. I have not been invited back. It's over."

"Okay, if you're not going to be a lawyer," said Mom, "you'll just

TEARS OF MY MOTHER

have to be a doctor. You can apply to medical school in Jamaica and start as soon as possible. Three of my friends' kids are getting their MDs in the Caribbean right now."

There was a moment of silence. "Mommy, I don't want to do that," I confessed.

"What *are* you going to do?" she asked.

The million-dollar question.

Mom left me and Yvo alone in my old room. I couldn't get a read on how she felt. Of course, she was *disappointed*. She was probably mentally adding up all the money she'd spent on my tuition over the years. Or she was numb, shocked into stone. My heart felt like a boulder in my chest. If Mom felt half as bad as I did, she was in hell.

For a week, I could barely get out of bed. When your whole life was pointed in one direction, and then you hit a mile-high wall, how do you go on? I was only twenty-three; I had no idea. Mom was relentless about my need for a plan.

"What are you going to do?" she asked. "Make a list! Give it to God! You will be a doctor or an engineer."

She was not going to allow me to sink further into my bed or into a depression. As I've said, Nigerians don't believe in being depressed. It's considered to be an excuse for not doing what you need to do. I was raised not to make excuses, but I simply wasn't capable of doing anything for a while there.

Yvo sat with me often during that week, but then she had to go back to medical school. I felt guilty just being in the house, adding to Mom's burden. She had her hands full with Darlington's many doctor's appointments, and with Jordan, now a kindergartener. Her disappointment in me was thick in the air. It made every room feel suffocating.

Mom tried to motivate me. "Med school in Jamaica is a good idea!" she said. "What about dentistry?" And, as always, "Give it to God."

I'd given my dream of being a lawyer to God, and this had happened. My faith wasn't shaken, but I couldn't figure out how this blow was going to turn into a blessing. Being around Mom and her relentless pushing only made me feel worse. I had to change the atmosphere, or it would get toxic.

I asked myself, "What would Mom do?" When Mom hit a promotion ceiling at work or dealt with racist bosses, she looked around for a new, better position, and always found one. The key was forward motion, to see myself getting beyond this. I might have been kicked out of law school, but it was not my destiny to be a failure. I had to change my energy, so I forced myself to get out of bed and do *something* that would get my feet moving.

My first thought was to pick up where I left off and return to Johns Hopkins to complete my master's degree in government. I'd done one year of a two-year program before pausing it to go to law school. I petitioned Hopkins to let me back in. Sorting out the logistics took a few weeks, but because I felt so emotionally drained, it felt like months.

I started taking classes again that fall. My stepfather was a great help to me during that time. My master's thesis was about impulsive political transitions in Nigeria—coups, assassinations, government corruption—and Darlington provided me with a deep background on the subject matter. If I asked him, "What do you know about Murtala Muhammed?"— speaking of the Nigerian general who led a coup and became the head of state, only to be assassinated himself—Darlington could rattle off dates, descriptions, and backstories (all without the help of Google). When I confirmed it in books, I was amazed by his recall. He never got a date wrong.

I worked hard and did well at Hopkins, but it felt like I was biding my time while I figured out my future. I never stopped praying throughout, but once I had a sense of agency again, I could go deeper in my conversations with God about what happened.

After a lot of prayer, an epiphany came to me: if I had become a lawyer and fulfilled Mom's dream for me, I would have been miserable.

My vision of making stunning courtroom reveals and saying, "Objection, Your Honor!" in designer suits was a fantasy, a TV script. It wouldn't have been my reality as a working attorney. One year of law school taught me that. I wouldn't call getting kicked out a subconscious act of self-sabotage. Absolutely not. I wanted to see it through. I'd given it to God, and my failure was God's way of rerouting me toward something better.

My longtime unspoken dream was to have a career in entertainment in some form, and I'd fallen in love with politics at the Obama rally in Houston. Could I combine entertainment and politics? What would that look like?

At dinner one night with Eddie, I said, "I was thinking that I want to go on TV and talk about the news, like Isha Sesay or Joy Reid."

He put down his fork and said, "Well, who will listen to you?"

It wasn't a nasty put-down. He just didn't understand why viewers would care about what I had to say compared with anyone else. He made a good point. What authority could I bring to the panel? I kept that thought with me as I progressed through my education, closing in on my first master's degree and continuing to figure out what to do next.

What choices could I make that fit my background and genuine interests?

The thought dawned on me: *I could get a PhD.*

A doctorate would satisfy my mom's degree requirement, and it would give me the necessary credentials to justify going on TV. People would listen to me if I were *Dr.* Wendy. I started looking at PhD programs that excited my intellectual curiosity. Meanwhile, Eddie decided that *he* wanted to be a lawyer. We both applied to schools in the Philly area, hoping we'd be accepted to a nearby (or even, God willing, the same) university. We'd been doing the long-distance thing for years now, and I hated it.

I applied to the University of Pennsylvania, Howard University, and Rutgers University (my stepfather's alma mater), and got into Howard and Rutgers. Rutgers offered me a full ride, including a job as a research assistant for the duration of my stay. I chose Rutgers and while there, I got a master's of science degree in public affairs and then earned a doctorate in public affairs and community development. The coursework for my PhD was about being a public servant and engaging with people in need. How could public servants—government workers, social workers, community organizers—best serve people? How could they ensure that low-income and immigrant populations had a voice and a seat at the table? It was all about helping individuals who couldn't help themselves.

Meanwhile, Eddie went to Rutgers Law School. Finally, we were at the same school, in the same city. God seemed to be routing us toward a life together.

It's funny how things work out. I was kicked out of law school because of Barack Obama. Several short years later, I became the director of family and community engagement for the Obama administration's antipoverty initiative, the DC Promise Neighborhood Initiative (DCPNI). There I created and launched the first comprehensive adult learning academy within an underserved neighborhood in Washington, DC. (*Yes I did.*)

If I'd been able to see into the future, I wouldn't have churned in anxiety and confusion after the law school debacle. I had no idea that I would evolve into the person I'd been inspired to become by Obama (and my mother). But now I understand that everything I went through was exactly what I needed in order to propel myself forward in life. That year of my life encapsulates the immigrant experience—from struggle to strength to success—that Mom had been living for decades. Having faced disaster and having pulled myself out of it, like she had so many times, I understood my mother better. Not as well as I wanted to. But maybe I could let go of that, too, and put my longing to be closer to her in God's hands as well.

FOURTEEN

My MRS Degree

On my twenty-sixth birthday, Eddie and I didn't do anything special, but he made plans for us the day after, May 22, 2010, a Saturday. "Pack an overnight bag," he said. "We're going somewhere nice for dinner." Good man, he knew I still had a childlike love for birthday surprises, going back to Mom giving me that hot pink mountain bike. I packed with stars in my eyes, wondering what he'd arranged.

The next day, he took me to a diner for a late breakfast. I sensed that something was off, because Eddie didn't eat a bite of his food. He is not a foodie like me, but if there is one thing he loves, it's a diner breakfast. The fact that he was pushing the food around his plate set off alarms. I asked, "*What* is going on with you? You're not eating."

"Nothing! I'm fine!" he said.

Now my antenna was really up, because Eddie did not talk with exclamation points. After breakfast we got into his car and drove from New Brunswick to Washington, DC, to the Liaison Hotel on Capitol Hill, a stylish, upscale boutique hotel.

We checked in and had only a few minutes in the room by ourselves when there was a knock on the door.

It was a makeup artist I followed on social media. Once, while looking at her work online, I casually mentioned to Eddie that if I ever got married, I'd hire this woman to do my makeup. And here she was, standing at my door.

She said, "Hi, Wendy. Happy birthday. I'm here to do your makeup for the evening."

First a fancy hotel, and then my favorite artist was going to make me gorgeous? It was like my birthday *and* Christmas. I said, "Come right in!" She had me sit in a comfy chair and worked her magic. I wasn't used to getting my makeup done by a professional back then, and it was such a treat. She coordinated my eye and lip palette to match my look for the evening, a custom-made coral one-shoulder asymmetrical dress that made me feel like a supermodel.

We got dressed for dinner—Eddie wore a charcoal suit from Zara with a white button-down and a coral pocket square to complement the color of my dress—and he called me a goddess when he saw me all put together. I sure felt like one as he escorted me down to the hotel lobby toward the Art and Soul restaurant.

"Hold up," he said. "Let me put this on." He showed me a black silk scarf he intended to tie around my head like a blindfold. I was up for it, as long as it was loose enough not to mess up my hair or flawless lashes. I promised to keep my eyes closed as he led me into a private dining area in the restaurant. Then he carefully removed the blindfold and said, "Open your eyes."

Standing in front of me were both of our families, close friends, and a professional photographer. They screamed, "Surprise!" After my initial shock and delight, I realized they were all dressed to match in black and white, and looked sensational. (You *know* how much I love color-coordinated events.) Eddie had encouraged me to pick a bright-colored dress because it would pop against all that black and white. *This man thinks of everything*, I thought.

No one had planned a surprise party for me before, and I was on cloud nine. My family swarmed in, and we laughed and talked exuberantly about how fabulous the space was and how we all looked. Eddie's brother, Greg, and his older sisters, Nora and Ify, greeted me with hugs and kisses.

"Are your parents here?" I asked, not seeing Eddie's mother or father. And because I didn't see his youngest sister, either, I asked, "Where's Oby?"

Eddie said, "They're not coming. I'm sorry, Wendy. Oby wanted to come, but Mom told her she'd be punished if she did." Oby was still in high school and was subject to her parents' rules. She had to obey them about everything, or she'd be grounded.

"Really?" I asked. "Damn." I knew Eddie's parents had their doubts about our relationship, mainly because Cecilia and Mom didn't get along. Still, I didn't let that put a dent in my excellent mood. I told myself, "I'll win them over eventually."

After dinner and dessert, Eddie pulled me to the front of the room. He said, "I want to thank everyone for being here tonight." Then he turned to me and said, "Wendy Onyinye Ozuzu."

As soon as I heard my first, middle, and last name, I thought, *Oh shit, it's about to go down*. He dropped to one knee. Everyone yelled and jumped out of their chairs. My tears started streaming (thank God for waterproof mascara). Eddie said, "Will you do me the honor of being my wife?" He opened up the Ascot diamond ring box and showed me a four-pronged solitaire ring with diamonds going around the band. It was the most gorgeous and elegant ring I had ever seen.

I yelled, "*Yes!*" and the room erupted. I always said that when I got engaged, I wanted my mom to be there. And she was, along with the people who mattered most to me: my sister, brother, and stepdad. That Eddie included our families and friends in this life-changing moment meant the world to me. Yvo had just gotten engaged herself. I was thrilled that we'd get to be fiancées together.

As soon as Eddie finished proposing, he directed my attention to the restaurant's windows: a white horse and open-air carriage was pulling up out front on the street. Our guests followed us outside, almost like they were giving us away, to applaud and wave as Eddie and I climbed into the carriage and rode off for a tour of DC's illuminated monuments on our monumental night.

Our fairy-tale life together began.

Unfortunately, every fairy tale has a villain.

Some Nigerian parents of Mom's generation make the mistake of preparing their children for the world that they lived in, not the world that we're living in now. According to Eddie's mom, when a son got married, his parents had a prominent place in the marriage. "Place" might mean a literal place in the son's home. But most Nigerian first gens don't invite their parents into their marriage. America is not designed that way. Still, Cecilia expected Eddie's wife, whomever she might be, to honor traditional roles. According to the old rules, the son's parents called the shots about the son's major life decisions. The son/husband was supposed to submit to his parents; the wife was supposed to submit to her husband, and to his parents. Cecilia's biggest fear seemed to be that if Eddie married me, the daughter of a nonsubservient, untraditional type, she wouldn't have a say in our lives.

The women in my family—my great-grandmother Nne and my mother, Susan—would not be okay with my being subservient to my husband's mother. As I mentioned earlier, Nne beat Angela's mother-in-law, Ifekewsi, with a bucket full of ashes to set her straight on that subject. On top of Cecilia's and Susan's personality clash, we also had to deal with the clash between traditional Nigerian culture versus first-gen sensibilities regarding our expectations about the parents' role in their kids' marriage.

My mother had been defying expectations and bucking convention her whole life, and that was not going to change when it came to her daughter's happiness in marriage. If anyone was going to tell me what to do, it would be Susan herself, *not* Cecilia. Mom was the alpha female. She had the ancestral strength of Nne and would always protect me and keep my mother-in-law from trying to control my marriage. Cecilia knew she'd get pushback from Susan, so her stance was, *If Wendy isn't going to be a traditional daughter-in-law, then Eddie should marry someone else.*

I've talked about how powerful parental approval—or disapproval—is for a first gen in their career. The pressure is *even more* intense regarding marriage. In Nigerian culture, you don't marry just your spouse—you marry the whole family. Parental approval is not just part of the process; it's the beginning, middle, and end of it. The groom's parents offer a bride-price to the bride's parents. If they accept the offer, the couple is thereby married.

The Osefos never offered a bride-price to my mother and stepfather. When Eddie asked them for their approval, they refused to give it. By proposing to me against his parents' wishes, Eddie defied his parents and our culture and traditions. He circumnavigated the entire bride-price process.

It hurt. The rejection and guilt of being the cause of the divide between Eddie and his parents was very heavy to bear. When it really sank in for me that the Osefos were not going to come around, I was cooking with Mom in her kitchen in Maryland. Emotionally wrung out, I said, "I hate this. I can't take the drama. Eddie and I don't need to get married."

Mom said, "My daughter, sit down." We took seats at the table where we'd had countless meals and conversations. "Look at me in my eyes."

"Yes, Mom."

"Do you want to marry him?"

"Yes."

"My daughter, you will marry him, and you'll marry him *well*, in front of *everybody*. I don't care what the outside world is saying. I support this marriage. Your father supports this marriage, and your stepfather supports this marriage. You are going to get married."

If it weren't for Mom's strength, I would not be with my husband today.

If I thought that Cecilia's disapproval had anything to do with me personally, it might have broken me. But it wasn't about me. I don't believe Cecilia would have approved of *any* woman for Eddie. Still, was she really willing to lose her son over this?

During our engagement, Eddie and I were living in an apartment on the fifth floor of a high-rise on Market Street in Philadelphia. (Mom accepted this living arrangement since we were engaged.) I'd had an infatuation with living in a city, because I'd mostly grown up in the suburbs.

The apartment was cute, a great "starter" place. It was a one-bedroom in name only. The wall between the bedroom and the living room was only chest high, so if I was sitting on my bed, I would still know what was going on in the rest of the apartment. The best thing about the place was the view. The living room windows were floor to ceiling and overlooked the entire city. It was beautiful at night with Philadelphia illuminated. We painted the walls ourselves in a honey gold. We spent many evenings on the living room couch, looking at the view, in the glow of our gold walls. We lived above a Trader Joe's, and I would buy all their quirky ingredients and cook dishes I'd never tried before. (If you haven't made Trader Joe's corn bread mix, I would say go out *today* and buy a box.)

We were happy and in love . . . with an enormous problem hanging over our heads. To marry me, Eddie was going to have to give up his family. Family is everything to Nigerians. Would he regret making such a huge sacrifice? Could we overcome such negativity?

In that apartment, I watched *The Real Housewives* for the first time. It was season three of *The Real Housewives of New Jersey* (RHONJ), when Melissa and Joe Gorga joined the cast. Joe and Teresa Giudice, an OG cast member, were brother and sister. The story line was that Teresa wasn't too happy about her brother and sister-in-law encroaching on her TV show and stardom, and she accused Melissa of driving a wedge between herself and her brother. According to Teresa, Joe married Melissa against the wishes of the Gorga parents, and that decision drove the family apart.

It was so relatable, because Eddie and I were facing the same situation. Although Melissa and Joe Gorga had my sympathies, it felt good to watch another family going through what we were. I wasn't alone. Joe and Teresa were first gens whose parents were immigrants from Italy. The parents were set in their old-world ways and the next generation was trying to respect the wishes of their parents, while blazing a trail for themselves. It just hit home for me. I hadn't expected the show to be more than mindless entertainment, but it actually reflected my own life and gave me solace.

In our academic lives at Rutgers, I was having great success, which did mitigate the effects of the family conflict. Eddie, however, was really feeling the pressure. Because his parents had turned their back on him, he felt like he had no room for error and studied obsessively. He would sit in front of a small wood laptop table from the moment he woke up until late into the night. I'd hoped we'd hang out more and roam the city together. But he'd seen what happened to me when I didn't make the grade in law school. He could not let that happen to him. The anxiety was doubled because of the drama with his family; if he failed, he had no one (except me) to go to for backup and support. There was a degree of loneliness sharing a one-bedroom apartment with someone who was just on the other side of the half wall, but in his own world of worry.

As his parents faded from our lives, Mom's presence became more prominent in mine. The law school debacle was behind us; she approved of my pursuing my doctorate. As for how to deal with Eddie's family, she told me, "Forget these people. God will handle them. You have to be strong."

It was nearly impossible to do that, though, while planning our wedding. I'd have fun dress shopping and sampling cakes with Mom and Yvo. And then, while watching TV with Eddie later on, his phone would ping with a text.

"It's from Ify," he said. "She says, 'I prayed on it, and I've decided not to come to the wedding.'"

He called her and asked, "Why are you doing this?"

It seemed that Cecilia had threatened her other children that she and her husband would withhold their blessing for their future marriages if they participated in ours. Knowing how important parental blessings are for Nigerian weddings and fearing they would be at the receiving end of this backlash, his siblings faced a difficult choice.

"I'm so sorry," I said.

"I'm sorry that she's doing this. At least the others are coming," he said.

A month later, after I'd auditioned DJs and chosen my centerpieces, Eddie's phone pinged again. "It's Nora," he said. "She's not coming, either. This is crazy."

A few weeks after that, I had my first gown fitting, and Eddie found out his third sister was backing out. All we could do was apologize to each other.

And then Eddie's brother, Greg, declined. Greg's turning his back on Eddie was, to me, the ultimate show of cowardice. The sisters bowed down to their mother, but Greg was a guy. It's a double standard, I know, but I expected a man not to go along with Cecilia's petty bullshit.

As a whole, I didn't think much of Eddie's siblings. They were cowering under parental pressure, as if they didn't have a mind of their own. I was raised by a queen who held her head high, a woman who would never force her children to choose between her and one another. How can you use your children as pawns to fight your battles?

"I can't believe they're all doing this," he said.

"Are you upset?" I asked.

Eddie is not an outwardly emotional person. If he showed any emotion, it was disbelief and disappointment. But he was not destroyed by it. The fact is, he just wasn't that close to his siblings or his parents. My mother instilled in Yvo and me, from birth, "We're all we have." We had internalized Susan's fierce family loyalty. Eddie's parents never embedded that message in him, and they didn't nurture close relationships within the family. They cut him off, but, as he said, "I'm not missing much, because there was not much there to begin with."

Originally, our wedding party had ten pairs of bridesmaids and ushers. With Eddie's family defections, it dwindled down to five. His siblings had made their choice. They would not risk their parents' disapproval of the spouses they hadn't even met yet. (Cecilia held true to her word, and she supported her other children's partners no matter who they were or how much they went against ideal qualities of a Nigerian spouse. One married a man who isn't Igbo. A second gave her husband US citizenship, and another had a child out of wedlock, the highest disgrace in our culture. But none of them were ostracized. Go figure.)

Mom was plugged into the Nigerian community, and she kept me posted on what she heard on her end. "Eddie's mother is telling people not to come to the wedding," she said. "Don't worry, Wen. They won't listen to her. Even if they don't want to come, they will anyway. They'll want to see what happens so they can gossip about it. I promise you, everyone is going to want to be at this wedding."

The Osefos' boycott sparked a whisper campaign in our community. People started talking about Eddie and me. If the start of our marriage was so terrible, they said, it was surely a sign of failure to come. Cecilia kept the gossip going by souring my name, calling me a harlot and other, more offensive words. She seemed determined to turn the entire community against me. Everyone knew what was going on, and veered toward one side of this rift or the other. Even one of my aunts asked Mom, "Why is Wendy marrying this boy? The mom doesn't want it. She's saying terrible things about you."

Some of Mom's friends said, "Wendy can have her pick. She doesn't have to marry Eddie."

They were right. We were both young; we could go on and meet other people. But Eddie and I were *in love*. We were (are) soul mates. When we looked into each other's eyes, we saw our past, present, and future *together*, our children's future, and their children's future. I was compelled to go through life with this man.

In response to those who said it'd be easier to just walk away, Mom said, "My daughter wants to marry him, so my daughter *will* marry him. And it'll be the wedding of the year."

Using the full force of her personality, she rallied her friends in Baltimore, Durham, and New York to support us. She was the bridge to Nigeria, and many of Eddie's relatives in his ancestral village of Umoji contacted her to come to the wedding and represent his family.

Yvo was my maid of honor, of course. She hosted my bridal shower at a swanky teahouse in Maryland, and my bachelorette party. She was at my side all year, and supported me every step of the way with a smile on her face.

A few days before the wedding, Yvo came to Mom's house. I was there, too, working on the gift bags for the wedding. I had them lined up on the floor of the living room. Yvo didn't seem outwardly upset, but I knew something was up.

She and her fiancé were having problems. As a result, she called off her engagement within days of my wedding. She still performed her maid of honor duties for me, which must have been painful for her. But Yvo is our mother's daughter; she put on a brave face, and no one knew that she was hurting. I never saw her cry or even break her smile. She never allowed anyone else to worry about her.

I was so wrapped up in wedding preparations and the Osefo drama, I didn't have the emotional bandwidth to comfort her in that moment. I should have been clued into what was happening in her relationship. I should have taken her to lunch. I should have packed a bag and stayed at her place for a week. We were always there for each other. By someone else's standards, my daily phone calls would have been enough. By our family standards, I wasn't there when she needed me.

At this time, Yvo was doing her residency program. Within the next few years, she'd start her own podiatry surgery practice, and be appointed by the state's governor to be the president of the Maryland Board of Podiatry, the first Black woman in history to hold that position. She would go on to meet and marry my amazing brother-in-law, Chyke, and have two beautiful kids. I hate to say it, but I am so happy her first engagement was called off, because I could not imagine her with anyone else but her husband. They are made for each other. So things worked out brilliantly for my superstar sister.

However, it still fills me with shame that I didn't show up for her when she needed me back then. She'd been my backbone since I was a baby, and the one time she needed protection and support from me, I wasn't available or capable of providing it.

The big day arrived. Just as Mom predicted, every person we invited came to the wedding. We actually had to turn people away at the door who weren't invited. That showed just how much Nigerians love to gossip and judge one another. It didn't matter if the guests were friend or foe. They just wanted to be there to talk about it with one another the next day. More than two hundred people celebrated our wedding with us.

We said our vows on August 20, 2011, at the historic Baltimore church St. Vincent de Paul. Vince, the guy Eddie introduced to me at that cookout years ago as his future best man, was in fact his best man. Mom and Darlington wore matching Nigerian attire in shades of orange. Mom's orange silk gele had to have been three feet tall. Together they walked me down the aisle.

Eddie and I changed out of our wedding clothes and put on traditional Nigerian attire for the reception. My gele in orange and grass-green silk with embroidered flowers wasn't quite as tall as Mom's, but it came close. Eddie's teal patterned dashiki was made with the same bold fabric as my sleeveless fitted dress. We wore matching orange beaded necklaces.

Even though it wasn't technically a traditional Nigerian wedding, we incorporated Igbo customs into it anyway, like breaking a kola nut and sharing it with guests as a sign of respect and welcome to all present. Also, a large contingency of the Umoji people from Eddie's village were in attendance, and they did a special presentation, demonstrating their personal support as well as the villages' endorsement and acknowledgment of our union.

Not every member of Eddie's family boycotted. Eddie partnered with his maternal grandmother for the mother-son dance. Eddie's aunt Maureen, Cecilia's sister, came as well. She pulled me to the side during the reception and said, "Wendy, you can't take it personally. It's not about you. This is who she is." I think it's telling that Cecilia does not talk to her own mom or sister.

I agree with the African proverb that family happiness takes a village. But from my first-gen perspective, that village doesn't have to include spiteful, hateful people. Moreover, that village is not about quantity but *quality*. Happily, Eddie could count on his excellent aunt and grandmother as the village members he could turn to for guidance and support. We all need our people. I'm just saying that we can choose who those people are.

By turning their back on us, Eddie's parents hurt him, but in the long run, they hurt themselves *far* more. Our relationship was tested, and we came out stronger than ever. Eddie's parents continue to deprive themselves of their son and their grandchildren. I can only imagine the pain they must be suffering from their self-inflicted wounds. But their pain is not my problem.

My mother is a traditionalist in many ways, like in her unwavering expectations for our career success. Her support during my engagement and wedding was an act of love. She made that magical day happen. She fought for us with such grace, such dignity. She never once doubted that her mission was righteous, that Eddie and I were meant to be together.

I am because of her. From her tears, I have become.

No matter what she did, Cecilia couldn't break us up or shake our commitment. In a way, her negativity brought Eddie and me closer. Psalm 23:5 says: God will "prepare a table before you in the presence of your enemies. I will anoint your head with oil, and your cup runneth over." God did exactly that. He blessed Eddie and me, and since the day of our wedding, our cup has runneth over with blessings.

So thanks, Cecilia. You had a plan, but God had a better one.

At the end of the reception, I gave Mom a hug and said, "Thank you, for everything."

She smiled and said, "You're welcome." A moment of deep gratitude and love passed between us, and I felt closer to her than ever.

FIFTEEN

A Birth and a Death

During Eddie's last year of law school, he got a phone call early in the morning from one of the partners at PricewaterhouseCoopers, a top accounting firm. He put the call on speaker, and we listened together as they offered him a job in Tysons Corner, Virginia. When we heard the news, we had to stay silent, but we were both doing the happy dance. He'd been under so much pressure, and getting that job was a huge relief. This was in 2011, post–Great Recession, when jobs for law school grads were hard to come by. And here he'd been offered a well-paid position before he'd even finished school. Our upcoming move coincided with my completing my coursework in my PhD program. The remainder of my research was independent. I could do it anywhere.

Between Eddie's graduation and his starting at a new job, we had a five-month period of limbo. We put our stuff in storage and moved into the basement of my mom's house. It was strange to go from a high-rise apartment to a basement, but at least it had its own entry. Mom didn't charge us rent and she did all the shopping and cooking for us. We enjoyed the aromas of her food wafting into the basement daily. Eddie could concentrate on preparing for the bar exam and I dug into research for my dissertation on how to engage low-income parents in their children's education. Mom's care gave us a chance to catch our breath.

Eddie and I celebrated our one-year wedding anniversary while living under Mom's roof. At our dinner out that night, I said, "I have a gift for you," and handed him a wrapped box.

"Thank you, Wen," he said, opening it.

He held up the first item in the box, a plastic stick with two pink lines in the small oval window. He said, "Is this what I think it is?"

I smiled, waiting for his emotions to catch up with his brain. The other item in the box was a black-and-white image that, without context, wouldn't make sense to anyone.

"It's a sonogram," I said. "That little white bean is—"

"It's our baby," he said, and immediately started crying. He swept me up in his arms. While kissing me, he said, "I love you! We're having a baby!"

During my first trimester, before we found out the gender, I spent a lot of time in church, begging God for a boy. In my heart, I always wanted a son. Was that longing genuinely in me, or was it the case of old traditions dying hard?

In Nigerian culture (then and now), a marriage is looked upon favorably by the community if not only the first but also the second and even the third child is a boy. Boys are status symbols. They're also considered to be a blessing from God.

My grandparents' first child was my uncle Fred. His birth was exciting—and probably a relief—for Angela and Albert after the chaos of their engagement. One boy down. They needed two more, and the marriage would be considered a success by the community.

Their second child was Winifred—not a boy. Their third child: Cordelia. After the second girl in a row, people in Nimo started asking Angela, "Why are you having all these girls?," implying something was wrong with her or the marriage.

Ekwy, the third girl in a row, came next. Her full name is Ekwutozina Chukwu, which translates as "Stop speaking down on God," an answer to the whispering among the neighbors who thought Angela must have offended God since she wasn't producing sons.

Nkiru, yet another girl, came next. Her name translates as "The one ahead is better," meaning that Nkiru was a blessing, but the child *after* her, hopefully a boy, would be even more of a blessing. To the increasingly loud whisperers, Angela's message in Nkiru's name was "be patient. A son is on deck."

The next child was Susan, my mother. Her Igbo name translates to "Let the will of God be done." With her, Angela gave up on the prospect of having a son. She believed that it was not in her destiny to bear another male child. Much to her surprise, Angela and Albert's last three children were all boys, starting with Chukwudi—which means "God is alive"—followed by Hyke and Ike.

My mother had two girls with Edwin. According to the Nigerian community, that alone was proof that their marriage wasn't blessed; her marriage to Darlington, however, produced a boy, so that got the thumbs-up. Mom didn't buy into these beliefs, and neither did I. And yet I prayed daily, "God, please give me a son, just to show everyone how right this marriage is."

When I was twelve weeks along, Eddie and I went in for my sonogram. The technician asked, "Do you want to know the gender?"

We both said, "Yes!"

"It's a boy," she said.

Whew! We smiled at each other and kissed, proud and relieved. Now his parents wouldn't be able to say, "You see? It's proof they're not going to last." By having a boy first, we headed off gossip. A small part of me, the part that bowed to Nigerian culture even as a first gen, saw it as a blessing from God that we would go the distance.

My pregnancy was a hectic time for us both. After Eddie passed the bar exam, we moved to Ashburn, Virginia, in October 2012. Our town house was a beautiful new construction with perfectly smooth walls and stainless steel appliances. I made it my goal to intricately decorate each and every one of its four levels. It was more than big enough for our growing family.

While my classmates were studying together for the comprehensive exam back in Jersey, I was alone in Virginia, getting bigger by the hour, without a tutor or academic support—and I had to teach myself statistics. I'm *not* a math person. But if I didn't get it right, I'd fail and that would be it. I remember telling myself, "You cannot fail this exam. If you do, the next time they allow you to retake it, the baby will be here, and you won't be able to study with a newborn." If you think your entire professional future, your livelihood, the honor of your family, and the expectations of your parents depended on your learning statistics, you'd figure it out. The stakes were *that* high. I aced the test because, truly, once and for all, *failure was not an option.*

As I took those comprehensive exams to become a PhD, I was so hugely pregnant I could barely pull my chair close enough to the table to write my answers.

I passed the exams and called Mom to tell her the good news. "I'm one step closer to getting my PhD." My dissertation remained, which would take another couple of years.

As a Nigerian, I did not let the years of hard work ahead intimidate me. It was what had to be done. Just like being pregnant, it didn't help to think about your body changing, the pain of childbirth or recovery afterward. You did what you had to do to get that degree or that baby. Nigerians focus on the goal and don't stress out about the steps they have to take to get there.

Mom said, "That's good, Wen."

She wasn't going to go overboard with her congratulations until I got the degree, and I didn't expect her to. After I'd received my second master's, she said, "Master's degrees are good. A PhD would be better."

But her tone was off. I asked, "You don't sound good. Is something going on?"

"Your stepfather needs surgery," she said.

My mother was a cardiac nurse, but no matter how hard she tried, she could do nothing to help Darlington's increasingly severe heart issues. His upcoming surgery was to insert a stent—a wire mesh tube—in his heart to keep the blood flowing. It would take place in December, not the best time of year to feel terrible.

The day of the surgery, carolers were singing outside my window when I called Darlington to wish him luck. "You're going to be fine," I said. "You'll be okay."

He was scared to go under the knife, and too emotional to speak. He said, "Wen." Just my name.

Hearing it put me right over the edge. I tried not to sob on the phone, and repeated, "You're going to be fine."

He made it through the surgery, but he was never the same. His physical and mental health continued to deteriorate. It turned into a vicious cycle of his not eating, losing weight, feeling weak, feeling depressed, not exercising, and he just got sicker and sicker. While life grew inside me, my stepfather seemed to be slipping away.

I went into labor in April 2013. In the delivery room, I kept saying to Mom, "I'm so scared."

She said, "Don't ever say that. You are a child of God. *Don't be scared.*"

For Mom, *fear was not an option.* Nigerian parents don't raise their children to be afraid. If you gave voice to things going wrong, that was what you got.

But I was scared! By denying my feelings, Mom was denying my truth.

After I safely delivered and held my newborn son, Karter, in my arms, I promised him, "I will be a warrior woman for you. My heart is open to you. I love everything about you." *Everything* included his fears, his weaknesses, and his dreams.

With my newborn, I stayed home most nights working on my dissertation and watching TV. One of my favorite shows was *Love & Hip Hop*. One night I was in my lounge pants, eating popcorn, sitting on our black leather couch, happily watching Harlem rapper Joe Budden have an argument with his then girlfriend, Tahiry Jose, when my phone rang.

"Mom?" I asked.

"Wen, it's me," said my brother, Jordan, then age eleven. Why was he calling me on Mom's phone?

"Jord, what's up?"

In the background, I heard my mother's voice saying, "Oh my God! Call 911!"

I sat up on the couch. "Jordan, what's wrong? What's happening?"

"Wen, I think Dad is dead."

Adrenaline kicked in and I was already running through the house, yelling at my husband, "Something's going on. Get dressed! Get dressed!" On the phone to Jordan, I said, "We're on the way."

Eddie and I threw on clothes, bundled up Karter, and headed down the steps of the house to get into the car. I remember I was on the fourth step when the phone rang again.

It was my sister. She said, "Wen, Ifeanyi passed away." Ifeanyi was his Nigerian name.

Don't be scared. "Oh my God. Oh my God." My brain was stuck on that one phrase.

Eddie asked, "What is it?"

I hung up the phone and a wave of coldness came over my body. It was November, around fifty degrees, but I started shivering.

We drove an hour and fifteen minutes from Ashburn to Baltimore with the heater cranked. When we turned onto Mom's street, a ghostly white ambulance came toward us, slowly and silently, from the opposite direction, sirens and lights off. I just knew my stepfather's body was in that ambulance.

He's dead and they're going to bury him in the cold ground. Another chill hit me full force, and I kept saying to Eddie, "I'm so cold."

We parked in Mom's driveway and ran into the house. Mom looked torn apart. She was sitting on the couch in the living room, rocking back and forth, her face wet with tears, her hair a mess. To see a woman who was ordinarily so put together in such a disheveled state made the death real for me. She'd never let anyone see her like this otherwise. I went over to her and hugged her with Karter in my arms. She pressed her face against my shoulder and sobbed. She said, "You just missed him. The ambulance took him."

The house was already filling up. Hyke, Yvo, and Chyke, her new husband of one month, had just arrived. I thought, *At least Darlington lived long enough to see us both happily married*. Eddie stood by awkwardly. My husband wanted to believe that everyone died peacefully in their sleep at ninety. So when reality conflicted with his optimism, he was at a loss for what to say or do.

Darlington was just fifty-six when he passed.

Jordan and I went into the kitchen and he told me what happened before he called me, and after. The three of them—Mom, Darlington, and Jordan—were watching TV. My stepfather said, "Excuse me," and went to use the upstairs bathroom.

Ten minutes went by, and he didn't come back downstairs. Mom called for him in Igbo, "Ifeanyi, where are you?" No response.

She went upstairs, into the master bedroom, and still didn't see him. She knocked on the bathroom door, no response. Finally, she opened it and saw her partner of fifteen years laid out on the tile floor, not moving.

Mom sprang into nurse mode and immediately started doing CPR. She'd brought people back to life before; she could work a miracle again. She yelled to Jordan to call 911, which he did, and then he called me. But it was too late. The man's heart just gave out.

In Nigerian culture, there are things that need to take place before a funeral. We would have to notify his village people, discuss with his family whether to bury him in the States or abroad in Nigeria, and gather all the groups and organizations he was a part of for them to participate in the wake. Due to these rites and customs, his funeral did not take place until several weeks after his death.

During this period of grief, I was broken. There were many things I would have liked to tell him, but I didn't get the chance. Back at home in

Virginia, I sat down at my kitchenette table, looking out at the view of our backyard, and wrote my stepfather a letter with pen and paper.

I wrote that he was the smartest and kindest man I'd ever known, and that I had the deepest love and respect for him. "I'm sorry I never told you that," I wrote, openly crying. "I'm sorry I never took your side when you and Mom fought." Taking Mom's side was my duty. The Nigerian way is that a child agreed with her parent's authority, period. But there were many times when Mom was wrong, and I should have been more objective. The thought that he felt unsupported by me still pierces my heart.

I folded up the letter and sealed it in an envelope. On the top of the envelope, I wrote, "My Daddy."

I've never called anyone Daddy in my life, including my birth father. After pouring my heart out in the letter to Darlington, it felt natural and right to seal it with that endearment.

The day of his funeral was abnormally cold for Maryland, in keeping with the coldness I'd felt since that first call from Jordan. It actually snowed the morning of his funeral, but it didn't stick to the ground. We were late leaving Mom's house to get to the service on time and in the rush, I forgot the most important thing.

"Oh shit," I said once we were seated in church. "I forgot the letter!"

One of my mom's friends was behind me in the pews, and she asked, "Do you want me to go back to the house and get it?"

"Yes, I have to give him this letter."

She raced to the house and back in record time and handed me the letter as they were wheeling the casket down the aisle of the church. I ran up to the pallbearers and said, "Wait! You have to open it! Open it."

The men stopped and opened the casket. My stepfather lay on a bed of white silk, in one of his dapper black wool suits. I placed my letter on his chest, the words "My Daddy" facing upward. Then they closed the casket and loaded him into the waiting hearse to take him away from me and us all.

So many tears were spilled that day. More tears than snowflakes. My only solace was that I got to give him my letter, and that he was buried with words of love right over his heart.

Before my stepfather passed away, Yvo and I thought we were entering a new phase in our lives. We had our husbands, and I had an infant son. We were going to focus on our own families, our careers, and not worry so much about pleasing Mom. But it didn't work out that way.

From the moment Darlington passed, my sister and I doubled down on caring for Mom. For starters, we took turns living with her in Maryland. Yvo and her husband would stay for a week with Mom. Then I would bring Karter and stay for a week. We all went back and forth like this for six months, despite having jobs and responsibilities of our own.

Mom never asked us outright to come. That wasn't her style. She would say something like, "I have no one to talk to," and we would drive out there because that was what good Nigerian girls do. We helped cook and clean, but our real purpose was to keep her company.

When I'm sad, I prefer to be alone. But Mom is a social butterfly. In her grief, she needed to be surrounded by people. You would think that her vast network of Nigerian friends would have been coming by the house hourly with food. But some of them shifted away from her after my stepfather passed.

In our culture, whenever someone dies young, people don't blame lifestyle, genes, or disease. They assume the death was caused by nefarious factors. Since Mom was closest to my stepfather, some people started looking at her differently, as if she'd somehow caused his death. This was utter bullshit. Mom had done everything in her power to take care of Ifeanyi. For every doctor's appointment, surgery, and medical procedure, Mom was by his side. Furthermore, Mom made sure he ate. She was his caregiver and put his health before anything. But Nigerians, with our deep-rooted faith, always try to find a bad connection when life goes against what we would expect. Despite all her sacrifices for her husband, Mom was not acknowledged for the good she had done.

Before the burial, we had an autopsy performed to prove that he hadn't passed away from foul play. No substances were found, no injuries or marks. The cause of death was unquestionably heart disease. Absolutely nothing sinister happened to him, but that didn't stop people from still gossiping.

Mom was strong during that period. She had the totality of our family history backing her up. The tragedies we've endured—kidnapping, war, violence, heartbreak, loss—are our family's legacy and the foundation of our strength. Nne's spirit and her fighter mentality live on in my mother.

Mom wasn't a coward and never hid her face from the community. If she knew a friend was spreading a rumor, she'd confront her. "If you think badly of me, I'm not your friend anymore," she would say. "Where were you when I was taking him to all of these doctor's appointments? Where were you when I was supporting the household because he couldn't find work?" A tragedy shows you who your real friends are. Mom learned that she didn't have as many as she had thought.

Despite her outward show of strength, I was concerned that she was undone by the loss. She took a leave from work that rolled from two months to four months to a year. She depended completely on Yvo, Jordan, and me to satisfy her deep social needs. The three of us collectively filled in the gap left by her deceased husband.

My sister took on the financial piece by supporting her and Jordan.

I took on the pampering piece, sending her flowers, spoiling her on her birthday, giving her frivolous gifts, taking her to get her hair done.

My brother became her companion. If there was a party or a wedding, he was her plus-one. He often didn't want to go, but she'd dress him up in a nice suit and drag him along anyway. And at the event, he would stay by her side the whole time.

In ancient Igbo culture, there was a basis for the family filling the gap for the bereaved. When a wife was widowed, it fell on the family to provide her with a replacement husband. A typical situation would be the dead husband's brother stepping up to marry the widow. In our own family history, a precedent was set eighty years ago. When my great-grandmother on Albert's side, Ifekewsi, was widowed, Albert "married" her to a young woman whose job was to be a "wife" to her. Not sexually, of course. The woman did everything for Ifekewsi, like cook and clean, and be her companion. Since this woman was considered married to Ifekewsi, she wasn't allowed to take a husband, but she could get pregnant and have kids, which she did. Her oldest son was named Danny, so she was called Mama Danny. In the Igbo tradition, a mother's name becomes the name of her oldest child. My village name would be Mama Karter.

Granted, in modern times, people don't do these kinds of things anymore. I love my culture and its traditions, but they don't always translate to modern life. We don't live in the village anymore. My stepfather's brother wasn't going to show up on Mom's doorstep with a bouquet and a ring. We aren't going to bring her a "wife" to cater to her every whim, or a new husband. The older generation's expectations of first gens are just not applicable in America.

For Americans, the family rallies around the bereaved for a period, around a year, and then there's an expectation that they'll move on with their lives on their own.

For Nigerians, the family is obligated to put the needs of the bereaved first, with no time frame attached. When my stepfather passed away, my siblings and I put Mom first.

I accepted this responsibility, but after several months, it started to wear on me. Around the first anniversary of Darlington's death, I was writing my dissertation, working on that Obama initiative, caring for Karter, and being a wife. On top of all that, Mom called me daily and inflicted guilt.

"I'm sad," she'd say.

The job of Director of Family and Community Engagement was high stakes. I had to produce report after report and answer emails as soon as they hit my in-box.

"I'm on a deadline, Mom," I'd say. "I'll come out as soon as I can."
The drive would take two hours with moderate traffic.

"Okay, Wen." Her tone was painful! It was probably the first time in
her life that she wasn't surrounded by people to talk to who she knew
cared about her.

An hour later, while I was scrambling to do my job, Mom would call
again. "Wen, when are you getting here?"

"It might be a while," I'd say. Now I'd hit rush hour and the drive
could take forever. It certainly felt that way with Karter squirming in his
car seat.

"I'm lonely, Wen."

I wanted to say, "My boss doesn't care that you're lonely." But instead, I kept my mouth shut and trucked over to Mom's. And then we'd
sit around while Investigation Discovery true-crime shows played in the
background and I counted the hours until I could go home and get back
to my own life.

Many times I tried to establish boundaries. "Mom, there will be
times when I have too much going on to come see you."

"I was always there for you when you needed me, Wen," she replied.

The transactional nature of Nigerian parenting was her trump card. I
was raised on the "I do for you, then you do for me" tradition. I saw how
Mom cared for Albert, how Winifred cared for Angela. That was the
deal. Mom needed me sooner than I anticipated, exactly when my life
was most intense. And yet she still expected me to magically appear at
her house at a moment's notice.

"I can't always control what's going on," I said. "I can't drop everything and come over." In the modern world, there are external factors,
like fixed work hours, conference calls, and traffic, that made it impossible to give Mom "village"-level attention and accommodation.

"But I'm sad," she replied. And that was it. I'd find myself getting in
the car, regardless of my other obligations.

We continued filling the gap, then and now, out of respect for those

old traditions. We don't have to be so obedient. We adhere to her imposi-
tions out of deference to her.

Did she understand that the world has changed? Did she understand
that her children could have easily chosen the American way and lessened her dependency after, say, six months or a year, by just refusing to
go to her whenever she called? None of our American friends would
have blinked if we had.

Growing up, I didn't feel like I had any choice but to live up to her
expectations. But when I became an adult, I realized I had a choice. And
still, even when I knew I didn't have to, I chose to be an obedient Nigerian daughter. I chose to abide by her traditions out of respect.

My first-gen sensibilities made me feel resentful, though. Did obedience engender respect? I wasn't sure. It would have been nice to get
some respect or appreciation from Mom in return, but I wasn't going to
hold my breath.

SIXTEEN

Becoming Visible

Darlington had been gone for over a year when Eddie and I, still living in Virginia, started talking about having another child. Since our first child was a boy, the pressure was off to have another son. Just one was enough to stifle any doubts. This time, I prayed for a girl. At the twelve-week mark, we had a sonogram and found out that I was carrying another boy. Oh well. I was disappointed, but Karter would love having a little brother.

We welcomed Kruz Fitzgerald Ifeanyi in March 2015. His second middle name is for my stepfather. As for his first name, people say, "Kruz is so cool," thinking it refers to a big car or a boat, or even Tom Cruise. Not even close. My son was born the Saturday before Palm Sunday, so we named him "cross," carrying on the tradition by giving him a religion-inspired name.

I passed my comprehensive exams with Karter in my belly. I defended my dissertation two years later very pregnant with my second son, Kruz. Each pregnancy came with an academic milestone. My kids were and continue to be my greatest motivation.

Speaking of my academic milestones, all told, it took ten years from graduating college to get my doctorate. Just to recap: My four degrees are (1) a BA in political science from Temple, (2) an MA in government from Johns Hopkins, (3) an MSc in public affairs from Rutgers, and (4) a

PhD in public affairs and community development from Rutgers. I was the first Black woman to earn this degree at Rutgers.

I'm not bragging. I'm stating the facts. And even if I *am* pumping myself up a bit, I have earned the right to do so. If a man talks about his accomplishments, he's just informing people. If a woman does it, she is a blowhard loudmouth. The double standard isn't right, and whenever I talk about my accomplishments, I'm doing my part to represent what's possible for women.

Although my mom's relentless demands amped up my stress and anxiety throughout this period, if she hadn't been pushing and pressuring me, maybe I would have given up. She taught me that failure is not an option, and I internalized it. I persevered for my own sake, but also for Mom's.

In the end, she didn't get one of each—a doctor and a lawyer. Mom got two doctors instead—one MD and one PhD—and now every person who thought we'd amount to nothing had to eat their words. And those words are: "Address me correctly, sweetie—it's *Dr.* Wendy to you!"

Mom said, "Congrats, Wen! Now you will get a great job." The goal posts were forever moving farther away.

My first academic job was at Goucher College, a private liberal arts college in Towson, Maryland. I was brought in as the inaugural director of a new graduate program in the art of management. I built the program from the ground up. But once I got it running, the thrill of being a director and sitting in my corner office wore off quickly.

I'd been an admirer of the career of author and TV host Marc Lamont Hill since I first heard about him at Temple University (he was also an alumnus). If he could start out poor on the streets of Philadelphia, and then graduate from the same college as I did, get his PhD, return to Temple as a professor (he taught media studies and urban education), and become a vocal force in the media, then I could, too. "I want to be the female version of Marc Lamont Hill," I told myself.

One day about a year into my employment at Goucher, a friend came to visit me on campus. "I had the hardest time finding your office," he told me. It just hit me: *Who will find me here?* The school didn't have a big platform, and the longer I stayed, the less likely it would be for me to jump into a bigger pond. Every semester that went by, I felt more unfulfilled, and even a little trapped. People who've grown up in a small town and dreamed of moving to the big city to be seen and heard can probably relate to my frustration. I wouldn't make my mark at Goucher.

I was one of two or three Black faculty and felt I had to be the voice for Black Goucher and speak for all the students of color. I'd tried to bring more diverse voices into the picture by inviting Black intellectuals to serve as visiting professors. One luminary I called upon was D. Watkins at the University of Baltimore, a brilliant writer who was just about to release his *New York Times* bestseller *The Beast Side: Living and Dying While Black in America* (his second bestseller, *The Cook Up: A Crack Rock Memoir*, came out a year later). He came for a week and taught my students about writing, which I greatly appreciated.

Another visiting resident was a successful writer friend of mine. This person taught my grad students for a week, Monday through Friday. And on Friday, they posted a picture of their Goucher ID on Facebook with the caption: "Now I can add college professor to the list of things I've done."

I saw that post and thought, *Wait, what? You taught a seminar for a week and now you're a college professor?* I'd already begun feeling disillusioned with Goucher. That writer's post—shouting, essentially, "Look at me and all the amazing things I am doing!"—compounded my feeling of being invisible.

I called Yvo to bitch about it. "I'm the director of the entire program and I've never boasted on social media," I said. "But this person was here for a minute and is getting all this love and admiration. Should I be doing more? Or am I doing enough and should be giving myself flowers for all the accomplishments I've achieved?"

I know this may be hard for some people to grasp, since I'm now known for shouting, "I have four degrees," every chance I got during my first season on RHOP, but I have never been one to toot my own horn unprovoked. My Nigerian culture made me think that what I was doing was nothing special. I would pump milk for my children, work nine to five as a director, cook dinner at night, and deliver a keynote speech all in one day. Yet I never once thought what I was doing was exceptional. One downside of being a Nigerian first gen is that we were taught that exceptionalism is the norm. So much so that we fail to give ourselves grace and acknowledge that we are doing great things.

Yvo got it. She said, "Wen, you're not *just* a mom. You are a professor, a director. You're amazing and you should let people know that."

My second mom was also a first gen. She saw things differently. I'd really become a doctor and a professor for my mother, and now, with my sister's endorsement, I resolved to put myself forward. That was the moment I started chasing *my* dreams.

But I couldn't just "go for it" like an American. I had to get a parental stamp of approval first. The next time I visited Mom, we sat down at the kitchen table for a talk. I had to work up the courage to say, "I'm not really happy at Goucher. I'm thinking of leaving to try something else."

"Something else?" she asked.

I took a big breath to get it out. "Maybe doing political commentary on the news."

She made a "that's crazy" face and a few displeased sounds. "You will stay at Goucher, Wen. You're a college professor."

"I don't know if teaching is what I really want to do."

"You have a good job and a career. Stay put."

Mom changed jobs constantly when I was a kid, reaching for a better situation, but always in her chosen career of nursing. As a rule, Nigerians are risk averse. The Nigerian handbook says to pick a lane and stay in it until death, so you never have to start over from scratch. Leaving a sure thing and going for it in a new career might mean failing, so Nigerians would rather just try to make sure they never failed. Sticking with the status quo might not result in a big leap forward in prestige or wealth, but I wouldn't lose what I had. When faced with a career crossroads, Nigerians will most always take the (narrow) path of least resistance.

But being a political commentator would satisfy all my interests and talents. With a doctorate and a professorship, I had all the authority I needed to give speeches and go on TV. I had fresh insights to bring to the table about the news and events of our times. Often, when you watched the news, you only saw people who were versed in politics. I had a strong grasp of politics as well as pop culture. Not to mention I did work in the community, so I knew what the people who would be most affected by policies actually wanted and needed in their lives. This unique perspective was my golden goose. I'd been dreaming about this, and now I was going to make it happen.

Even though Mom was not on board, I used my Rolodex to get the names and numbers of some event organizers and TV producers. Then I cold-called them and gave my pitch. I started to get booked for keynote speeches, panels, conferences, regional TV, and fringe national TV spots.

In the beginning of my public speaking career, I booked all my TV appearances and speeches myself. Later, I had a short stint with a media booking agency, but that didn't last. I had done a better job for myself. Even now, I don't have an agent. So often, people who aspire to get into the field think they need someone "to put them on." The truth is, no one will ever advocate for you with more conviction than yourself. Do not wait for someone to discover you. Instead, work your ass off and the rest will follow.

IN JUNE 2015, there was a mass shooting at the historic Emanuel African Methodist Episcopal Church in Charleston, South Carolina. Nine people in a Bible study group, including the senior pastor and a state senator, were killed by a twenty-one-year-old white supremacist named Dylann Roof. It was yet another incident of racial hatred and murder in our community and on our streets. At the same time, Donald Trump was running for president on a platform of bigotry. It was a frightening time to be a Black professor on a college campus in the South.

That massacre felt personal to every African American, and the Black students at Goucher looked to me to help them through the pain, shock, and fear they were experiencing. We prayed together and waited for the college to put out a statement, to say *something* to condemn white supremacy and gun violence, and to support the Black population on campus. I wasn't looking for much. An email. A freaking tweet. But they didn't issue a statement of any kind.

If I felt invisible as a faculty member, I could only imagine how my students, who called the school home, were suffering. Many of them sought me out, crying, needing to express how they felt about the events of the day, but also the fear and fury of being Black in America. I was one of very few on campus they could turn to for guidance. It was all-consuming.

It felt to me like Goucher simply lacked the necessary support structure for people who looked like me. I needed to go somewhere that encouraged and welcomed a public discussion of racism in America and the rise of white supremacy that was emerging at that time. Goucher was never going to be a strong voice in that discussion. To be part of it, I had to get out of there.

I saw a job posting at Johns Hopkins University. I had gotten one of my master's degrees there a few years before, but I wasn't really plugged into Baltimore intellectual circles. I got in touch with D. Watkins, who was at the center of Baltimore's Black academic community. I mentioned that there was a job opening at Johns Hopkins, and before I could ask him for help, he said, "Hey, do you want me to reach out to anybody?"

I exhaled. "Yes, that would be great," I said.

That connection opened a door. I still had to walk through it.

The process to become a professor at a university as prestigious as Johns Hopkins is not for the faint of heart. I prepared a package of writing samples, references, and bona fides, and was then invited to an all-day academic interview.

Since this would be a step up as a professor—still in my lane—Mom was all for it. She, Eddie, and I talked about strategy at Mom's house the night before the interview.

My main question—the one that could really make or break this process—was, when would I be able to pump? I was still breast-feeding Kruz, normally pumping every two hours when I was at work.

Mom said, "You can't. You have to hold it in. You don't want them to disqualify you because you are a new mom."

Eddie said, "She's right. Can you get through eight hours without pumping?"

"Oh my God," I said, clutching my chest. "This is gonna suck."

Just to be clear: I'm not saying that anyone at Hopkins would discriminate against a new mother. But it was common knowledge, and a widespread American practice, that employers were hesitant to hire or promote pregnant women, mothers, even women of childbearing age. Will you go on maternity leave and never come back or need extra personal days when your kids were sick? No one would have such concerns for a man, even if he was a new father. Women have to operate under different circumstances when looking for a job, because motherhood might be a mark against us that takes us out of the running. The bias might be conscious or otherwise, but the risk was real. At this or any job interview, if I said, "I have to take a forty-minute break now to pump," how seriously would they take me? All eyes would drop straight to my boobs. They'd think of me as a mother first, an academic second.

It wasn't fair. As Mom would say, "So is life. Get over it."

My breakfast with the dean was at 9 a.m. sharp. I arrived at 8:30 a.m., sat in my car, and pumped until the last minute, as much as I could.

After our breakfast, I made a presentation to faculty members in the department.

Next, I went on a tour of the school.

I met with students for an hour to take their questions.

I had lunch with the dean, followed by another presentation to more higher-ups at the university.

I wore three breast pads so I wouldn't leak through my white shirt. I remember glancing down at my chest every few minutes to check. I wore a black blazer, but as the day wore on and my boobs were getting progressively bigger, I wasn't sure I could even button it. Oh my gosh, it was so absolutely painful.

I got back to the car at 5:30 p.m. My engorged breasts and I could barely fit in the front seat. I pumped in the car for an hour. *Sweet relief.* I filled the bottle, dumped it into an empty Medela container, and then filled it again. While pumping, I thought back on the day, and whether my concern about leaking or overfilling had an impact on my presentation (a question that no man will ever have to contemplate).

Fully engorged breasts and all, I must have made a good impression. I was offered the job in the Department of Education at Johns Hopkins, where I've now been since 2016. Would I have been hired if I'd talked openly about being a new mom? We'll never know. I'd like to think so.

I didn't just wake up one day with my doctor wings and fly right into a position at one of the most prestigious universities in the country. They don't just hand out doctorates and professorships like turkey chili samples at Target. I had to work my ass off, write and defend countless papers, pull all-nighters, all the while leading and creating humanitarian side projects, giving birth, nursing, and dealing with nonstop family drama.

No question, the move to Johns Hopkins gave me more credibility to speak as an expert, and I got more offers to do TV and speaking gigs. I started writing political columns for *The Hill*, raising my profile another notch.

My visibility was increasing. I could feel myself emerging from the shadows, and my true self taking shape. Only by being visible could I hope to achieve my goal of making my mark on the world. Nigerians tend to toil away, doing incredible things, outside of public view. I knew I could make the biggest impact by representing us on a bigger stage. Every speaking engagement and column was a small step that brought me closer to the kind of visibility I'd always secretly dreamed about.

My giant leap forward in the public arena came in 2016, thanks to the orange goblin himself, Donald J. Trump.

On Tuesday, November 8, 2016, Eddie and I watched the election returns come in on the couch of our town house in Maryland. At around 10 p.m., he said, "I don't know where this is going, but I don't think it's going to end well. I'm going to sleep."

I wasn't willing to give up just yet, but as the night wore on, I said out loud to an empty room, "Hillary is going to lose."

Spontaneously, I pulled out my computer and started writing. I had to channel my feelings productively or I'd explode. Before midnight, I finished a draft of an op-ed called "Donald Trump Didn't Win. Hatred Did."

At the wee hour of 2 a.m., I gave my finished product a quick polish and submitted it to an editor at *The Baltimore Sun*. They loved it and posted it that day. It reads like the midnight rant it was: "The reason for Trump's success has been hate. Not just the type of hatred that aligns with Trump's views, but the deep-seated hatred that manifests as a result of having a Black president for the past eight years, the deep-seated hatred of having to endure the social movements triggered by the killings of Black people at the hands of law enforcement, and need I say it, the deep-seated hatred resulting from the prominence of the Black Lives Matter movement."

It mentioned the Bradley effect, what happens when a white candidate is challenged by a minority candidate (in this case, a woman) and voters say they're undecided when they know they're going to vote for the white guy, because they don't want pollsters or their friends to think they're racist or sexist. I examined the concept of a "white-lash" against a Black president, BLM, Black protesters on the streets, a Black country singer onstage at the Country Music Awards. I used the word "deplor-ables."

I just *went there*, and readers responded. The op-ed went sort of viral and I was asked to come on TV to talk about it. My phone hasn't stopped ringing ever since.

Every time I knew I'd be on TV, I called Mom to tell her when to tune in. "You did great, Wen," Mom would say. "I'm proud of you, Wen." But no matter how I performed on TV, to her, my real job was being a professor. As long as I taught classes, I could talk politics on cable news. It was okay to go out on a limb, as long as you keep one hand on the trunk.

This new avenue of my career diverged from the narrow path, but I took it anyway. I pushed for it against my mother's advice. She instilled the value in me to work hard and find a way to get past obstacles. I'd in-ternalized the messages so well that I didn't need anyone to push. I could do that all on my own, in any direction I wanted.

SEVENTEEN

The Lion's Den

*W*hile juggling two kids and my new job at Hopkins, I had a short-term health crisis. My body was trying to pass a kidney stone and, in the process, I got sepsis. I ran a high fever and had to be hospitalized to get the infection under control. On my second day in the hospital, while I was still woozy from the fever, the booking agent I worked with at the time called me. "Are you available to do a spot tomorrow on Fox News?" she asked. Fox News, a.k.a. the fuel that kept the Trump dumpster fire burning, was the number one cable news channel. It would be the biggest commentary spot I'd done so far.

"I can't take the show," I said reluctantly. "I'm in the hospital."

After we hung up, I turned to Eddie, who was at my bedside. "Fox just requested me. They're never going to call me back now that I said no to the first invitation."

"If they want you today, they'll want you tomorrow," he said.

"No," I said, changing my mind. "I can do it. I *have* to do it!"

I sat up in bed. *I can do the spot bedside. No, I should check myself out*, I thought. I swung my legs over the side of the bed like I was going to stand up and walk out of there.

Eddie and Mom, who was also in the room, practically jumped across the bed to stop me.

Under strict doctor's orders from Yvo, I didn't do the spot, but then I moped about it for the entire eight days I was in the hospital.

It was a needless worry. Eddie was right: Fox called me again a few days after I got home, and I've been appearing on the network regularly ever since. Those spots put me at a new level, and that led to invitations from CNN and MSNBC.

Mainly, I appeared on Fox News. A big misconception is that Fox News does not invite people of color to do their shows. The reality is that a lot of them choose not to accept. Some people of color refuse to go on the network because, after appearing on it once, they got death threats. One Black woman I know went on Fox, and the next day, someone sent a bag of manure to her mom's house.

I thought, *If I don't do it, who will?* I said yes to Fox News and will keep doing it, despite the fact that I disagree with their editorial content, and despite the death threats that I get every single time.

Uncle Hyke would read the comments online and say, "Who said it? Who's talking about my niece?" As always, ready to go to war.

Well, I didn't go on Fox News expecting praise. Appearing on Fox gave me an opportunity to be what I never saw on TV as a kid: a Black female immigrant with a hard-to-pronounce last name and a chocolate face. My objective was to represent African immigrants to an audience that didn't know us yet feared and hated us, and to say what needed to be said. On TV, I never saw anyone with the same viewpoint as me. And I love that. I embrace that. Young women of color need to see themselves on TV, on scripted and unscripted shows and in positions of authority, as newscasters, reporters, and anchors. Women need to see others they can look up to and emulate. Fox gave me the platform to be what I didn't see in the media growing up.

I am always paying attention to the way I represent myself on camera. Recently, I wore braids on the air on Fox News. It was a deliberate choice, and the comments that flooded in were just as you would predict. We live in a crazy world, that a woman in braids can enrage certain people. My attitude is, keep wearing them, keep representing, until they get used to it . . . and then they'll have to come up with some other thing to foam at the mouth about.

Though it's not just hair that's an issue. From the start, some of the makeup artists at Fox, not very talented ones, applied foundation that made my face three shades lighter than the rest of my body. This happened to me time and again. Was it because they didn't have the right shade for my skin tone, or was it an assumption that dark-skinned people want to lighten up? Or was it to make me more palatable to their viewers? I have been very adamant about my makeup matching my skin, and always ask, "Does my face match my neck?" I don't let that slide.

I remember how important it was for me to see dark-skinned girls and women on TV when I was growing up, and how rarely I did. It was like we didn't even exist. My mission to get more visibility spoke to the need to see people who looked like us on TV. I'd never want my daughter, Kamrynn, to think that because of her dark skin she wasn't beautiful or worth being seen. By showing my Black face on TV, I'm doing my part to change that flawed cultural beauty standard and traditional absence on-screen.

But being visual isn't enough. When I go on TV, I speak from a place of positionality. I speak as the mother of Black boys. I speak as an immigrant. And that's just the beginning. I don't go on TV to say, "This is how *I* feel." If I'm talking about health care, I reach out to my mom and sister. If I'm talking about immigration, I ask Mom, my uncles, aunts, and my Deferred Action for Childhood Arrivals (DACA) students, "How does this make you feel?" If I'm talking about the harassment of unarmed children and Black men, I call my friends who look like Trayvon Martin and George Floyd and say, "What is your take on this?" The police are not necessarily killing people who look like me, but they are killing people who look like my husband. So let me get *his* opinion.

I don't know a lot of other pundits who do that. You see commentators give their opinions based on their own experiences. I have opinions, too, but guess what? They're not always relevant or helpful. I also try to be a vessel for other people's message, the people who are most often ignored and silenced, unseen and unheard.

PREPANDEMIC, FOX NEWS would send a car to my house and drive me to the DC bureau to do an appearance. You sit in the green room and wait your turn along with the other guests. The room isn't green, by the way. It's like any other waiting area, with chairs, tables, beverages, and a platter of fruit and cheese. It's pretty generic, like an airport lounge or doctor's office.

In December 2017, I was sitting in the green room, and Lindsey Graham, the US senator from South Carolina, walked in like he owned the place. The room was a bit crowded, with five or six people sitting in chairs. I was the only Black person in sight.

Senator Graham went up to every individual in the room, introduced himself (as if we didn't know who he was), and shook hands. He lingered over a young blond woman. "What's your name?" he asked. "What's your profession?" He chatted with her and she seemed flustered by the attention of a famous and powerful man.

After he'd spoken to every other person in the room, he got to me. He looked me up and down, up and down. I felt his eyes piercing me.

He looked at my heels, Louboutin.

He looked at my dress, Gucci.

He looked at my hair, flawless.

Then he started from the bottom and worked his way back up.

The entire time, he didn't utter a word. It was excruciating and embarrassing. The whole time, the rest of the room was silent.

Then he handed me an empty paper cup and said, "Throw this out for me."

I was sitting in a green room meant for commentators only, the only Black woman, and he handed me his garbage and expected me to clean up after him like the maid. I was speechless. Do janitors wear stilettos to work? Do they have camera-ready makeup? He knew I wasn't "the help." But I believe he wanted to humiliate me and assert his power over me as a white man.

It was one of many times at Fox News that I asked myself, "Why am I doing this again?" The answer was to continue to fight for and speak up for the underserved. And it was *not easy*.

Lindsey Graham made me feel like trash. It sure felt like his *goal*. And this was not an isolated incident in the green room there. Working as a commentator at Fox often made me feel insignificant and invisible. Hardly anyone acknowledged or spoke to me, even people I'd worked with many times. They wouldn't look me in the eye or would walk right past me.

For the record, one of the only people at Fox News who made me feel welcomed and respected was Tucker Carlson. He's not my cup of tea on a personal or political level. Far from it. But he treated me well and championed me. During my appearance on his show, he discussed health care, and he listened and engaged in a meaningful conversation. Ainsley Earhardt was another notable champion of mine. Occasionally she would be in hair and makeup and catch my segments. She would shoot over a warm text complimenting my work. While our politics may not agree, our hearts did. She is one of the kindest and most genuine people I've ever encountered.

When I started my punditry career, I hoped that I'd wind up on MSNBC. I visualized having my own show on MSNBC to talk about the news of the day from an immigrant's perspective. But I didn't get that opportunity (at least not yet). I got Fox News. God routed me there for a reason, so I'll keep going in this hostile environment. When I need an extra dose of courage, I turn to one of my greatest influences, Ruby Bridges. I have her picture framed in my office. In 1960, at age six, Bridges was the first student to desegregate the William Frantz Elementary School in New Orleans. In the photo she's in pigtails, a pinafore dress, black Mary Janes, and frilly socks as she's walking into the all-white school while being escorted by federal marshals with guns. A white mob was screaming at her, holding up signs with despicable messages that no child should ever see. This little girl was so poised, her head held up high, as she made history.

Every time I look at that photo, I'm reminded of why I do this. If Bridges could do it at six with the whole world screaming at her, calling her names, and throwing tomatoes at her, just to get an education, I can tolerate some rude-ass bitches in the green room.

When people say, "Are you scared? How do you do it?" I tell them I do it because I'm a grown woman who refuses to back down.

I had a revelation a year or so later during another rude encounter with a conservative talking head. I was a guest on *The Hill's Rising* hosted by Buck Sexton and Krystal Ball. I sat on a panel with Amber Athey, a writer for the right-wing publication *The Daily Caller*. (Look her up: Athey would later apologize when old tweets surfaced that were perceived as antisemitic, homophobic, and racist. This did not surprise me.) Athey tried to equate being a foreigner with being an illegal alien. I pointed out that *resident* aliens voting in California were not the same thing as *illegal* aliens.

I looked at her for her response and was surprised to see her hand shaking . . . seemingly in fear. Talk about white fragility! She was terrified of a fact-check. It was the typical "I fear for my safety because this 'aggressive Black woman' has made me uncomfortable." In my mind I was like, "Girl, please! Give me a break. We are pundits. Our job is to challenge each other ideologically, not make cupcakes and drink tea." But I was thrown by it. What did I say or do to make her so scared? It dawned on me that many whites in America fear Blackness. I thought that some just hated us. In that moment it became very clear that Blackness itself is often viewed as a weapon.

Sidebar: Buck Sexton only spoke to Athey. Again, it was almost like

I was not there. I've learned not to take it personally. They fear me. Their disregard makes me tough. It's become a source of strength.

Once again, I led the way in my family, and couldn't turn to my mom or sister for guidance on this divergent path. I was on my own here. They always had this beautiful bond over health care. They'd make corny jokes about blood pressure, and talked in medical shorthand, like, "Yeah, my patient was V-fib." I would listen and nod awkwardly, having only a vague idea what they were talking about.

However, once I started playing on the big stage, Mom reveled in my new success. Her favorite thing was to watch me on Fox News and cheer me on. Not only did my name and occupation flash on the screen under my face ("Dr. Wendy Osefo, professor at Johns Hopkins University"), I looked great and spoke the truth about what was happening in our country. As I've said, Nigerians have two topics: people and politics. For Mom to see me talk about the greatest democracy in the world, for everyone to see, made her so happy.

Trump adviser Katrina Pierson and I debated whether we should remove Civil War monuments in the aftermath of the white supremacist rally in Charlottesville, Virginia. To my surprise, Katrina said that slavery was a great part of American history (Google it). Mom called me as soon as I went off camera. "Yay, Wen-Wen. I love it! Go get her!"

I relished going up against all the talking heads in that predominantly white space and kicking ass. I get joy every time the host has to refer to me as "Dr. Osefo" while referring to my white male counterpart simply by his name. But I especially loved facing off with Kayleigh McEnany. She is the exalted Republican millennial darling at Fox News. There were rumors about East Wing interest in her, and then West Wing meetings (she would eventually become Trump's press secretary). They often put me up against Miss White Thing to debate issues like socialism, immigration, feminism, and Russia's involvement in our elections. The producers loved the visual of a blue-eyed blonde sharing a split screen with me, a melanated goddess. Beating her on the air played into my competitive nature. Every time we were paired for a debate, I thought, *I'm going to demolish her simply to make a point.*

Yes, I know it's petty, but it kind of makes up for all the times I was called an "African booty scratcher."

EIGHTEEN

Mama Drama

Several years after our wedding, Eddie was invited to his sister Nora's baby shower as a gesture of goodwill. We were cautiously optimistic about seeing his family again and hoped this could be an opportunity to turn things around. We brought Karter and Kruz so they could meet their paternal grandparents, aunts, and uncle. The boys would also be a good buffer. They're the life of the party. With those two around, how could anyone be cold to us?

We arrived at the banquet hall and walked inside. The hall was set up so Eddie's whole family was seated immediately to the right of the entrance. The rest of the crowd sat at tables facing them. So opening the front door was like walking onto the stage where a tense drama was already in progress. Everyone there knew the history, that Eddie and his parents hadn't spoken in years, that they hated me and tried to stop our wedding. So when we came through that door and walked onto that figurative stage, the whole room went silent. The "audience" stared at us, waiting excitedly for the fireworks to begin.

We said hello and waved. Still crickets.

With lots of eyes on us, Eddie and I led our sons toward a table with four open seats. As we went through the room, we could hear whispers:

"Look who showed up."

"Wow, I can't believe they came."

We didn't prep the boys for this because we didn't know what to expect. Also, they were too young to understand the conflict. Once Eddie was telling them a story about his childhood and he mentioned his mom. Karter said, "You have a mom?" Eddie explained that he did have a mom and a dad, and siblings. Fortunately, Karter didn't follow up and moved on to a new topic of conversation. It might've been a good idea to give them a small warning, though, because even our boys knew something was off in the room. I'd never seen them so quiet. Children have a sixth sense. They know when something is up.

We sat down at the table with some elders from the community. I recognized them and said hello. They didn't speak, only smiled and nodded. It was incredibly awkward. For a while, we sat there and tried to eat. The tension was too thick to cut. Eddie said, "Let me just say hi to my family and then we can go."

"Let's do it together and get it over with," I said.

We made our way back through the whispering crowd over to his parents and siblings. Nora, for one, hugged him warmly. She had invited us! It was her olive branch. His parents were rudely standoffish. Like everyone else in the room, I watched Eddie try to get them to look at him or speak to him. They refused to acknowledge him at all. It's almost as if they cared more about showing the crowd their stubbornness than embracing their estranged son.

Seeing that made my heart tight. I moved in to support Eddie and show the crowd that we were not intimidated by his parents' cruelty. I said hello to my father-in-law and gave him a loose quasi hug. It was like bumping shoulders with an oak tree. He refused to speak to me, much less hug me. His literal cold shoulder was pure theater. It felt rehearsed.

If it were me, and I was shunned by my family in front of a roomful of people, I would have broken down and run out of there. Eddie kept a smile on his face, but I knew he was hurting.

I maneuvered the boys in front of Eddie's parents. "These are Karter and Kruz, your grandsons."

They barely looked at them. It was extremely tense and painful. These people wouldn't embrace their own flesh and blood out of pure spite.

"Let's go," said Eddie. We stayed for no more than forty-five minutes. Once we were back in the car, I sighed with relief. I said, "Thank God that's over."

Eddie said, "I'll never make you do that again."

Karter said, "Did we do something wrong?"

"Absolutely not," I said. I wasn't sure how to comfort him without trashing his grandparents. I think I said, "It's not you, it's them." The phrase gave me comfort, so it would probably work for the boys.

Although it was awful, I was proud of my husband. It took a lot of courage to walk through that door, knowing that it would probably go badly. We showed up. Sometimes that's all you can do. That baby shower goes down in the ledger of life as "We tried."

It was the last family function on his side that we've attended.

Emotional detachment is an area of child-rearing that Eddie and I have completely rejected. Our home is warm, loving, and vibrant. We express emotions to our kids, we share our feelings with each other. We ask each other questions like, "Who's your favorite rapper?" and "How do you feel?" We let ourselves, and the kids, be sad or scared, and they come to us to make them feel better. Eddie and I would not have it any other way.

His parents were a lost cause. They made their decision and weren't going to budge. A dutiful Nigerian son, Eddie abided by their wishes to have nothing to do with us. As for his siblings, we harbored some hope that they might one day come around. Our strategy was to just live our lives, do our best, raise our children, and avoid the drama.

MY FOX NEWS appearances continued, since there was always a need for someone with a black face to comment on the latest antics from

Team Trump. During the Christmas holiday in 2018, I was booked on Fox News' *The Story with Martha MacCallum*. Usually I went to New York by myself, did the spot, and went home. But this time, I thought, *Let's make a weekend of it.* Around the time I was planning for what now would be a family trip to New York City, I got a call from a woman, a connector type who loved to make introductions. She asked, "Would you ever consider doing reality TV?"

"Sure. Why not?" I replied. Mom loved my political commentary. Being on a reality TV show would be okay with her, *as long as I didn't quit the day job.*

The woman said, "I want you to meet the producer of *The Real Housewives of Potomac* in New York."

I'd never seen a single episode. In fact, outside of a handful of episodes of other *Real Housewives* series and that season of RHONJ when the Gorga family was being torn apart by Joe's decision to marry Melissa, my knowledge was limited. I hoped the Gorgas found a way to reconcile. My own family situation with the Osefos was as tense as ever. If I joined this show, maybe viewers might see our troubles and feel less alone in their own family drama. I'd bring a unique perspective to it as a Nigerian first gen, caught between two worlds.

"I'm actually going to be in town in a week or two, so let's set it up." Incredibly, she arranged for a meeting at the Truly Original production office on the Lower East Side of Manhattan for the following week.

So much for steering away from drama.

Eddie, Karter, Kruz, and I took the Amtrak to New York City. We got a room in a beautiful hotel right in the Theater District, just a block from the lights, energy, and dozens of costumed superheroes in Times Square.

On the day of the interview, I had my makeup done in the hotel room, then I got dressed in a white suit, along with a red fedora and a Chanel bag, and called an Uber. Mom's voice was in my head: "Always wear earrings. Always wear lipstick. Never leave the house in your head scarf!" I knew I looked and smelled great, and that Mom would approve of my interview outfit. That alone gave me confidence.

At their offices, I was introduced to a group of people ranging from production executives to executives in talent acquisition. I'd been in TV long enough to know that, going by the titles of the people sitting in front me, they weren't playing. These were the top people, the decision makers. This made me take the opportunity more seriously and got me excited.

We sat in a glass-walled conference room and got right down to business. "Tell us about yourself," said the lead producer.

I opened my mouth and shared it all—my childhood as the daughter of a single Nigerian immigrant, how my warrior mother raised me to be the best, make no excuses, and honor the family. I talked about my two kids, my four degrees, my two jobs as a professor and TV pundit, my love for my sexy husband, food, music, and fashion, my unique position of being a first gen with my roots in Nigeria and my branches in America. They asked plenty of questions and I answered them all. I had a good time, actually. I was shocked to see that two hours had gone by.

At the end, they shook my hand and said, "We'll be in touch."

In the Uber back to the hotel, I called Eddie and said, "I think it went well."

According to the decorum my mother taught me, I sent each person I met a thank-you email. They responded right away. A few steps later and I was offered the opportunity of a lifetime.

My appearing on Fox News as a political commentator was not looked down upon in the Nigerian community. I was talking about politics and the plight of immigrants. All acceptable, even honorable. They loved it because my professorship and professionalism was on full display.

However, being on a reality TV show was going to be a very hard sell to the Nigerian community. Although we as a people are comfortable talking about our accomplishments in science, medicine, and the law, the worlds of entertainment, the arts, and even sports were uncharted territory for my parents' generation.

When Nigerian entertainer Davido told his father he was going to be a singer, the older man said, "No. You're going to go to medical school." Davido chose to do his own thing and now he's a multimillionaire international sensation. I wonder what his father says now. I look at Davido as a trailblazer in the entertainment industry, as someone first gens can point to when our parents say, "Med school! Law school!" When Uzo Aduba started portraying Crazy Eyes, a lesbian inmate with mental health issues on *Orange Is the New Black*, I'm sure many Nigerians were offended. Aduba went on to win two Emmy Awards for that role. Would that make old-school Nigerians change their tune about discouraging an acting career? Doubt it. But Aduba is a hero to first gens.

I'm not comparing myself to Davido or Uzo Aduba. I'm saying it's hard to be the first. I became the first Nigerian in *Real Housewives* history, and my goal from the outset was to use this platform to celebrate Nigerian culture and Black excellence. When Andy Cohen made a point of describing me as "the first Nigerian Housewife," it wasn't just for the optics. Doing a show like *Real Housewives of Potomac* is so far outside what is considered safe for Nigerians, hardly any of us would have even considered it.

Like most Nigerians, Eddie had a lot of questions before he endorsed such a huge risk. He and our kids would be filmed as well, so his agreeing to do the show was a huge leap outside his comfort zone. He said, "This will be either the best decision or worst decision of your life—the jury is still out on that." In the end, surprisingly, Eddie agreed to try it.

I called Mom and said, "Have you heard of *The Real Housewives*?"

"Yes, of course." She lived in the Nigerian bubble, but not on Mars.

"What would you say if I told you I'd been asked to join the cast of *The Real Housewives of Potomac*?"

"Do it and do it well," she said. "*But don't quit your day job!*"

No other parent from Mom's generation would have even considered it. But it would be okay for me to switch into a different lane only as long as I stayed on the same highway. I'd be a Housewife, but a *professor* Housewife, a *doctor* Housewife.

Before I signed on, I prayed on it. That's my go-to. I always pray before making a decision. It's not a quickie, like looking skyward and saying, "God, if you can hear me, please give me what I want."

When I "pray on it," even if it's a small matter, I hit the rosary for a solid twenty minutes at least once. For something big—like any issues related to taking a new job, buying a house, raising a child—I prayed multiple times, seeking clarity and guidance.

My pre-RHOP prayers were variations of "Is this is for me? How can I be successful?"

It's not like I woke up one day with the dream of being on reality TV. I wanted to be the next Anderson Cooper on CNN. I wanted to be the next Sunny Hostin on *The View*. I prayed to God to give me MSNBC. But He gave me Bravo, and because I was routed in that direction, I thought it meant this opportunity would be greater than anything I'd imagined.

My prayers brought me to the conclusion that this was right for me and that I'd successfully represent myself, my Black family, my worldview, and my Nigerian culture to millions of viewers. It was a God-approved plan. I accepted the offer.

That night, I asked Eddie, "How do you think your family will react when they see us on TV?"

"They'll be shocked."

Part of me hoped that his family would see our marriage, children, lifestyle and think, *Hey, they're doing really well. We were wrong to say marrying Wendy would ruin Eddie's life. We should seek forgiveness and welcome them back.* Maybe it was wishful thinking. But if they saw our happiness with their own eyes, we might be able to come to an under-standing and clear the air.

Like my work on Fox, I would not take the *Real Housewives* plat-form for granted. I could show millions of viewers what it looked like to be a proud wife and mother. I could show how to juggle multiple jobs, the unique pressure of being a first gen, that all female professors do not walk around in tweed blazers and knee-length skirts.

Our mandate, as first gens, is to find opportunities to be the best. Well, here was a whole new realm for me to excel in, one that no first gens had tried before. I understood that Housewives were not perfect people. That would be extremely boring to watch. Mom's generation of Nigerians would rather die than broadcast their imperfections and prob-lems on TV. But as a first gen, I knew that hiding imperfections and burying problems didn't make anyone feel better. I would go on TV and show that we have real human moments, like everyone else. It could be freeing for other first gens to see me embody that on TV. Not only that, but by being the first Nigerian first gen on reality TV, I could open the door for others in our community to come into the field, too.

After I accepted the offer, I had some news for the producers: "By the way, I'm pregnant."

The third time around, we decided not to find out the gender. The due date was August 22, 2019. That alone convinced me the baby would be a girl. Only a little diva would attempt to steal my shine and arrive just *two* days after our wedding anniversary. What's more, I was told that filming RHOP was going to start around then, too.

We moved houses that summer on top of everything else, and I often forgot to eat and drink enough water. Dehydration became a problem, and my doctor gave me a few stern lectures about it. "If you don't drink more water, it could hurt the baby," he said. I'd never before been issued a warning during my previous pregnancies, so I was con-cerned enough to follow the doctor's orders, hydrate and avoid stress (when possible).

Mom visited our new house in July from her new house in Pittsburgh, Pennsylvania. She had moved there for a job opportunity as always, but also to get away from the house she lived in with Darlington. She wanted a fresh start. (Change was Mom's normal, too.)

We'd only just finished unpacking and arranging our furniture and putting on the finishing touches. Not a smudge on the cream walls. Not a stain on the upholstery. Every appliance in the kitchen was spotless, without a scratch. I intended to keep it like that, perfect, for at least a little while. My aesthetic is clean, classic, cozy. I want to feel clarity and calm in my house, like it's an oasis and sanctuary for just us to escape the craziness of the world outside.

Around the time we moved into our new home, Yvo set the date for a baptismal party for her son Blake. Mom saw this an opportunity to christen not only my nephew, but our new house. "We should celebrate Blake's christening with an after-party at your house," she said on the first day of her visit. "Let's throw a huge party and invite everyone! I can cook for a hundred people in this kitchen."

Forget that I was hugely pregnant. Forget that I'm an introvert and throwing parties was her thing, not mine. Forget that a party would be stressful. Eddie and I were looking forward to enjoying our house's newness for as long as possible, and to keep people out of it for that very reason. But Mom's approach was to fill the house with cooking smells, music, and laughter.

I said, "Not yet, Mom. No parties. We only just got here."

"That's ridiculous. Why have a big house like this if you aren't going to entertain?"

Every day, she brought it up, and our disagreement evolved into a culture clash. A good Nigerian daughter should do whatever her mother told her to do. I wasn't just saying no to a party, I was disrespecting her wishes and breaking from her traditions. Honestly, I would have been flexible about anything else, but not about throwing open my doors to a hundred people while I was eight months pregnant. After a tense week,

Mom headed back to Pittsburgh. Her facial expressions and annoyed sounds made me feel terrible about holding my ground, even literally on my own ground.

On Friday, July 19, Eddie and I ran some errands with the boys. When we got home, Eddie took our cockapoo, Zoey, out for a walk and I went to our laundry room and bent down to transfer some clothes from the washer to the dryer. When I stood upright, a gush of water poured down my leg.

With the boys, my water was broken by the ob-gyn in the hospital. I'd never had this experience before. I must have shouted, "Oh my God!" because Karter and Kruz ran in. They saw the puddle on the floor and were as surprised as I was. I wasn't due for over a month.

I called Eddie and said, "Baby, my water broke."

I called Mom and said, "My water broke! We're headed to the hospital!"

"Oh my God, you're joking, right?" she said with a chuckle. "Okay, I'll get a flight." Mom may not be perfect, but she made sure always to be by our side during delivery of our children. This would be no exception. In fact, throughout my life, Mom was there whenever I needed comforting when sick. When I was younger, I had digestive problems and sometimes needed to be given IV fluids. The nurses always had trouble finding my vein, and Mom would say, "Move out of the way, I'll stick her." Her reassurance during those times, and my labors, was a huge comfort.

At the Howard County General Hospital, my ob-gyn told us, "I'm concerned that your water broke so early. With the protective amniotic sac broken, there is an increased risk of infection. We'll have to deliver the baby now."

"I'm thirty-four weeks and five days. Can we wait a couple of days? What if I just crossed my legs really tight?" The hospital policy said that if a baby was born before thirty-five weeks, it had to go into the neonatal intensive care unit (NICU). I was shattered and terrified. A premature baby was serious.

"Let's get you checked into the hospital, watch, and wait," he said as a compromise. "We'll be prepared to deliver anytime, but we won't induce you just yet."

My family had my back, as always. Yvo came to the hospital and picked up the boys to watch them. Eddie stayed with me. Mom arrived the next morning and came immediately to my room.

As soon as she was at my bedside, she said, "Let's pray." Together, like we had when I was a child, we recited our prayers, one for each bead on her rosary. When we finished, she said, "Wen, it will be okay. The baby will be healthy." She'd seen so many early labors in her years as a nurse, so she wasn't just saying the words to keep me calm.

"How do you know?"

"I know," she said with conviction.

Her certainty was a comfort. The ritual of prayer gave me strength for what came next.

With Mom and Eddie by my side, the contractions began on their own, and I progressed quickly. My doctor came in to examine me and said, "It's time."

I started pushing. Suddenly, D'Angelo's love song "You're My Lady" came on Pandora. I thought, *That has to mean something!* Four pushes later, the baby was out.

"It's a girl!" said the doctor.

Eddie just broke down in tears. I was crying. The baby was crying. We were thrilled to have a daughter to complete our family. She was so small, only four pounds, fourteen ounces. Eddie hugged us both.

"She has to go to the NICU now," said one of the nurses. I hated to let her go, but we had to. When the nurse took her from me, I felt an instant visceral ache.

Mom left to relieve Yvo and take care of the boys. Eddie stayed with me and said, "The baby is so beautiful."

"She just came early," I said. "There's absolutely nothing wrong with her."

"Of course she's fine," he agreed. She was here, and she was fine. We were going to be all right.

After seventy-two hours, I checked out of my own hospital room, but I refused to leave the building. I moved into a drab, unoccupied ten-by-ten administrative office and slept on a cot they wheeled in for me. I used the public bathroom down the hall. When I wasn't resting in there, I was at my daughter's side. She slept in an isolate, a preemie-size crib in a plastic tent. Our first family picture was of my husband holding Kamrynn with a feeding tube in her nose flanked by Karter and Kruz, surrounded by machines.

On day three of Kamrynn's life, Yvo called to check on me and the baby. She had two babies of her own by then, and her own medical practice. She asked, "Are you sad?"

"No." Why would she ask that?

"I know it's really hard to have a baby in the NICU. I'm sorry you have to go through that."

Until that call, I'd only allowed myself to feel optimistic. Her comments changed my mood. I didn't care if Nigerians weren't supposed to give into their fear or show weakness. I realized I was terrified. I broke down and cried in that office.

As small as she was, Kamrynn *was* fine. Her organs were fully developed, and she wasn't born with any abnormalities. Her life was never hanging in the balance, thank God. Not all the children in the other cribs were as fortunate, and their parents were in hell. One child had been in the NICU for three months with severe birth defects. I was just so broken for his mom and dad. Every baby was hooked up to beeping heart monitors. When the beeping changed or stopped, it was pandemonium with nurses and doctors rushing in, the anguished cries of parents. I prayed over Kamrynn, and prayed for each child, each parent, for hours a day.

On a strict schedule, the nurses came over to do a series of tests. Along with vital signs, they would prick Kamrynn's tiny little foot for a drop of blood to check her glucose. She would start crying, and that set me off, every time, every hour on the hour. I told my husband, "I'm so tired of them poking her." But I also knew it had to be done.

I became an expert hand washer and sanitizer. Before you entered the NICU, you had to wash your hands for sixty seconds, use a hard bristle brush to get under your nails, and wipe down your phone and anything else you might touch. We bought a ton of Lysol, Clorox wipes, and antibacterial soap to keep ourselves and the house clean for when we brought her home. (Eight months later, when the pandemic hit, we had a stockpile in storage.)

It occurred to me that Eddie's family had no idea that he'd just had a daughter. If they did know, did they care? When our sons were born, he felt his parents' absence. When our daughter was born, we were used to it. What did shock and upset me during my long days in the NICU was the fact that my mother was absent. Susan had not shown her face at the hospital since the morning of the delivery.

I sat in a chair by Kamrynn's crib and held her tiny hand, wanting my mother to be there to hold mine. Granted, my emotions were raw. But Mom's no-show felt like pouring salt on a gaping wound. Yvo came to the NICU, and on day five, I asked, "Does it bother you that Mom isn't here?"

"It's upsetting, yes," she replied.

Was this Mom's way of punishing me for disrespecting her on her last visit? Why else would she be avoiding me? She wasn't staying away because it would be too disturbing to see Kamrynn like that. Mom had seen much crazier stuff over her thirty years as a nurse. Nothing freaked her out.

"Do you think it's possible she's staying away because she's still mad at me for refusing to have that party?" I asked my sister.

"Are you kidding?" asked Yvo. "I don't think that's the case."

It ate at me until, on day six, I called Mom and said, "Where are you? Why haven't you come to sit with me and Kamrynn?"

"You needed me to watch over the boys, and that's what I've done," she said. "I cook for them. I make sure they're okay." She had a knack for turning things around. But I wasn't buying it.

"You asked me what I *needed* you to do. I didn't think I needed to tell you to come to the freaking hospital to support me with my week-old baby in the NICU."

"Please, Wen," she replied. "I just want to help you. If you don't want my help, if you don't want me here, just say it."

I was asking her why she hadn't shown up, and now I felt accused of telling her to leave. How had it gotten turned around on me? I could count on my hand the number of times I had ever confronted her about her behavior, and it was always the same. She never took ownership of her behavior, and always managed to flip it on me.

The more I thought about it, the sadder and angrier I became. Everyone was starting to lose it a bit. Kruz was really feeling my absence. At four, he was too young to understand what was going on. So when Kamrynn fell asleep for the night, I drove home to see my boys.

Eddie opened the door for me at midnight, and I dropped into his arms, physically and emotionally exhausted. In the shower, I let out the primal cry of a mother who wanted her baby. My husband had never heard me make such a sound before (neither had I). He was waiting for me on our bed and wrapped me in a warmed bathrobe.

While I wept, he said, "Tomorrow, you sleep in and get some rest. I'll go to the hospital and bring our daughter home."

If it were only that easy to just check a baby out of the NICU. Each preemie had to clear certain benchmarks and maintain them for forty-eight hours before being released from the unit. One benchmark was breathing on her own. Another was regulating her body temperature. Another was eating without regurgitating. The last benchmark was sitting in a car seat without experiencing any vital sign disruption. Kamrynn was good to go on all counts and was nearly at the forty-eight-hour mark.

On day seven, true to his word, Eddie let me sleep in, in my own bed, and went to get our Kamrynn. While waiting for final clearance, he tried feeding our daughter. Since I'd been doing it the whole week, Eddie didn't have much practice. He held her head at the wrong angle, and she choked up her milk.

The nurse saw it and said, "We have to keep her for another forty-eight hours."

He called me and reported the bad news. "I'm so sorry," he apologized, clearly devasted.

"She was about to come home!" I screamed. "How could you screw that up?"

Eddie said, "I feel terrible."

I was furious at him, but truly I blamed myself. Long ago, I'd convinced myself that if I slacked off at all, bad things happened. Exhibit A: getting kicked out of law school. The one time I took my eyes off the ball, it cost me a career. I told myself back then that I would never do that again. But I left the NICU for one night and let someone else carry some of the load, and things went left.

I'd been taught that hard work was the only safety net we had, the only protection from ruin. Working myself into the ground was the only thing that would save my daughter. One of my favorites sayings is, "Pray as if everything depends on God. Work hard as if everything depends on you."

Objectively, I knew that I couldn't control when my daughter was going to come home. But I couldn't control my thoughts, either. My brain was telling me, *If something goes wrong when I should have been on the watch, I have only myself to blame.*

When Mom finally showed up at the hospital on day seven, I was not there. I was back home, taking a break and spending time with Karter and Kruz. A part of me feels like the only reason she went at all was because Yvo and Eddie got involved and pressured her into going.

I'd always tried to live up to her expectations because I knew that if I failed to do so, her disappointment would kill me. What about her living up to my expectations? Did I have any right to expect her not to disappoint me? During that hell week, the woman who'd been my champion for my whole life let me down. It was crushing.

My bitterness was temporarily forgotten when we brought Kamrynn home on day nine. She's been perfectly healthy and happy ever since, a source of joy like no other. I wish the story of our daughter's time in the NICU was about family unity, love, and support. Sadly, Mom being MIA added a layer of pain and stress to an already excruciating experience.

Three weeks later, while still embroiled in the hurt and anger within my own family, I started filming my freshman season of *Real Housewives of Potomac*. The drama was only just beginning.

Aunt Cordelia at her graduation.

Grandfather Albert in his police uniform.

Grandmother Angela.

Uncle Fred.

RIGHT: Mom, Edwin, and Yvo, in Nigeria. (I was in Mom's belly.)

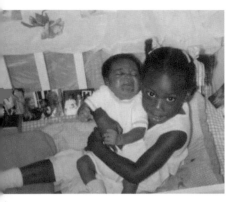

ABOVE: Yvo holding me, in Nigeria.

LEFT: Me celebrating my first birthday, in Nigeria.

RIGHT: Yvo and me, in Nigeria.

FAR RIGHT: Mom, Yvo, and me, in Nigeria.

Me at Mom's college graduation, North Carolina Central University (NCCU).

Darlington's chieftancy ceremony in Nigeria.

Mom and Darlington's wedding.

Mom and her siblings (left to right): Nkiru, Hyke, Winifred, Mom, Chuldi, and Ekwy. (Ike not pictured.)

Mom at Aunt Ekwy's house in the Bronx.

Yvo, Mom, and me.

Me in front of our house on Fargo Street in Durham, North Carolina.

Yvo, Jordan, and me.

Eddie and me at his fraternity's cookout, in 2007.

Mom and Darlington walking me down the aisle.

Eddie and me on our wedding day, August 20, 2011.

Me and Kamrynn, in the NICU.

Our first photo as a family of five, in the NICU.

Me and my three kids, December 2020.
PHOTO BY MIGUEL DJONTU

Mom, Kamrynn, and me.
PHOTO BY MIGUEL DJONTU

NINETEEN

All Apologies

$\mathcal{P}$eople see the RHOP show on TV and they think, *How hard can it be? They just sit around and talk.*

That is true. It is a lot of sitting and talking. It's not so easy to keep a conversation going for five hours with cameras in your face the whole time, all the while knowing viewers are going to watch it. Reality TV is *work*. Not everyone can be high energy and on point for that long. Not everyone can open themselves up and reveal the good, bad, and ugly parts of their life. You have to say, "There goes our privacy. Here comes our quirks and imperfections." You are allowing people to see you, and to judge you. I've gained the utmost respect for everyone who has done reality TV. Being entertaining is a skill, and it takes a lot of courage to be vulnerable.

My goal from the outset in appearing on RHOP was to expose viewers to the life of a first-gen Nigerian immigrant. Eddie, the kids, and I represented a dark-skinned family on TV, the kind I longed to see growing up and never did. My kids, all three of them, were as charismatic as could be. And Eddie, well, the man is not only fine as all hell, but truly the kindest soul. I went into the experience thinking, *People are going to love me.* Why wouldn't they? I was Black Girl Magic.

While filming, I focused on my political activism, being a proud Nigerian who was outspoken about my accomplishments, and my beautiful family. Since I came into the show as newbie in season five, my goal was to observe the relationship dynamics among the other cast members, and react to their story lines by upholding my values. I believed I was staying above the fray.

But while the drama unfolded in front of the camera, I was dealing with stress behind the scenes as well. A couple of months into filming, the cast was called to the Andrew Mellon Auditorium in Washington, DC, to shoot the opening credits (my tagline: "The professor has arrived, and class is officially in session") and the cast photo. The shoot took all day. Eddie was at work and our nanny, a woman named Linda, was taking care of Kamrynn.

I asked Mom, "Can you pick up Kruz from school and Karter from the bus stop and bring them home?" Mom was between houses and living with us for a four-month stretch then, so it wasn't a big ask.

"Of course, Wen," she said.

"The bus arrives at exactly three forty-five. Please be early."

"Okay, okay."

I pushed her to be early because we had some bad history around this situation. When I was a child, Mom was always the last parent at school pickup. I would stand there, watching every other parent pull up, collect their kid, and drive away. There'd be four kids left, then three, then two. And then just me.

"Is your mom coming?" asked the teacher. "Is there anyone I can call for you?" She couldn't leave until I did. Her impatience and sympathy were agonizingly embarrassing.

Finally, Susan would drive up and I'd be flooded with relief. If the wait had been a half hour or more, I would be so upset that I'd start crying as soon as I climbed into the car.

"Why are you so late?" I would ask.

Her tone always had an edge. "It's not like I was partying or taking a nap. I was working at the hospital and couldn't clock out sooner," she said. "I had to wait for the nurse on the next shift to arrive. I can't just leave my patients without someone there. You think I want to work two jobs to afford to send you to this school? I work all week for you. I do in-home care on the weekends for you. I'm working hard to make a better life *for you*."

I felt even worse. "I'm sorry for complaining," I would say.

The day of that photo shoot, I had an anxious premonition that history was going to repeat itself and that she'd be late to pick up the boys. As soon as the cast was allowed to leave, I got into the waiting car and asked the driver to rush back to my home, an hour and a half away.

My phone buzzed with an alert from the Ring app. Someone was ringing the doorbell at my house. I opened the app and saw on live video Karter pressing the button. Behind him, my neighbor's car idled in the driveway. The nanny was home, thank God, and she let Karter in. I called the house and spoke to my son. "What's going on? Where's Grandma?"

He said, "Grandma didn't pick me up. Brian's Mom asked if I needed a ride and brought me home."

Livid, I called Mom. She picked up on the second ring and before she could say a word, I went *in*. "I *told you* what time to pick him up! Why weren't you there? How could you do that? He's just a little boy."

The thought of Karter standing alone at the bus stop sent me right back to the embarrassment, frustration, fear, anger, and guilt I'd experienced as a child in that same situation. Because of that, I'd always been compulsive about being on time for pickup so Karter would never face it. My mother's lateness triggered a deep rage in me.

Look, I worked three jobs to make a better life for my children, too. And I was early every single day for the bus.

After I finished yelling, Mom said, "I was late because I picked up Kruz and took him to Chick-fil-A so he'd have a snack for the ride home. I grabbed food for Karter as well."

She didn't say, "I'm sorry."

I believed she meant well. Her lateness was, as she always explained it to me, for the betterment of others. The air went out of my anger, but not completely. She wanted to be a hero to Karter and Kruz by getting them fried chicken sandwiches. But I didn't need her to be a hero. I needed her to be there on time. Did the ends justify the means? I wished she'd asked herself which mattered more.

I was still stewing in anger when she said, "Remember how I used to surprise you at school with lunch?"

I sighed. "Yes, Mom."

It happened often during my elementary school years. I'd be sitting in the cafeteria with all the other kids. Out of nowhere, Mom floated into the room, smelling like vanilla, her red lips forming a smile when she found me. She unpacked a paper bag with the logo of my favorite restaurant. The other kids huddled around as she took out containers with smothered pork chops, mashed potatoes with gravy, green beans, and a big cup of lemonade. It was a feast that she'd brought just for me on her day off. Other times, she surprised me with a McDonald's Happy Meal, when it came in a box with two finger holes on top. The other kids were so jealous! They'd say, "Your mom is so cool! I wish I had your mom."

The surprise food deliveries—and how they made me feel—warmed my soul. They happened far fewer than the number of times I stood waiting for her at pickup. I can't really say which affected me more, Mom's magic or her lateness.

Mom was equal parts love and pain. She could be so caring and loving, yet so dismissive of my feelings. But complaining to a Nigerian parent about their behavior was not something children were allowed to do. It took Susan fifty years to confront her mother about her grievances, and she never got the validation she wanted from it.

Would I ever confront my mother about my grievances? What kind of validation could I expect? In Nigerian culture, a parent can do no wrong. Even if a parent is objectively in error, they will never, ever say, "I'm sorry," to their children. That is not in their vocabulary. A child is not owed emotional comfort, much less an apology. A parent would never humble themselves to a child. Would a king or queen say, "I fucked up. Can you ever forgive me?" to one of their subjects? No. In a Nigerian family, the parents are royalty, and the children are subject to their rule.

American parents, from what I've seen, aren't so big on apologizing, either. When the kids become adults, they work it out with their therapists. Nigerians, as a rule, don't believe in going to therapists—although this is now changing with first gens—so we wind up internalizing the powerlessness, humiliation, and frustration we experienced as children.

Eddie and I are big on talking and communicating with our kids and using the golden words "Thank you," "You're welcome," and "I'm sorry." We have integrated appreciation, acknowledgment, and apologizing into our form of child-rearing because we didn't get that, and we know the price that is paid. The kids should know that it's okay to admit we made a mistake. If they hurt someone's feelings, saying "I'm sorry" is the right thing to do.

The same week Mom failed to pick up Karter on time, I came into the kitchen and saw a glass of milk spilled all over the table and dripping onto the floor. I assumed Karter was the culprit, and I yelled, "Karter! You have to be more careful!"

Linda, our nanny, said, "I spilled it, actually. Not him."

Without hesitation, I turned to my son and said, "I'm sorry I yelled at you. You didn't do anything wrong. I made a mistake. I apologize."

There. Is that so hard?

Ironically, the inability of some of my cast mates to say "I'm sorry" to each other was a major theme on my debut season (and every other season). I watched their drama play out while staying out of it for the most part. Bravo started airing previews in the summer of 2020.

One of my aunts saw the trailer and said to Mom, "Tell Wendy to stop arguing on TV."

Mind you, I was not arguing; the clip was of me telling a cast mate to "address me correctly, sweetie." This was the same aunt who told Mom that my sister and I would never amount to anything. She never gave me kudos for getting a PhD. She never offered me words of affirmation about working at Johns Hopkins. Among that generation, saying "congratulations" was as rare as "I'm sorry."

I didn't consider myself close with that aunt, so I ignored it. But then, a very close member of my family told me, "Wendy, you need to leave this show. It's beneath you. These people are beneath you. You're a professor."

"As a professor, I can only affect my students," I explained. "On one season of *Housewives*, I can expose millions to the immigrant experience."

"And lose your dignity in the process. You can't represent our culture when you're dealing with those ridiculous people," replied the family member.

The Nigerian community didn't seem to understand the trade-off, and the early feedback was disapproving. I expected that. Once they saw the actual show, I figured they'd change their tune.

During the Covid lockdown, I threw a watch party at our house on August 2, 2020, for my debut episode. It was small, just immediate family, some friends on Zoom. Yvo made cutouts of my face and glued popsicle sticks on the back to use as handles. We had cakes and cupcakes and made it as celebratory as we could during a pandemic. Mom and Yvo couldn't wait for the show to start.

Mom asked, "You wore earrings in every scene?" One of her everyday glam rules.

"Yes, Mom," I said.

"And lipstick?"

"Of course!"

"It's going to be amazing. You're going to change the trajectory of *Housewives* as we know it!" Yvo said.

The episode aired and we thought I looked good and represented myself well. Then the comments and tweets rolled in:

"Why does Wendy mention her degrees so much?"

"Wendy is an elitist."

"Just because you have four degrees doesn't make you better, Wendy."

"Shut up and sit down, Wendy."

Right from the start, viewers were put off by me. So much for Black Girl Magic.

Having four degrees doesn't make me *better*. But why was it preferable for other cast members to talk about how rich they were and how much money they spent? I was attempting to tell the audience, "Wealth is one form of currency. Education is another. Money can buy you nice things and open doors for you—so can a quality education."

Among Nigerians, education is the baseline requirement for respect in the community. It's where you *begin*. My mother's generation came to America to go to college, and then devoted their lives to making sure their children went to grad school. I was raised to believe education was my most valuable possession. Historically, African Americans risked death and beatings to get an education. If slaves learned to read and write, their hands would be cut off, or they'd be lynched. There's even the saying, "If you want to hide anything from a Negro, put it in a book." Sorry (not sorry), but there is nothing wrong with being proud of one's accomplishments.

I was a new kind of Housewife, an immigrant from a developing country who placed a high value on education as a direct reflection of my upbringing and became a top university professor with a PhD. I stood up to say, "This is how we do, and it's working out great for us," but people didn't get it, even though I made my Nigerian heritage a major focal point in my scenes.

As the season wore on, the mean tweets kept coming:

"Here comes another Nigerian taking our jobs."

"Who does Wendy think she is?"

"Go back to Africa, Wendy."

By trying to be aspirational about education (as opposed to aspirational about money), I got crucified.

The comments weren't *only* negative, though. People seemed to appreciate seeing a dark-hued Black family on TV. I was the darkest cast member of RHOP by at least three shades. Not only were most of my cast mates light-skinned, but two of them had green eyes (real ones!) and three were blond. Now anyone could tune into Bravo and see my family in our chocolate glory in living color on TV. We looked like hundreds of millions of Black families all over the world. And yet, on American TV, we were a rarity.

While I appreciated the praise, insults tend to cut deep while compliments bounce off. I thought I'd been in the lion's den as a Democrat on Fox News, receiving death threats and called the N-word. All I can say is social media is the Devil.

I had my dark moments with it. After I cried to my husband about Instagram and Twitter, Eddie asked, "What are the issues, and how can we remedy it?"

"The comments," I said.

"Don't read the comments," he replied.

"The recaps."

"Don't read the recaps. You just have to laugh at it," he said. "Don't take it so seriously. Let's try to have fun with it."

His attitude was optimistic, as always. Even at my low points, scrolling through comments obsessively, feeling worse and worse, I appreciated my loving, solution-oriented husband. The game for him was figuring out how we could make the experience positive. I struggled with that. Of course, I thought about quitting. (I'll bet every Housewife thinks about it at some point.)

What hurt me the most? A lot of the people who attacked me were the very people I have spent my career defending: immigrants, women, people of color. After Eddie and I shared a very short version of the conflict with his family on the show, Nigerians of Mom's generation sent me hateful messages, all with the same core sentiment: "How dare you talk about your husband's family on TV? Shame on you!"

They believed I should hide that sorrow from the world. Sorry, not going to happen. Being a Housewife means being transparent about all aspects of your life, and that includes the not-so-pretty ones. I was being authentic because when we share our own flaws and troubles, it provides comfort for others who may be going through the same thing. Just as Melissa and Joe Gorga's story helped me years ago, my story might help someone else.

Of course, I wondered how Eddie's family was taking all this.

In October 2020, after the season had been running for two months, we found out. I got a Google alert on my phone and clicked through to the link to an article with the headline "Exclusive: Wendy Osefo's Nigerian Family Cursed, Shunned by Villagers, PLUS Her Massive Debt EXPOSED!"

Reading this felt like a knife sliding into my back. It quoted an anonymous "in-law" who made the bogus claim that Eddie's family rejected me because of an ancient tribal curse. It was textbook xenophobia, no different than Donald Trump saying Nigerian immigrants should go back to their "huts." The language was designed to make Africans seem primitive and backward—and it seemed to come from someone in Eddie's own family. What's more, the same source said that we were $1.5 million in debt, and that Eddie hadn't tried a case in years. We did have student loans, like millions of other Americans, but the quoted number was an insane exaggeration. As for Eddie's career, not all lawyers try cases (duh). The vast majority never step foot in a courtroom.

I seethed while reading this article, furious that a relative, even an estranged one, would put this poison into the world. It took everything I was proud of and tried to demolish it. I see value in my education, so the source said, "But you're in debt." I was grateful for my family heritage, so the source said, "You are outcasts and cursed. We don't want you."

I forwarded the link to Eddie. He called me immediately and said, "I'm so sorry."

"You don't owe me an apology," I said.

The two of us are very good at saying "I'm sorry." I said, "You've done nothing wrong."

"The source was a member of my family," Eddie replied. "They tried to ruin our wedding and now they're trying to ruin this opportunity."

"They can't hurt us," I said, feeling stronger already.

Later that night, we said our prayers as a family as always. Right before the kids' bedtime, we got on our knees and recited the Lord's Prayer. Once we finished the prayers and put the kids to bed, Eddie and I closed the door to our bedroom, and we hashed it out. "Let's do a process of elimination," he said. "It's not my parents. They're too old to leak stories to a blog." The source used slang terms like "thirsty," which his elderly parents wouldn't know.

"Your brother?" I asked.

"I don't think so," he said. "I can't see him doing this."

"Your sisters?" I asked.

Just a few years ago, Nora had extended an olive branch to us by inviting us to her baby shower. Oby, his youngest sister, was a teenager when the family split happened. We had heard some whispers about how his sisters were handling our being on reality TV by possibly creating fake social media accounts just to trash us (but I have no idea if that is the case) and snapping at people who asked them about us.

"If I trusted them, I would feel betrayed, but I haven't trusted them for a long time," he said.

I said, "Are they ever going to stop coming at us with all this negativity?"

He sighed. "There's nothing we can do."

"I'm sorry," I said, feeling terrible yet again for being the catalyst for his family's cruelty.

"I'm fine, Wen," he said. "I lost them years ago."

My mother's take on the blog? She laughed at it. "The outcasts aren't from Anambra State," she said. "And if we were cursed, then I wouldn't have ever married, my mother wouldn't have married, my grandmother wouldn't have married. No one would have come to your wedding. I wouldn't have founded my organization. I promise you that not one Nigerian will believe this article."

She was right. No one took it seriously. Since Mom lived in her Nigerian bubble, the blog didn't affect her at all. But I had one foot in America, where people believed what they read in the media. It had no basis in truth, but that didn't matter. A Nigerian saying goes, if someone throws cotton balls from the top of a mountain, you can gather up some, but not all. The American saying goes, a lie can travel around the world before the truth puts on its shoes. This "exposé" was a brutal lesson about being in public life. People can say anything about you, and others will buy it.

I was complaining about it on the phone with Mom and she said, "They're just jealous, Wen."

"I thought I already knew how petty and spiteful people could be *before* I appeared on reality TV."

Mom said, "I guess your education isn't over yet."

Well, the upside of my celebrating Nigerian culture and achievement on TV: while some of the elders in the community might not like the show itself or my being on it, they saw that Eddie was killing it financially, we are still soul mates and best friends, and we have three beautiful children. Ten years ago, Cecilia and her husband predicted that marrying me would destroy their son, and that we'd never last. Now people in the community were asking, "Was any of that true? Have they been lying all this time? How trustworthy are they?" The blog was another attempt to discredit us, but it only served to discredit *them*. (The irony: if any member of Eddie's family had reached out over the past ten years, he would have welcomed them back with open arms, with or without their offering an apology.)

When Mom appeared on the show, she became the topic of conversation in Nigerian circles as an outlier. As traditional as she was about her parental expectations, she defied other Nigerian cultural standards by getting divorced, raising two girls on her own, and being on TV. Viewers loved Mom and wanted to see more of her. Sure, some traditionalists in the community made comments about her life choices, but her overall reception was positive.

Unlike me, she didn't give a damn about any of the criticism. She'd faced worse, when she split with Edwin, and after Darlington passed away young. And what could anyone say to her at this point? She'd achieved her life goal: to raise her two daughters to be successful. RHOP went a long way in showing just how successful we were. It gave Mom her redemption on a much bigger scale than she ever could have imagined.

Unlike Mom or Eddie, I couldn't just brush off the negativity. For the first time in my life, I was angry with God. I gave voice to it privately, usually in my head. My end of that conversation went something like this: "I prayed to you, and I asked you if this was right. I was willing to walk away from the opportunity if it wasn't right. They could have picked any woman in Maryland. They didn't have to pick me, and you allowed it. If you knew that this would be my experience, why did you let me do it?"

I want to be clear: I'm not a brat, and I do not expect my life (marriage, kids, career, anything) to be perfect. *Nothing is perfect.* Praying is not a bargain you make with God for a great life, a guarantee that things will go your way, an insurance plan, or even due diligence. That's not how my belief in God works. I know that God's children face some of the hardest battles because he knows that as his children, we will get through it. I live with the expectation that I will have hard times, and I will be okay because of my faith. I was just so taken aback by how people perceived me.

NOVEMBER 3, 2020, Election Day, came at the midpoint of the tele-vised *Real Housewives of Potomac* season. It was a milestone. I had come into the political fray on the same night four years before when I stayed up late and wrote that op-ed for the *Baltimore Sun*. Like most Democrats, I was a nervous wreck during the election. I dreaded having to write another analysis, this one called "Hate Wins Again," which was the sorriest, saddest article I could ever write.

When I voted early the day before, people standing on line at the polls were predicting that Trump would pull it off. My mind went dark. I believed that if we had *any* chance of beating Trump, the only candidate who could do it was Joe Biden. It was almost as if Democrats were on their last legs. If Biden couldn't eke out a win, we were screwed.

I was doing segments constantly in the lead-up to Election Day and was very low on sleep. Between appearing on TV segments and political panels, I was burned out. I decided to take a break on the day itself and book segments only after the election was called. I didn't know that it'd take four days.

On Saturday, November 7, I was at home with Eddie, the kids, and Mom. I'd put on a poppy-red sundress to give myself some energy after the emotionally draining week of waiting and praying. We had CNN on in the background while we sat at the kitchen table, as always, just talking.

Mom pointed toward the TV and said, "Look! Something's hap-pening."

Eddie and I turned toward the screen. He increased the volume. Wolf Blitzer was saying, "After four long, tense days, we've reached a historic moment in this election. We can now project the winner of the presidential race." Eddie took hold of my hand and we all held our breath. "CNN projects Joseph R. Biden Jr. is elected the forty-sixth pres-ident of the United States, winning the White House and denying Presi-dent Trump a second term."

I *screamed*, jumped up, fell to the floor, and broke down in tears.

Eddie and Mom were screaming, too. The kids came running in, saying, "What happened? What's going on?" They started running and ripping around the room, feeding on our energy. We had informed the kids about the electoral process, so they felt a sense of victory as well.

I wasn't crying because Biden won. I was crying because Trump lost.

Every person who voted for Biden and Kamala Harris (my AKA sister) shared in this victory. Every person who made calls and volunteered at polling locations, who went to socially distanced rallies, deserved to take some credit. For me personally, it felt like it was the culmination of my political commentary career.

For four years, I had gone into enemy territory and described Trump as xenophobic and racist, and explained how his policies affected people who look like us and came from "shithole countries" like Nigeria. I often felt like my message to the Fox audience fell on deaf ears. But I kept at it, speaking on TV and doing lectures across the country about how our people, our democracy, was under attack, and begging, begging, begging them to vote, not just in the national election, but in local ones, too.

When Biden was finally declared the winner, I felt like my words mattered and that people had actually listened. If all my efforts changed *just one vote* or encouraged *just one person* to register to vote, that was enough. My message made a difference.

I could not stop sobbing! Eddie helped me up off the floor and gave me a hug. He'd never seen me react this way to an election. I was elated when Obama won in 2008, but I didn't turn into a wet mess.

He asked, "Why are you crying?"

It was joy, relief, gratitude, and exhaustion. It wasn't until that moment that I fully understood the toll being one of the only Black faces on Fox News had taken on me. I was carrying that weight.

So often, we see images from the civil rights movement, the women's suffrage movement, and numerous pivotal moments in history. When we see these images, one of the first things we say is, "I wonder what

I would have done if I were living during that time?" The truth is, you would have done exactly what you are doing right now.

History has a strange way of repeating itself. There is always a segment of the population that is marginalized. Ask yourself, "What have I done to be a voice, an ally, a conduit for a marginalized group?" When I look back at November 7, the day that hate lost, I know I did the best I could. When my kids ask me what I did to save our democracy, I will simply pop in my media reel and tell them to take a seat.

The election got me out of my own head and realigned me with my purpose.

I'd originally signed on to RHOP for the same reason I appeared on Fox News, to represent the immigrant experience, regardless of the feedback I received. Seeing the big picture turned my attitude around. I prayed on it and told myself daily, "I will be damned if I let trolls tell me who I am. I've been speaking up for underserved populations and I'm not going to allow miserable strangers to distract me from that mission."

As soon as I turned my attention away from myself and toward others, I felt only gratitude for the opportunity of being on RHOP, excited for where it would lead, and what change I could effect in the world. I had that purpose going in, but it got lost in the hate. I thanked God for helping me find it again and reclaim it.

I want my children to know God because of all the good that relationship can do. Just as prayer has carried my mother through her most challenging times, it's been my not-so-secret source of strength, too. And I needed a lot of strength to carry me through my first year on RHOP.

Being the first *anything* comes with fear, misunderstanding, and hate built in. But I am my mother's daughter. I took on the responsibility of being the first regardless of the risks. Hundreds of first-gen Nigerians have messaged me, saying I've inspired them to take risks and rattle the steel trap their parents put them in. They wrote that they never thought they would see one of us on reality TV. By being on the show, I've inspired them to chase their own dreams in whatever direction they want.

By doing something uncharacteristic for Nigerian first gens, I *was* actually in total alignment with our culture and values. Prayer *did* carry me through, even if I wasn't aware of it at the time.

God's GPS for me and for all of us isn't any of our business. We just have to honor it by doing our best and always turning our love light toward others, with gratitude and intention. The path we're on will one day make sense. The struggles we face along the way will be worth it. We need to ask, "What have I learned on the journey?" and "How can I use the knowledge once I've reached the destination?" No matter how tough things get, God does not hate you. He is simply preparing you. For that, we can only say those other magic words: "Thank you."

TWENTY

Fed Up

*W*here I live in first-gen America, it isn't strange or unusual to have a nanny. My mother disapproved of my hiring one from the start. She couldn't afford to when we were little, and even if she had the money, she wouldn't have done it. Yes, Nigerians of means back home have help. But for immigrants in America, the thought of hiring a nanny was unheard of. Distrust was a factor. Mom would say, "You don't know who they are, where they come from, or their families' background." So was tradition. In Nigerian households, when childcare was needed, aunties and uncles stepped up (like Winifred and Hyke). Older siblings became second mothers (like Yvo). You did not bring a stranger into your home and treat that person like family when actual family members were around. It takes a village to raise a child.

But my family was not in the village anymore. I needed in-home help.

"I can do what she's doing. Why is she here?" Mom asked me of Linda, the nanny, whom we hired two years ago when I was pregnant with Kamrynn.

"It's your time to relax. Your job is to enjoy life," I said.

"How much do you pay her?"

I never answered that question because it wasn't her business. I heard she asked Yvo about Linda's salary many times, and my sister finally made the mistake of quoting the going rate for nannies in the area.

She called me and said, "You could pay me half of what you give the nanny, and I'll take care of your kids."

The problem with that idea was that whenever Mom babysat, she'd make sure to tell me in detail just how busy the day was and all the things she'd done, code for "I worked *so hard* and this is the thanks I get." Mom thought the nanny had a job that she could do, but the job itself was harder than she wanted to work.

Besides that, Linda wasn't just the nanny. She was like a nonfamilial family member who ate with us, hung out with us, and lived with us in her own "apartment," a bedroom in the basement with an en suite bathroom. She was kind and gentle, and an amazing cook. Linda had a signature dish, a crispy, succulent, salty fried shrimp, that we all loved.

Although I loved Linda's food, and I appreciated the help, I felt a bit guilty that she made dinner so often. In my culture, the mother is responsible for cooking for the family every night. As a working mom who was juggling three jobs and being a homemaker, it was (is) a challenge to accomplish this seven nights a week. When I put too much pressure on myself, I wound up cutting corners. And when I rushed, even the simplest of my recipes did not taste the same. Mom taught me that your ingredients make your dish, but it is the love you put into cooking that transforms the ordinary into a meal people will never forget. After Kamrynn was born and I started being a Housewife, my food wasn't showing my love like it should have been.

For a long time, if I couldn't cook for my family, I felt like a failure as a mother. The older I get and the more obligations I take on, the more I've begun to realize that setting a certain bar for success and feeling like a failure if I can't reach it is detrimental to my well-being. The point isn't to heap blame and shame on myself, an unfortunate by-product of my Nigerian upbringing. Instead, I tell myself that DoorDash exists for a reason. I have a nanny to cook when I can't. I can send my husband out for Chick-fil-A. As a first gen, I'm trying to let go of the unhealthy expectations I've internalized, and I'm learning to give myself grace.

And yet, even the slightest hint of an accusation that I was failing at this duty rankled me. Mom always asked, "Are you eating? Do you need me to cook for you?" Just the offer made me feel like she knew I wasn't cooking as much as I'd like to. It was a nice offer, but I reacted to it like a dig.

"You don't have to do that for us," I told her. "Making dinner is part of Linda's job. And we love her food. She makes this incredible fried shrimp dish—"

"Are you saying you don't love my food?" Mom asked. Now my polite refusal was a criticism.

"Just because I love someone else's food doesn't mean I don't love yours. We all love your food."

Mom didn't need to defend her title as Best Cook Ever. She knew we adored her food. But this tiny encroachment on her turf made her dislike Linda even more.

Mom lived with us for a four-month period while she was between houses. While I was working, Linda and Mom were spending way too much time together at our place and really getting on each other's nerves.

Linda came to me one day and said, "I don't know if I can stay in this job anymore. Your mother doesn't like me."

"What? No!" I said.

"She gives me dirty looks," said Linda, embarrassed.

"I'm so sorry."

"And she makes rude comments, all the time, about everything, like how I load the dishwasher and fold the laundry."

"It's going to stop, I promise," I told Linda.

Once I'd clued into the dynamic between them, I could see exactly what Linda was talking about. While Linda prepared dinner that night, Mom said to her, "Don't you know how to chop an onion?" The tone was openly hostile.

I pulled Mom out of the kitchen and asked, "Can you please be nicer to Linda? She's just doing her job."

"Okay, Wen. Of course, Wen."

And then we returned to the kitchen and Mom proceeded to shoot Linda withering glances and make bitchy little sounds all night. I said, "Mom!"

"What? I didn't say anything." Like she ever needed words to get her point across.

Linda could only take so much. Not long after, she gave us two weeks' notice. Her reason for leaving was that she had to go back to her home country, but I suspected Mom's barbs were a major contributing factor.

I naturally thought that now that Mom had driven my nanny away, she'd stick around to fill in the gap. But that was not how Mom played it. She announced, "My new house is ready for me to move into, so I'm leaving this weekend, on Saturday."

"Mom, Linda's last day is Monday," I said. "I'm having surgery on Thursday." I was scheduled to have a breast augmentation and a Brazilian butt lift (BBL). "I can't change the date."

"Well, I can't change my plans," said Mom.

She was leaving me to recover from surgery without childcare. Once again, it felt like punishment for disrespecting her by taking the nanny's side over hers. I shouldn't have been surprised, but I was.

Desperate for help, I wound up using a service that sent revolving-door babysitters. Kamrynn was sixteen months old, and she cried constantly because she didn't know these women. After a breast augmentation, I wasn't supposed to lift anything more than twenty pounds or put my hands over my head. But my baby didn't care about the doctor's orders. She wanted to be held. I carried my baby on my hip and lifted her in and out of the bath and her crib. I lived in constant fear of tearing my stitches, bleeding, and getting an infection.

In a passive-aggressive replay of Kamrynn's birth, Mom never came to see me during my entire postop recovery. She professed to be all about loyalty and being there for each other. I was raised to believe that we are all we have. But when I needed Mom, she wasn't always there for me. In fact, by her needling Linda and driving her to quit, Mom made my life much harder. It made me reevaluate our relationship. For a few months, I didn't reveal the personal details of our lives. I kept our conversations very superficial, just the bare minimum to stay in touch, but even further from intimate disclosures than usual.

I certainly didn't tell her about my new nanny search. After trying out dozens of candidates, we finally found a wonderful woman named Mosun, who moved into the basement apartment. Even after she'd been with us for a while, I was afraid of a replay of the Linda situation and kept Mom away. The two women eventually met, though. Kamrynn had a cough, and I was worried about my premature baby's lungs during the pandemic. I called Mom, as a nurse, for her opinion on how Kamrynn sounded. Mom offered to come along to see the pediatrician with me. Mosun came, too, to hear the doctor's instructions firsthand.

Mom played it cool with Mosun all day, but that night, when Eddie brought home takeout for dinner, she got weird. He made sure to get a sandwich for Mosun, who always ate with us. And he ordered extra everything else so there'd be enough for Mom as well.

With five bags of food on the table, I asked, "Mom, do you want something to eat?"

She said, "No. I'm leaving in a minute."

Five minutes later, I saw her eating the leftover fries on my son's plate. There were plenty of fries still in the bag.

She watched Mosun dig into her sandwich and said, "Oh, wow. They got you a sandwich."

I said, "Of course we did. We got you a sandwich, too. Do you want it? Have you eaten? Are you okay?"

She said, "In our culture, you don't ask someone if they want to eat. You just give them the food. You didn't even offer it to me."

"That's not true. As soon as we walked in, I asked you."

"I didn't hear you."

"I asked and you answered."

"No, you didn't."

My sons' eyes were nervously going back and forth between us. I could tell Eddie would have liked to slip quietly out of the room. Mosun just kept eating her sandwich, knowing it was wise to stay out of it.

That sinking-gut feeling from childhood hit me again. Mom didn't only criticize the nannies. She picked at me constantly, too. Eddie confirmed later that I absolutely offered her food as soon as he arrived with it and she distinctly refused. Along with her passive-aggression, she was gaslighting me. But in the past, when she told me everything was okay when it clearly wasn't, she was trying to protect me. But this was outright lying to give herself something to complain about.

Was this a Nigerian thing, or a Susan thing?

A bit of both.

The cultural part: Mom disapproved of the nanny because according to her tradition, we shouldn't need to hire someone to do what she could do for us. Also, she was offended that the nanny was offered the same food as she was. As the elder, her position in the tribe should be elevated. If the nanny got a sandwich, Mom should have been offered cake. (It didn't matter that all of us had the same food that night.)

The Susan part: she had a "what about me?" personality. Her gele is always the highest in the room. At any family gathering, she carved out the center of attention, even if the event was to honor someone else. When I hosted a "sip and see" party for Kamrynn on RHOP, Mom gave the first speech and dominated the evening, as if it were her show. It had always been her show. Even when Mom was literally *on my show*, it was her show.

When I was growing up, the kitchen was Mom's favorite stage, and she didn't like to share it. She never allowed Yvo and me to cook with her at her side when she made dinner night after night. Mom took pride in it and insisted on doing it herself. Food is her love language. She believed that food brought people together, and she served her love in every dish. We ate her food and received her love. That was the dynamic.

I agree that food is love. But as a parent, I believe that *cooking* together is where the magic is. I can't keep my kids out of the kitchen, and I wouldn't have it any other way. Cooking together means sharing the effort and the journey into a world of spice and heat. Over a cutting board, people chat about everything and nothing, the kind of shooting-the-shit conversations I never had with my mom and sorely missed. Cooking together is how you get to know someone and create heart-warming food and memories with them. That's true in *any* culture.

At the next family gathering at Mom's new place in Pennsylvania, the table was laden, as always, with all her signature dishes . . . and a brand-new one for her: Linda's fried shrimp. Mom had never made it before in her entire life, so why now? Was it her way of apologizing for driving Linda away and giving us the dish we missed? Was it because she acknowledged how great it was, and she just wanted to add it to her repertoire?

No. It wasn't about the shrimp. It was about the love. Mom needed to claim our love for Linda and her cooking for herself. It struck me the wrong way. She'd already won that war. And this seemed like rubbing it in.

A month or two later, the Covid vaccines became available, but they were nearly impossible to get. Older members in our community were desperate for the protection, but they weren't tech savvy and struggled to navigate the online vaccine portals. This was Mom's chance to shine. As a nurse, she had connections. She told our people, "I got you," and became the vaccination hookup queen for five whole Nigerian families. She even scheduled an appointment for Mosun.

She infuriated me one day and made me burst with pride the next. To the world, she was a hero. Among her peers, she inspired awe. Not only revered by her peers, Mom was beloved by mine. While she was in the world, I felt nothing but awe over everything she'd done, how she looked, smelled, cooked. But privately, in the microcosm of our relationship, she drove me nuts.

WE STARTED FILMING *Real Housewives of Potomac* season six—my second season on the show—three weeks after my surgery, and with everything on my plate, including writing this book, the months of shooting went by in a blur. When the trailer for my second season dropped, Eddie moved all his meetings to sit with me, hold my hand to make sure I was okay. Tenderly, he said, "Remember what we talked about. We're not going to repeat what happened last year."

Throughout the day, he came upstairs to ask, "Hey, babe, just checking. Are you okay? Don't read the comments. I love you. *Don't read the comments.*"

My sophomore season addressed issues of female identity and being a professional working woman. I was still very much a professor, but after my mommy makeover surgeries, I was reclaiming my own identity as a woman with substance who was proud of her body. Women should not be put in a box. Yes, a woman can be educated, but she also has the right to feel sexy, and her sexiness is solely defined by her. I was telling the world, "I'm still Dr. Wendy, but I got my groove back."

My intelligence and substance were unchanged by my physical tweaks. I could have double D breasts *and* a high IQ. That wasn't too hard to understand, right? A woman could be everything and style herself in a way that was authentic to herself. And if that didn't jibe with people's preconceived notions, the expectations were what needed to change, not the woman.

Being defined by others is an area of sensitivity for all women, but especially people of color and immigrants. People make assumptions about you based on your appearance, good or bad, that have nothing to do with reality. As a professor, I've been told by colleagues that my nails are too long or my hair is unprofessional. Back in the days of on-site learning, way before I had new boobs, I walked into the classroom for the first lecture of the year in a conservative suit and went to the front to start the lesson.

My students glanced back and forth at each other, and a brave one asked, "Where's the professor?"

"I don't know," I said. "Where is she?"

My students had a picture in their head of what a professor should look like, and it wasn't me (even in the conversative suit). And yet I was a professor, and this was how I looked.

A news producer once told me, "You're a great commentator, but you'll never make it until you cut your hair at least six inches shorter."

Another told me, "You can't wear red lipstick."

Another: "No one will take you seriously with those nails."

I didn't change my hair, makeup, or nails to fit their dusty old mold, and these same producers keep calling me anyway.

It seemed like in any context that I entered, people tried to enforce their expectation on me about how I was supposed to look or how I was supposed to live. Nigerian kids get enough pressure from their parents, they don't need it from the world as well. By cramming us into a box, society snuffs out the light of authenticity we were all born with. How we choose to represent ourselves matters politically and personally. Most important, my choices were mine.

I was just *fed up* with being judged by my cast mates, with Mom about nannies and cooking, and her inability to say "I'm sorry." And incredibly, being so angry got me over the hump of my own fears about confronting Mom about past hurts.

The last time I intended to try, while she cooked soup for us in my kitchen, she dropped the "Don't live for your kids" bomb on me, and my courage evaporated. This time, it'd be different. This time, I was going to say what I needed to say and be glad I did, regardless of outcome. I was also going to have an audience . . .

On camera, while filming for RHOP, I said to Mom, "It really hurt when you were always the last mom at pickup."

"Why are you saying this to me?" she replied. "How can you do that to me?"

She immediately went into all the ways she had sacrificed her own life for that of her children, reiterating the same explanation she gave me as a child, that it wasn't like she was out partying—she was late because she was working to provide a better life for her kids, and so on.

I get it, Mom! I had heard all that many, many times before. But just once, an apology would be nice. I got no satisfaction in confronting her, and once again, she turned my old grievance into a new one for her.

We mutually agreed, without our having to say a word, to cool off and not talk to or see each other for a while. After the "you weren't there for me" confrontation, Mom and I didn't speak for two weeks, which had to be a record for us. When Mom finally called me to check in, she happened to catch me in a bad way. I'd been running on fumes for days on end and was exhausted. We had just wrapped filming my sophomore season of RHOP. It was a crazy rush to finish because we were filming during a pandemic, and everything took twice as long. It was also the end of the academic year at Johns Hopkins, and I had to submit grades for my students, who'd been remote learning at home. It all weighed heavily on me.

Mom said, "How are you?"

I was too exhausted to pretend to be strong. "I'm tired and just so hungry," I said.

"I have all this food I cooked for your brother."

"It's okay, Mom. You live an hour away. I'll cook for myself."

The next morning at 7 a.m., there was a knock at my door. Mom was standing there, with a dozen food containers. She must have gotten up at dawn to get to my place so early. "Good morning, Wen. I've got some extra spicy stew and rice that I made with oxtail. Your favorite."

She handed me a week's worth of soul-nurturing Nigerian food and gave me a kiss. "You can never say I don't love you," she said.

Food is the highest form of love, and she drove all that way just to feed me when she knew I was stressed out and in need. As I received this bounty from my mother, in that moment, I felt completely loved. Only Mom could give me that feeling.

And you know what? I ate it all and felt better.

Again, it wasn't the food per se. Offering me food was her way of saying, "I hate to see you unwell. I care about you. Let me help."

When I *really* needed her, she did come through for me.

I hated the emotional roller coaster of our relationship, veering from highs and lows. When and how would it ever stop?

TWENTY-ONE

The Empty Nest

$\mathcal{W}$hen Jordan finally went off to college after a year's delay during the pandemic, Mom found herself alone, truly alone, for the first time in her life. Yvo and I had families, careers, and good Nigerian husbands of our own. We did what she expected, and the result of her pushing us to be successful was that we were extremely busy with less time for her or need for her help.

"Wendy, I'm not feeling well. I'm going to die," Mom called to tell me while I was waiting to appear live on a TV news show. I'd just been given a five-minute warning from the producer.

"It's just a blood sugar drop, Mom." I'd heard her say this recently, and it always turned out fine. "Please, call your doctor if you're really worried. I have to go. I'll call you this afternoon."

A couple of hours later, I was finally able to check my voice mail and found three messages from Mom.

"Wen, call me. I'm in bad shape."

"Wen, why aren't you calling me back? It's an emergency."

"Wen! This is serious! Where are you?"

I called her back and she yelled, "I could have died! I called you from the doctor's office! You don't care about me!"

"Of course I care," I said. "What happened?"

She unloaded her story (she did *not* almost die, by the way), and I let her tell it without interruption. It didn't matter if I talked at all, really.

She just needed someone to listen. For my entire childhood, she had been invulnerable, a warrior. But lately she'd shown me nothing but vulnerability and need, and it freaked me out. Was she changing, or was I reacting differently to her?

Once she was talked out, I called Yvo. "The busier I am, the needier she gets," I said. "She expects me to put her first, but I want to put *my* kids first, like she did."

I understood that Mom's life had changed significantly since her warrior-woman prime. Her kids were grown. Her husband was gone. She stopped working full time years ago. In a new stage of life, Mom was struggling to find her footing.

"You think it's bad, I *work* with her," said Yvo. Mom's part-time job at my sister's medical practice was just something to do, and it gave her a small income. It couldn't compare to the professional gratification and purpose she once had as the director at a hospital.

"I wish she could relax and enjoy retirement," I said. "Just spoil her grandkids and be content."

"Wen, Mom has never been content," said Yvo. "She wants too much."

It was true. Her heart was filled with want, for attention, accolades, material objects, and status symbols paid for and provided by us.

I could only imagine how much it hurt to sacrifice your whole life for someone only for that person to leave. In Mom's case, "that person" was me and my sister. And my brother. And my stepfather. There's a Nigerian saying, "People speak from where their shoe hurts them." It was clear that Mom's hurt was rooted in loneliness. I tried my best to be there for her as much as I could, calling her to listen daily, always saying, "I love you." But I was not doing enough, because she always needed more.

A transactional relationship was written in the Nigerian parenting handbook: "We took care of you, now you take care of us." The way this traditionally played out, back in the village: adult children invited their parents to live in their house and to help care for the grandkids.

Mom bucked this cultural norm. We'd offered, but Mom insisted on staying by herself in her own house (a.k.a. the empty nest), watching her true-crime TV shows and gossiping with her friends. She absolutely loved and adored her grandchildren, but between our nannies and the kids' social calendars, her involvement in their lives didn't take the load off us. Still, she expected the "village" (Yvo and me) to take on the responsibility of providing for her. Yvo carried the bulk of it by paying for her necessities. I sent her cash for the extras, life's luxuries. She didn't ask outright. That's not how Mom played it.

She would call me to say, "My hair is a mess."

That was my cue to say, "Make an appointment, and I'll pay for it."

"Nothing fits," she would complain.

"Go shopping, on me," I replied.

"I miss my sisters."

"I'll book you a flight."

From her perspective, these weren't gifts, they were obligations.

Eddie and I were saving for our children's future, investing in different projects, and paying our bills. Eddie happened to be very good with money, so we were okay. I shouldn't have been hesitant to give so much of our money to my mother. It was part of the deal; I knew I would be responsible for her one day. But I was reluctant to do it anyway.

At the crossroads of appreciation and sensibility, I struggled. On the one hand, first gens *were* indebted to their parents for all they sacrificed for us. Our parents left their homeland and came to a foreign country not just for the betterment of themselves, but for the betterment of their children. They left *everything* they knew and loved for us.

Moreover, how could first gens not want to repay our parents for everything they'd done? Every racial slur they endured? Every difficulty they went through working minimum-wage jobs? It was our duty to repay them, support them, and let them know that all their hard work was not in vain. But at what cost? At what cost does appreciation overshadow our own sensibility that we were taking on more than we can chew?

I knew I owed Mom my life. She pushed me to become a doctor and a professor. She instilled in me the drive I needed to become successful. Thanks to her effort and support, I married Eddie and had three beautiful kids who are my everything. Most other Nigerian parents would have encouraged me to let him go and marry someone else because of his parents' disapproval. I give her a lot of credit for making the wedding happen. But didn't she owe it to us not to drain us financially when we had our own children's financial security to consider?

For the majority of my adult life, I'd lived in this conflict. Mom deserved the world. She deserved comfort in her old age (although she was not yet sixty) and, by all means, she deserved a weekly mani-pedi. But by giving her *whatever* she wanted, I sometimes compromised my own happiness.

I am now rewriting the Nigerian parenting handbook to engage with my kids on an emotional level. I would never tell my child, "Don't be scared," for example. The way out of fear was not denying it existed. It was acknowledging it and accepting that it was just part of being human. Asking, "How do you feel?" followed up with, "Why do you feel that way?" was a smarter strategy for correcting a child's bad behavior than the traditional Nigerian tactic of yelling and hitting.

My son Karter recently pulled a girl's ponytail at coed soccer camp. A traditional Nigerian parent would have grabbed him by the arm and spanked him while yelling: "Do [smack] not [smack] do [smack] that [smack] again [smack]!"

Eddie and I made a conscious decision not to spank our kids. Instead, I asked, "Karter, why did you pull that girl's hair?"

He said, "I just did."

"What were you feeling at the time?"

"I was just playing around," he said.

"Well, you know that's not how you play with others," I said.

"Yes."

"So will you think before you do that again?"

"Yes."

By talking to him about why it was wrong, he learned how to handle himself in the future. That's a lot healthier than just yelling or punishing.

As a curious person, Karter loves talking. He always has questions, and answers for my questions. These kinds of conversations are interesting for him, even when we talk about tough stuff, like his own behavior. When you ask a child about their thoughts and feelings, and then listen to their responses, they feel seen and heard. We all need that, and getting validation from a parent is huge.

I knew Mom loved me; she told me every day. She always gave me great practical advice. She beat down the doors of heaven with her prayers on my behalf. But to this day, she talked to me like a child who was expected to obey. She didn't see me as a grown woman with three jobs and three kids of my own. Sure, Mom laughed with me, cursed with me, had cocktails with me. But one thing Mom had never done, or seemed interested in doing, was getting to know me. Not just on a surface level, but the real me, my vulnerable side. The Wendy who was strong, but anxious; the Wendy who had accomplished a lot, but feared failure. The missing element in our relationship was the deep connection shared by equals.

We had a fundamental disagreement about priorities. Mom's advice not to live for my kids was code for "Make sure you live for yourself." On the face of it, her telling me, one of her children, that she regretted prioritizing me, was just mean. But I sort of understood where she was coming from. She had sacrificed her whole life for her children, and now those same children were living their lives, and she was alone. It's not that Mom regretted all she had done for us, but she was at a crossroads and had to start wondering, when would she start living for herself? Unfortunately, old-school Nigerian parenting focused on children and rarely put emphasis on self. Here she was in middle age without having truly lived her own life. For this, I felt sorry for her.

Every instinct I had told me that my kids should be my top priority. They needed me more than Mom did. Giving to them, teaching them, being there for them, was the greatest joy and satisfaction I'd known. Apparently, Susan and I had very different experiences and expectations for motherhood. I wasn't raising my kids with my own redemption or bragging rights in mind. I was raising them to be happy and fulfilled.

Yvonne, Jordan, and I, and other first gens, are the end result of our parents' traditional Nigerian parenting. Our success was their purpose. But now I had my own purposes that diverged from my mother's, and the conflict was causing resentment on both sides.

As the adult child of a traditional Nigerian parent, I'd done everything that was expected of me. My issue now: When do we stop living for our parents and start living for ourselves?

It was about time that I found out.

TWENTY-TWO

From My Mother's Tears

Over our thirty-seven years together, my mother and I have gone through different chapters. When I was young, she was a goddess to me. I worshipped her and thought she was the strongest, coolest person in the world. When I was a teenager and young adult, I started to see her as a human being—an amazing one—who had fought and won against the odds for me. In my early adult years, our relationship became contentious, and turned into a battle of who I am versus who she wanted me to be. Now, in my late thirties, I want to be my mom's friend. I want to know the intimate parts. She did a great job parenting me, but I'm not a child anymore.

Every mother and daughter's relationship evolves over time. Along with normal growing pains and generational conflicts, immigrant mothers and their first-gen daughters contend with cultural differences as well. For a period, those differences were pulling us further apart. It took me recognizing our cultural clash as the root cause of our declining relationship for me to begin to accept Mom for who she is.

In the old-school Nigerian culture, the parent is the parent, and the child is the child, forever. I'd like to see a more American evolution from the parent-child relationship into a friendship of equals, where it's okay for her not to get angry if I hold her accountable. Motherhood was great for her when we needed her, ate her food, and worked hard to meet her expectations. But now that we don't need her for our basic necessities, she doesn't like it. It's more like she needs us now, and no matter what we do for her, it often feels like it's never enough.

Which begged the question at the heart of our relationship: What did I owe her?

I prayed on it and came up with some answers to guide my side of our interactions going forward.

I owe her gratitude for all she'd done for me. That's a given.

I owe her compassion. While I was growing up, I didn't get much compassion and empathy from her. That was not the Nigerian parenting style. But as a first gen, and an adult child who longed for grace from her, I have resolved to give my mother the compassion and empathy she didn't give me.

Life hardens everyone, and it seemed to have hardened the person I loved and admired the most. My mother had lost nearly everything. Cordelia. Her parents. Her first and second husbands. She'd raised three children in a foreign land. She'd worked for decades building a career that was now just a memory. She'd endured so much and now seemed dissatisfied with where she'd landed, despite all she'd done.

It was hard to empathize with a woman who seemed determined to be discontented. But it wasn't for me to say how she should feel, or to resent her for not feeling the way I wanted her to. I'd show her compassion by accepting her discontentment instead of wishing she'd change.

It was unfair for me to want her always to be the warrior woman of my childhood. She was older, and vulnerable. She raised me not to show weakness, so naturally, when Mom called to complain about her health, my reaction was, *How dare you, my hero, my warrior, be weak?*

In the future, when she showed me her vulnerability, I wouldn't roll my eyes or try to get her off the phone. I'd *really* listen and let her know that she was heard.

I owed her caring. For years, I'd resented having to support her while also trying to build a secure future for my family. But supporting her was part of the cycle of any parent-child relationship. She cared for me, and now I was blessed with the opportunity to care for her. It was a matter of reframing. I'd inject emotion into the transaction. I'd take care of her because of love (easier to find with a compassionate frame of mind), not just because it was my responsibility.

Recently, I took her to New York City to celebrate her birthday. I rolled out the red carpet for her. She went shopping, ate at the most fabulous restaurants, and stayed at the ritziest hotel. As we were in the car being chauffeured home, I heard her on the phone telling her friends about the amazing two days she just experienced. As we passed the Hudson River in the darkness of night, tears streamed down my face. The same way I cried from joy when she bought me my pink mountain bike at the age of ten, I cried that I was able to provide Mom with this experience. I realized this is exactly what I should do as her daughter. Give her the life that she sacrificed everything for me to have. If it was not for her sacrifices, I would not be in the position to provide for her in this way financially. Mom deserves all the flowers because it was she and her sacrifices that allowed me to be where I am today. No more hesitation on my end, just gratitude that I can give her the world.

I was ready to step into a cycle of caregiving that had begun generations before, and would continue long after I was gone. Whether Mom saw me as an adult or not didn't matter. I was an adult, and I would take on the duty of caring for my mom along with my sister. As her daughter, I was obliged to provide for her now. My goal as a mother and a first gen who aspired to be authentic and real was to make peace with doing whatever she needed me to do, regardless of the limits of our relationship.

As for what I don't owe my mother, I have a short list.

I don't owe her obedience. Not anymore.

After months of stalling, I was ready to tell Mom that I'd made a major decision for myself that she wasn't going to like.

I'd decided to increase my appearances on friendly networks like

CNN and shift my focus toward political commentary exclusively, which meant I'd have even less time and energy for my professorship. If my mother had her say, I'd focus on my teaching exclusively.

For Mom, professorship gives me credibility and stability. A lot of Nigerian parents want their sons and daughters to become doctors and lawyers for the title and prestige as well as the financial security. People will always get sick, so it's safe to become a doctor. People will always sue each other, so the world needs lawyers. People need an education, so teachers will always have opportunities.

And there was the prestige factor. My mom never got tired of saying, "One of my daughters is a professor at Johns Hopkins and my other daughter is a surgeon." No one predicted that Mom would raise successful daughters. Her own siblings said as much (as fate would have it, of all our cousins, Yvo and I are the most successful). A part of me believed that I was always shaky on taking a leap in my career because I didn't want to compromise her status as the Champion Mom. She earned that. She deserves that. Who was I to take it away?

Some status comes with being a political commentator, though, right? Who wouldn't want to say, "I'm Don Lemon's mom"? But does the world need pundits? Is that job secure? Probably not. But if I didn't go for it now, would I ever? The time had come for me to tell Mom the direction I wanted to go in, and it'd take me off the narrow path she put me on decades ago.

Mom was over at my house, back in the kitchen, back at the stove, cooking my family our favorite foods. Yet again, I sat in a green armchair in the corner of my kitchen, awkwardly fiddling with my hair, looking for an opening to tell Mom what was on my mind.

If I didn't seize the moment, it wouldn't come. "Mom, I have something to tell you."

She made a "hmph" sound that said, "Don't get heavy on me. I can't deal."

I ignored it, which was a small triumph in and of itself. "I think I'm going to take a break from being a professor." It all came out in a rush. Every word made me feel so much lighter.

"Stay being a professor and you'll always have that," she said. "If you leave, you're making a huge mistake. What would you do instead?"

"Focus more on my commentary," I said. "Do more speaking. Who knows? Maybe one day I'll transition to commentary and have my own daytime talk show."

"Oh my God," she said.

"It's a dream, Mom. But it'll never happen unless I try."

"What if nothing works out?" she asked. "What if you're left with nothing?" Mom had always been cautious about the what-ifs of life.

"Don't worry, Mom. We'll have enough money to take care of you."

She put her knife down on the counter and looked hard at me. "That's the reason you think I don't want you to quit your day job?"

Well . . . she did ask for a lot from us. "I know you want me to keep my professorship so you can brag about it to your friends." Whoa! I said it before I could stop myself. The filter was really off now.

She shook her head, made a pained expression and many exasperated noises. "You don't really know me at all," she said.

Yes! That was what I'd been saying. "You're right. I don't."

"I want you to be successful *for you*," she said. "For a long time, yes, I wanted you to be successful for me, too. I still do. It makes me proud to see you do well. And I deserve a lot of the credit for pushing you so hard . . ." She had to get that in. "Look, Wen," she continued. "I tell you what to do because it's what I think is best. But I believe in you. You know what's right for you, even if I think it's wrong. And I do think it's wrong to leave your day job."

Wait, did she just say that she believed *in me* to do what was right *for me*? "Can you repeat that?" I asked. I needed to get a recording to play for Yvo.

"I'll be very disappointed if you leave your professorship," she said. "But I can't stop you."

There it was. The cutting of the strings. I would not get her approval on this decision, but enough had shifted in our relationship over the years that she acknowledged her control over me was waning. Mom must have known that I'd been feeling the strain, and that something had to give. The emotional imperative—my fear of disappointing her—was, suddenly, significantly lessened.

"Can I help you with that?" I asked her, gesturing to the cutting board and the onions that needed chopping.

She paused and then said, "Sure. But don't cut them too thin."

"Yes, Mom." I picked up a knife and, for the first time, we stood side by side. I wouldn't exactly call us equals. I wouldn't say we had the friendship I wanted. But we were moving in the right direction.

In the long run, by being appreciative, compassionate, and caring of my mother *now*, I'd be a better mother by modeling these qualities. My goal in motherhood was to build individuals who were ready not necessarily for the world that I birthed them into, but the world they would eventually live in. They would need the life skill of compassion in all their relationships.

While praying on all this, I've come to recognize my frustration with Mom's demands as a struggle against a deeper understanding of myself. I had felt as though Mom was too much for me to take on, along with everything else. What I realized, though, was that she'd already provided me with the strength to be the daughter she needed me to be now.

From my mother's tears, I am the woman she raised me to become.

TWENTY-THREE

Tears for My Children

The original wave of Nigerian immigrants in the late twentieth century constantly reinforced the message to their first-gen kids: "We came to this country with twenty dollars and the clothes on our backs. We came here *for you*. We made something out of our lives from nothing. You have no excuse."

Their stories of sacrifice, struggle, and survival are the background of our lives. Mom and her siblings told them to us over and over. Some had to drive a taxi because that was the only job they could get. Mom was a nurse so her daughters would become doctors. The goal was for the next generation to be the best version of their parents. Mom's era of immigrants created a first generation to be proud of. But we're not necessarily going to raise our children the same way.

Just as my mother is a reflection of her upbringing, I am a reflection of her. As one of the subjects in this great immigrant experiment, I've tried to put a modern spin on Nigerian culture, to be ambitious while also opening my heart to my sons, daughter, husband, sister, brother—and, especially, my mother. For my children, I want to be a role model and show them that emotional connection is just as important as professional and educational accomplishment. I aspire to show them that happiness comes before success, not the other way around.

Using Mom's rules—no excuses, failure is not an option—has made Nigerians the "model minority" in America. Our parents applied intense pressure on us to chase success since birth. Relentlessly pushing children as a parenting style is rooted in Nigerian DNA. It's passed down from one generation to the next, just like any other inherited trait. It's nurtured as well. My mother has been the dominant external motivator in my life. Because she taught me to adhere to her rules or risk losing her approval, I internalized them, and I push myself.

And I'm going to push my children to be the best people they can be as well. That means I'll pressure them to work their asses off at school, first and foremost. I'm not so sure about enforcing the same excellence-only intensity on extracurricular activities. Of course I want my children to excel at what they choose to do. My kids will be allowed to discover what they enjoy doing. And I'll enjoy watching them, whether they're the absolute best or not.

"No excuses" means being accountable. Don't blame anything or anyone for your not advancing toward your goals. I have a mantra that goes, "Excuses are tools of the incompetent." I have lived by this for the majority of my life.

There is no denying that systemic racism exists in America, and years and years of oppression within the Black community have affected upward mobility and generational wealth. The question then becomes, how do Black people manage to succeed within an environment that was built to destroy them? Nigerians put forth the belief that success is attainable no matter what your family's socioeconomic status is, and regardless of whether you are born into privilege and wealth. My siblings, husband, and I were raised to achieve even in an outwardly racist and discriminatory environment that is designed to keep people of color down. Some might say we exceled because of nature, the strength and ambition that is in our DNA. However, I believe our achievement is due to nurture, that we were brought up always to find a way to succeed, that no matter what circumstances we were put in or what obstacles we faced, success was about the will to succeed and work our asses off, regardless of what challenges we faced.

My mother told us, "Failure is not an option." Her approval hung on our successful outcomes. My parenting perspective is, "Failure is not an option, but if it happens, it's an opportunity to learn and grow." My approval isn't an issue, regardless of outcomes.

As for the "narrow path to success" (doctor-lawyer-engineer, marriage, kids), obedient first gens stayed on it and were so successful we became the "model minority" despite the color of our skin.

The true test of the Nigerian immigrant success story, though, is going to be my kids' generation. I suspect that second gens aren't going to be held to the same standards on the same terms as first gens were. What you're going to see in the next couple of decades from Nigerian Americans are success stories on divergent paths. Second gens will include the best doctors and lawyers, but they will be the best chefs, writers, and artists, too.

First gens are still going to instill the parenting wisdom of past generations. I have already heard my mother's voice coming out of my mouth, saying to my boys, "Did someone in the class get an A? Then that means it's possible for you." We're still going to instill high standards. But I think we're going to loosen the reins on what success looks like. Not only professionally, but in terms of emotional connectedness and their ability to work less and enjoy life more. The children of immigrants have the dual perspective of taking the best things from the old traditions and blending them with the best of the new world we live in. The same could be said for any parent, anywhere. When you know better, you do better, whether you're a child of an immigrant or not.

The defining mission of my life for its first three decades was to become a doctor or a lawyer. Mom's asking, "What do you want to be when you grow up?" wasn't a real question. It was a cue, the preceding line on the already-written script.

When I ask my kids, "What do you want to be when you grow up?" I'm genuinely curious what they have to say. And when they open up to me, I listen.

However, I uphold Nigerian tradition by making it clear that I do have unwavering expectations for them to be successful, just not necessarily as doctors, lawyers, or engineers, but as people. We've been having these conversations about professional dreams since the kids were two- and three-year-olds. It doesn't matter if their answer is movie star or firefighter, as long as they understand that they have to be excellent in their chosen field. The expectation of success will still be there for second gens. It's just that the fields for success have expanded. The most important aspect of my upbringing that I will reinforce with my kids without any hesitation is the idea that we are all we have.

When Karter, Kruz, and Kamrynn read this book when they're older, I hope they see how deeply they are loved and how much I hope their relationships with each other will give them strength for their whole lives.

I said before that Mom, Yvo, and I are a triangle, the strongest shape in nature. My kids are a triangle, too, with the boys at the bottom and my daughter on top. Together, they form a triangle of love, hope, and happiness. No side is more important than the other. In order for them to function, they have to operate as a unit. As much as I pray for their career success and educational attainment, my greatest hope for them is always to have each other. They are best friends, and with each other's love and support, there's nothing they can't achieve.

My philosophy of child-rearing is that it's like a relay race. Your job when the baton is passed to you is to run as far as you can so you can ensure your children start life on a more level playing field than you did. My mom started her race in Anambra State, Nigeria, and passed it off to me in America. I just hope I ran far enough to pass the baton to my kids so they never have to experience the struggles I faced in my childhood, and more important, for them to run so they can pass the baton to their children. Everything I did was for them, everything I sacrificed is for their betterment. My kids will be their ancestors' wildest dreams!

Like my mother, I work so hard, and I feel the strain. Sometimes I think, "Why am I doing this?" And it's always for the same reason, so I can pass something to my children, give them security, and know that they have a safety net.

Immigrants start in their new country at a huge deficit. They often come with nothing, like my mother. They don't know the new culture. They're surrounded by people who often speak a different language, and they have to make their way. The goal is just to get a footing, to obtain something that resembles the American Dream. For some, it may be buying a home. For some, it may be graduating with a degree. For my birth father, it was getting a managerial position at a fast-food restaurant. Just getting to square one was the goal of my mother's generation, so they could pass the baton to us, the first gens, so we could take it from there. I deeply appreciate my mother and can finally see the connection between her decision to raise us in America, her unyielding expectations, and my living the beautiful life I have today.

I hope that we as first gens have done enough for our kids, so the second gens will be winning Oscars, Grammys, and Emmys, and become the creative forces of the Nigerian community. My generation will make it possible for our kids to achieve beyond their imaginations and know that they can accomplish anything they put their minds to.

To my children and all of those in their generation, remember that the sky is not the limit, it is the view. Make your mark on the world and do not let anyone tell you what you can and cannot achieve. The baton is in your hand now; run as far as you can and never look back.

ACKNOWLEDGMENTS

*T*hank you to every person who made this book possible. Valerie Frankel, Cherise Fisher, Karyn Marcus, and Rebecca Strobel, I am forever grateful to you ladies.

To my mom, the woman who made me who I am. No words are big enough. Thank you for sacrificing everything for your children. I hope I have made you proud.

Yvo, my sister and best friend. You have never turned your back on me and I am forever grateful. The greatest gift our parents gave me is you.

Jordan, my baby brother. I pray Yvo and I have paved a better path for you. The world is yours.

To my husband, I would choose you again each and every time. Thank you for loving me unconditionally.

Karter, Kruz, and Kamrynn. My heartbeats. My perfect triangle. Everything I do is for you three. I have never loved anyone more and I never will. I'm blessed to call you mine.

To the country that birthed me, and the people who raised me, you hold a very special place in my heart.

Dr. Wendy Osefo is a Nigerian American political commentator, public affairs academic, philanthropist, and television personality. She is an assistant professor at Johns Hopkins School of Education. She is also a cast member on *The Real Housewives of Potomac*.